The Living of These Days

OTHER BOOKS BY

HARRY EMERSON FOSDICK

THE SECOND MILE

THE ASSURANCE OF IMMORTALITY

THE MANHOOD OF THE MASTER

THE MEANING OF PRAYER

THE MEANING OF FAITH

THE MEANING OF SERVICE

CHRISTIANITY AND PROGRESS

TWELVE TESTS OF CHARACTER

THE MODERN USE OF THE BIBLE

ADVENTUROUS RELIGION

A PILGRIMAGE TO PALESTINE

AS I SEE RELIGION

THE HOPE OF THE WORLD

THE SECRET OF VICTORIOUS LIVING

THE POWER TO SEE IT THROUGH

SUCCESSFUL CHRISTIAN LIVING

A GUIDE TO UNDERSTANDING THE BIBLE

LIVING UNDER TENSION

ON BEING A REAL PERSON

A GREAT TIME TO BE ALIVE

ON BEING FIT TO LIVE WITH

THE MAN FROM NAZARETH

RUFUS JONES SPEAKS TO OUR TIMES, AN ANTHOLOGY

GREAT VOICES OF THE REFORMATION, AN ANTHOLOGY

A FAITH FOR TOUGH TIMES

WHAT IS VITAL IN RELIGION

The Living
of These Days

AN AUTOBIOGRAPHY

by
Harry Emerson Fosdick

HARPER & BROTHERS
Publishers: New York

Library of Congress catalog card number: 56-10207

Contents

	Prologue	vii
I.	The Family Background	1
II.	Boyhood and Youth	24
III.	Revolt against Orthodoxy	48
IV.	Preparation for the Ministry	63
V.	Learning to Preach	83
VI.	A Professor at Large	113
VII.	The Fundamentalist Controversy	144
VIII.	The Riverside Church	177
IX.	Winds of Doctrine	229
X.	Ideas That Have Used Me	267
	Epilogue	312
	Index	321

Prologue

BIOGRAPHY and autobiography have long been my favorite reading, but I have always shrunk from the idea of writing a "biography by mirror." Nevertheless, the urgency of friends has been strong, and I am now yielding to it. My friends have argued that my autobiography need not be merely "first-person-singular-ish," that I have lived through a long generation, reflecting its religious life and thought, and that from my youth my problem has been the endeavor to be both an intelligent modern and a serious Christian. Write about that, they have said, depicting the life story which lies around it, for that problem is central to many people.

After long reluctance I now surrender to this friendly importunity. It is true that I have lived to a ripe old age through one of the most fascinating eras in history, and I have had a fairly good seat in the bleachers from which to observe some aspects of the amazing spectacle. If I could write an autobiography which would convey the intimate *feel* of this last three-quarters of a century—especially its religious life—as a Christian minister from a typical American background experienced it, that might be worth while. I shall still have to

write about myself—perhaps at times fulfilling the definition of an egoist as one "who wades me deep in conversation"—but at least my main intent can be to share with the
reader the experience of living through these past threescore
and eighteen years, which have radically changed the world.

My indebtedness to friends and to members of my family,
who have rekindled my memories and enheartened me when
zeal ran low, is very great. Especially I am thankful to
Eugene Exman, of Harper & Brothers, long my personal
friend as well as my publisher, who with endless patience
has persuaded me that this autobiography was worth writing,
and whose suggestions have been refreshing and stimulating.
Also to Professor Robert L. Calhoun, of the Yale Divinity
School, goes my cordial gratitude. While he is not responsible for any views which I express, he has given me significant help with his clarifying criticism and good counsel. Nor
can I forget the debt I owe to Robert James McCracken, my
successor in the pulpit at the Riverside Church, who encouraged me to write these memoirs and who has aided me with
his judicious advice. For such knowledge as I have concerning my lineage, I am indebted in part to Lewis L. Fosdick's
book, *The Fosdick Family*, published in 1891, but most of all
to my brother, Raymond, the genealogist of our tribe, whose
recent volume, *Annals of the Fosdick Family*, tells the whole
story.

As for this autobiography's title, taken from a line in my
hymn, "God of Grace, and God of Glory," Elton Trueblood,
professor of philosophy at Earlham College, is responsible
for that. I had intended at first calling it "What a Genera-

tion!" but I have accepted Dr. Trueblood's suggestion. The
title really is a prayer:

> Grant us wisdom, grant us courage,
> For the living of these days.

As I send this book to the press I recall Leslie Stephen's
remark: "A dull autobiography has never been written." I
seriously question the truth of that statement, but I find it
very encouraging.

H.E.F.

The Living of These Days

Chapter 1.

❦

The Family Background

To THE YOUTH of today the Victorian era seems ancient history, but the lifetime of its representative characters —Gladstone, Disraeli, Tennyson, Browning, George Eliot, Ruskin, Carlyle—overlapped my boyhood, and I was out of college before Queen Victoria died. It is difficult for me now to imagine that my life's span reaches so far back. Indeed, having been born in Buffalo, New York, on May 24, Victoria's birthday, one of my earliest recollections is crossing the Niagara River into Canada to let the Canadians celebrate my advent by shooting off firecrackers for the Queen.

In the eighteen-seventies—I appeared in 1878—although American culture was strongly influenced by British standards, Americans did not always think affectionately of the British. The Revolutionary War had been fought a century before, but in my boyhood we still were fighting it, and few books then stirred me more than *The Boys of '76* and *The Blue Jackets of 1812*. It is said that when the French Revolution broke, Robert Burns drank a "jubilant toast" to the "last verse of the last chapter of the Book of Kings," and we were still drinking it when I was young. For America was a new country, fiercely independent, proud of its democracy, its

1

spacious frontiers and open doors, its invitations to adventure
and its opportunities for the common man. The rural population, with its self-sufficient agriculture, its isolation and self-
reliance, far outnumbered the urbanites. When I was born
we were mainly a nation of farms, with nearly forty million
of our people, out of fifty million, living in the wide open
spaces or in villages with less than four thousand inhabitants;
Dakota, Montana, Idaho, Wyoming, Washington, Utah, New
Mexico and Arizona, comprising one-third of the present national area, were not yet states; and prairie schooners, which
I remember seeing, were still moving west.

To be sure, industrialization had started with a boom after
the Civil War. I have become used to the fact that the first
successful transatlantic cable was laid only twelve years before I was born, and that two years before my birth, at the
Centennial Exposition a primitive telephone was exhibited,
all believers in whose practicality "sensible" people called
"dreamers." Because as a boy I rode many a time on trains
that were stopped by hand brakes, I find it credible that the
automatic air brake was not patented until 1872. Because
throughout my boyhood milk came in large containers from
which we dipped it into our family pails, I can believe that
not until 1878 did a milkman in Brooklyn conceive the idea
of selling it in bottles. Because I visited Thomas Edison in
his laboratory while he was still in the full swing of his in-
ventive work, I can believe that he produced the phono-
graph the year before I was born and made possible the
incandescent electric light the year after. But I find it hard
to imagine how recently, in my childhood, had begun the
manufacture of machine-made shoes, ready-made clothes,

sewing machines, washing machines, mowing machines, typewriters, and how recent was the birth of such industries as meat packing, flour milling, steelmaking.

This restless, ambitious, forward-looking America which I knew in my boyhood had been created by plain people, by families of common folk, often by "dispossessed persons" from foreign lands, and one cannot understand that America without looking at it from the family angle. I tell the story of my lineage now with the more relish because, while far from being dramatic or important, it is typical of countless undistinguished households which helped to lay the foundations of our nation.

In Suffolk, England, in the early sixteen-thirties lived a man named Stephen Fosdick. His ancestors probably had come from the little village of Fosdyke in Lincolnshire—still there with its windmills and dykes, a few houses and stores, and a church. The village took its name from the Fosse Way, an old Roman Road, and since *fossa* in Latin and *dyke* in Anglo-Saxon mean much the same thing—a ditch with a levee or causeway—the settlement called Fosdyke probably marked the place where the Fosse Way, supported by dykes, crossed the Welland swamps. Who the "de Fosdykes" were who moved from Lincolnshire to Suffolk we do not know, but they were evidently farmers or artisans. Stephen was a carpenter, and at fifty-two years of age he left Wenham Magna in Suffolk for Charlestown, Massachusetts. Either then, or a year or two later when he briefly returned to England, he brought with him to the new country his wife and eight children.

The records show that during the decade before Stephen
Fosdick emigrated, Suffolk County had been having a rough
time with poverty, the fear of war, and the press gangs that
forcibly conscripted men for military service. While these
ill conditions doubtless furnished part of the *push* which
sent Stephen to America, there was evidently a *pull* too—
the lure of religious liberty in the new country. Archbishop
Laud was then playing tyrant in England, using every se-
verity he could think of to compel religious conformity, and
there was angry rebellion against him in Suffolk. The clergyman at Wenham Magna, James Hopkins, was a "liberal," and
we have a letter that he wrote to his friend John Winthrop,
then governor of the New England colony, in which he
said: "If I cannot enjoyce my libertie upon God's tearmes
as I have done, I have a purpose to make myselfe a member
of your plantation and when I come I hope I shall not come
alone." This demand for freedom, represented by Wenham
Magna's clergyman, probably explains why in 1634 some
six hundred of Suffolk's citizens made up their minds to
emigrate to New England and almost certainly Stephen
Fosdick was a member of this large company.

In the Charlestown Town Record the earliest notice concerning him runs as follows:

Stephen ffosdick   1635 Vth month, 11th day
                    Stephen ffosdick was
                        yielded to have
                    ye houseplott next
                    Good Convers, his new
                    house upon condition
                        to build A

good house upon it,
and to pay good
Richeson A daies
work.

Stephen was made a member of the church in Charlestown and a freeman of the Commonwealth in 1638, but he
soon found that religious liberty in New England was not
broad enough to satisfy his needs. In 1643 he was fined
£20, probably for reading heretical Anabaptist books, and
was excommunicated from the church. The civil penalty
involved in this sentence was remitted a few years later
and the fine reduced to £5, but he was not restored to
church membership until 1664, about three months before
his death in his eighty-second year. Those twenty-one years
of excommunication from the church which my first American ancestor endured were a major tragedy to him, involving severe social and economic penalties, but I am proud
of him now, especially because in spite of excommunication
he evidently made his way and established himself as a
solid citizen. He even left an estate inventoried at £500,
which in those days was affluence.

My lineage comes down through John Fosdick, seventh
child of Stephen, and, like his father, a carpenter. His
son, Samuel, moved to New London, Connecticut, about
1680 and there married Mercy Picket, a great-granddaugh-
ter of Elder Brewster of the *Mayflower*. He seems to have
been a citizen of some consequence, one of the patentees of
the Township of New London, a leader in the church, a
deputy in the General Court of Connecticut for six years,
and a captain in the militia. He owned a prosperous farm

on Plum Island, a town residence on Fosdick's Neck—now
Shaw's Point—and a house lot comprising what is now
nearly the whole block between Golden and Tilley Streets;
and concerning his estate one commentator says: "A glance
at the inventory of Captain Fosdick will show the ample and
comfortable style of housekeeping to which the inhabitants
had attained in 1700."

His son, also named Samuel, was a blacksmith in the
old-fashioned sense of craftsman in iron work, making
hinges, bolts, nails, fire tongs, and mending metal instruments and utensils. His craft probably accounts for the fact
that he moved to Oyster Bay, Long Island. The history of
Queens County suggests this explanation: "No blacksmith
was found fit to mend their utensils and wares. . . . The
records show that for many years the settlement of a blacksmith in the village was considered a public concern." At
any rate, the second Samuel established himself in Oyster
Bay and handed on his trade there to his son, Samuel the
third.

The Revolutionary War ruined the fortunes of my ancestors in this Oyster Bay family. At its beginning they were
well-to-do; at its end they were wrecked. The British occupation desolated Long Island and after the war Samuel
the third, an impoverished man, retired to the farm of his
eldest son, Silas, in Dutchess County, New York, where he
died in 1792, aged eighty-two, having worked in the harvest
field the day before his death. We still possess two memen-
toes of this blacksmith ancestor—a tomahawk, bearing the
date of 1769, left with him by an Indian to be mended and
never called for, and an old colonial musket.

My great-grandfather, Solomon, was the twelfth child of
Samuel the third. Moving with his father to his older
brother's farm in Dutchess County, New York, he became a
carpenter, and following the call of his trade through New-
burgh, Rockaway and Amsterdam, he settled at last in
Rensselaerville in 1811. Thence, in 1819, in a covered
wagon, he moved his family across New York State to the
present site of the little village of Boston, about twenty
miles south of Buffalo. There the Fosdicks and the Algers,
who apparently had preceded them, built their cabins,
whose huge rough-hewn logs are still to be seen in the
foundation of more than one of the community's early
houses. My grandfather, John Spencer, was carried as a
baby in that covered wagon. He could recall the days when
the family lived in a log cabin. He labored as a pioneer in
making that frontier outpost habitable, and as a carpenter
he helped build its early houses. Then the call for teachers
to instruct the children came and he answered it.

Together with his brothers, Morris and Jesse, my grandfather had attended Griffith's Institute in Springville, ten
miles over the hill from their home—the boys, so family
tradition says, walking the twenty miles daily. His home
must have been intellectually above the average. The records indicate that his Quaker mother, Anna Thorne, was
an extraordinarily able woman. She came from a long line
of Quaker ancestors, reaching back to the days when her
great-great-great-great grandfather in 1657 had signed the
famous Flushing Remonstrance, defying Governor Peter
Stuyvesant's edict against showing hospitality to a Quaker
even for a single night. She had had a good education, was

an avid reader—"She lived with Shakespeare and the Bible," said one of her granddaughters—and she had an important influence on my family's subsequent history. At any rate, my grandfather became a teacher, and in the basement of the church in Boston they still show the room where his first classes were held, and where he taught for a salary of $37.50 for the school season. From that little room he moved out to be a leader in public education, and finally superintendent of education in Buffalo.

In my grandfather's boyhood western New York was taking on new life. Only five years before his arrival there the British in the War of 1812 had burned Buffalo to the ground—only one house left standing—but five years later construction had begun on the Erie Canal and, when the canal was opened in 1825, it made Buffalo one of the chief stations for emigrants from the east to the Great Lakes country. How thrilling the canal was in those days is indicated in a letter from a contemporary traveler: "Commending my soul to God and asking His defense from danger, I stepped aboard the canal boat, and was soon *flying* toward Utica." To be sure, the canal had been stoutly opposed, even on religious grounds. In one Quaker meeting a solemn voice had said: "If the Lord wanted a river to flow through the state of New York, he would have put one there." Then, after a profound silence, another member rose and said simply: "*And Jacob digged a well.*" I have often wished, in facing similar situations, that so brief and crushing a retort could be found to religious reactionaries.

At any rate, in 1819 when my family headed for western

New York, the Erie Canal was under construction, and I suspect that this was one reason for their trek. Then the railroads came. The first train in our country to be drawn by a steam locomotive made its initial run in 1831 from Albany to Schenectady. Just when my grandfather took his first ride on a railway I do not know, but his experience was probably similar to David Crockett's in 1834. "This was a clean new sight to me," wrote Crockett, "about a dozen big stages hung on to one machine, and to start up hill. After a good deal of fuss, we all got seated and moved slowly off, the engine wheezing as if she had the tizzick. By and by she began to take short breaths, and away she went with a blue streak after us. The whole distance is 17 miles, and it was run in fifty-five minutes."

My memories of my grandfather, John Spencer Fosdick, are clear and distinct. He was a rugged, vigorous, determined character. He had come up the hard way and he had in him the austere stuff which that demands. He used to tell us how he had taught himself Latin—his Latin grammar propped up on his carpenter's bench with a block of wood. His bristling hair and full beard were setting for a pair of unforgettable dark eyes that seemed to look clean through us. He could be as gentle as a May morning, but always behind affection was an inherent sternness. Once when the "hired man" accidentally broke a toy gun of mine, my provoked father said "Damn" in my grandfather's presence. I can see yet the way my grandsire turned his blazing eyes on my father and can hear the concentrated rebuke in the way he said "Frank!" And I was profoundly impressed when my father took it meekly, as though Sinai had thundered. A man once came into my brother's office in New York and said: "I don't know whether I want to shake hands with you or not. Your grandfather gave me the thrashing of my life and I have always held it up against the whole Fosdick family." "What did you do to provoke it?" my brother asked. "Nothing at all," he replied. "It was completely unprovoked. Your grandfather had the habit of kicking his shoes off when he came into the schoolroom in the morning and slipping his feet into a pair of carpet slippers that stood beside his desk. One morning we boys got there early and nailed his carpet slippers to the floor. He thrashed every boy in the class."

Nevertheless, from all that I have gathered across the years, listening to many grateful reminiscences of my grandfather's teaching, I judge that such a scene is no adequate picture of his methods. He doubtless shared his generation's rough techniques for enforcing discipline, but he also had a prophetic foresight that surprisingly went beyond them. In a lecture to teachers in 1860, he described a typical parent demanding more corporal punishment in the schools. "I'd thrash everyone who disobeyed my rules or missed their lessons," the parent said. "That's the way I do at home and that's the way I want you to do." On which my grandfather made this comment:

A number of years ago I visited such a school. When I came near the door I thought there was no school, all was so still. But as I entered the door the cause of this unnatural stillness was explained. The teacher held in his hand a new rawhide, which kept the order, but a single glance at the class convinced me there was no happiness there. . . . Come with me to a school I know well. A breathless silence pervades the room. As the teacher kindles into earnestness and eloquence, the children kindle into responsive enthusiasm. Whenever his eye meets theirs he sees the glow of the fire he is lighting in their hearts, and his own gathers new warmth in return. . . . Such a man is fit to teach, and you could scarcely break the spell by which he holds his pupils, though you should give them for playthings shining fragments, broken off from the sun.

That sounds like my grandfather as I knew him. He was a dynamic person, fiercely independent himself, and secretly admiring independence in others even when he seemed most dogmatic in his opinions and stern in his judgments. He was the first Baptist in our family, converted doubtless in the whirlwind evangelistic campaigns that swept western New York in his youth. His father and grandfather had been Episcopalians, and before that the family had been Congregationalists. Just what it was in the Baptists that most impressed him I do not know; the literal meaning of *Baptizo*, immerse, was doubtless part of it; but I suspect that he was attracted by their independent individualism. He was certainly a self-reliant character. In Buffalo he became a vigorous campaigner against alcoholic intemperance; much of his spare time he spent visiting convicts in the prisons—had not Jesus said: "I was in prison and ye came unto me"?— and he risked public disfavor and legal punishment by being the last station on the underground railroad, rowing escaping slaves across the Niagara River to liberty in Canada. My father recalled stormy nights when a signal was tapped on a windowpane, and his father rose from bed and went out to row another boatload of black refugees to their freedom. As his custom was, he had a text for this defiance of the Fugitive Slave Law too, Deuteronomy 23:15: "Thou shalt not deliver unto his master the servant which is escaped from his master unto thee."

My grandmother Fosdick was adorable. I stood in holy awe of grandfather, but I loved her warmly. She, too, had been a schoolteacher. Her father was Reverend Jacob Blain, a Baptist minister. That is, he was a Baptist minister until the church excommunicated him. He did not believe in hell. The kind of God who could operate the hell of his generation's orthodoxy was too much for his credulity and he said so. He wrote a book, *Death Not Life*, proving, so he thought, from the Scripture itself that the impenitent wicked are annihilated, not damned, and pass not into eternal torture but into extinction. For that, the Dearborn Street Baptist Church in Buffalo drove him from its ministry.

Oliver Wendell Holmes once remarked: "He is a wise man who chooses a good grandfather." I have done many foolish things, but my memories of my ancestral background confirm my claim to at least that initial act of wisdom.

Believing in public education in my grandfather's time was not so simple as it is now. In those early days tax-supported public schools faced sturdy opposition. Education of children was properly a family's responsibility, said many; if the poor did not educate their children at home or in private schools, that was their fault, not the public's. Free public schooling, said some, invaded the field of individual initiative, furnished gratuitous education to those "who were better suited to their station without it," and did not

meet the nation's real need for an adequate reserve of
laborers who could very well dispense with education. Many
then regarded public schools, to use our present phrase, as
"creeping socialism."

My grandfather Fosdick's whole life was a fight against
that kind of nonsense. Horace Mann, who died in 1859, had
led a stirring crusade for the idea that education of the
children was the public's responsibility, and I am proud of
the part my family played in that crusade in western New
York. During the sixties and seventies public education
gained powerful momentum and the school system of the
nation was firmly established.

When my grandfather retired from his work in Buffalo,
he accepted the principalship of the Academy in Westfield,
New York, sixty miles to the south, where he bought a farm,
and so unwittingly made possible my own fortunate home.

Beside a syringa bush in front of her home in Westfield
a sixteen-year-old girl, Amie Weaver, stood one day in 1870,
when a swanky young college sophomore breezed up the
street. That was the first time my father and mother saw
each other. Judging by photographs and family traditions,
he was a gay, high-spirited youth. His father had come to
Westfield while he was a student at the University of
Rochester—the first Fosdick in my lineage who ever went
to college—and it was on his first vacation visit to his new
home that he saw that charming girl beside the syringa
bush.

She must have been charming at sixteeen. She was always lovely to look at. She was a village girl, her life cen-

tered in her home, the Academy where she graduated, and the church where she sang in the choir. Her father, a mild, placid, amiable man, without any business ability, was the village grocer, and failing at that, he became an itinerant peddler of general merchandise. I recall him in later years, settled in Buffalo on a small salary that he could count upon, still a gentle, shy, dreamy man, singularly appealing and lovable, of whom we children were always fond. My mother's mother, on the contrary, was an unusually up-and-coming aggressive person, strongly tinctured with the ideas of the contemporary feminists. The first attempt to organize women as a group to obtain equal rights with men had been made at Seneca Falls, New York, in 1848, where a small convention, called together by Elizabeth Cady Stanton and Lucretia Mott, declared war on the whole inferior status of womanhood. My grandmother Weaver caught the fever, and throughout my youth she made our family aware of the insurgent demand of women for revised ideas of their legal and political status and for recognition of their just right to public activity in social causes. How well I recall the apathy, the derisive indifference and the positive opposition with which this emergence of the feminists was greeted! A prominent educator once heard Susan B. Anthony make a speech. It was not so much what she said that shocked him as the fact that a woman should make a public speech at all. "Miss Anthony," he said to her afterward, "that was a magnificent address. But I must tell you that I would rather see my wife or my daughter in her coffin than hear her speaking, as you did, before a public assembly."

The Weavers—anciently Wevre or Weever—were an old

English family, claiming descent from a Norman gentleman, Baron de Wevre, who came to England before the Norman conquest and who was granted a manor in Cheshire by King Edward the Confessor. The first of the family to arrive in America was Clement Weaver, who landed in Massachusetts the same year the Fosdicks came, 1635, but who fifteen years later moved to Rhode Island, very probably seeking religious freedom among the Baptists and Quakers there. For a hundred and fifty years afterward Rhode Island was the home of my mother's ancestors, until in 1800 her great-grandfather, a cooper and farmer, moved to New York, where later her grandfather, a farmer, settled in the village of Portland, near Westfield. Like the Fosdicks, these folk were plain, hard-working pioneers, and their political slant is doubtless indicated by the fact that my mother's father was named Andrew Jackson Weaver. On both sides of my family I have a strong tradition of nonconformity.

The Fosdicks and the Weavers, save for their church relationships, moved in different circles in Westfield, and when that young sophomore appeared, no one would have predicted that Amie Weaver would capture him. When she first saw him he wore a tall, pearl-colored plug hat, and swung a cane. A tintype taken at that period shows him with jet-black curly hair, handsome eyes, and sideburn whiskers. Mother used to say: "Nothing like him had ever been seen in Westfield." The tradition is that when he began surrendering to her charms the Fosdick family at first objected. "Frank," his mother said to him, "you leave Amie Weaver alone; she is too good for you to fool with." Frank, however, was not fooling, and when he graduated from the university and began teaching in Buffalo, the path that began at the syringa bush led to the marriage altar.

My grandfather had been a teacher in Buffalo for twenty-seven years, 1842 to 1869, and my father took over where he left off and went on for fifty-four years more, 1872 to 1926. When in later days I walked down the street in my father's company, I found it convenient to take off my hat and keep it off, for so many boys and girls in the city had been trained under him and under his father before him, that his progress called out an almost continuous salutation.

When my memories begin, we were living on Pennsylvania Street in Buffalo, near the Circle. Where the First Presbyterian Church now stands, I picked wild flowers. Where Hudson Street now runs, circuses annually set up their tents, and from our back fence we could see the wild excitement of Barnum's "Biggest Show on Earth." All recollections of that early home must antedate my seventh year and, vague and fleeting though they are, they bring back clear pictures of a happy household. My father and mother were friendly folk. Neighbors, church folk and school colleagues were frequent visitors. My mother played the piano; my father played the flute—and by ear the piano also; everybody was supposed to sing, and music was a familiar resource and pleasure.

The earliest memory to which I can give a date is June 9, 1883, when I had just passed my fifth birthday. The awesome sense of something ominous hung over the house all that day. I was banished to the back yard; none paid attention to me; I felt like an outcast for guilty deeds unwittingly committed; and when the day ended with everyone else in celebrant mood, I recall yet my bewildered endeavor to understand it all even when they showed me the newborn twins, Edith and Raymond.

A strange assortment of recollections comes from those first six years—going to school for the first time at the Buffalo Normal; sitting in a front pew at the Prospect Avenue Baptist Church, drawing pictures while E. E. Chivers preached and my father led the singing; being bullied by a neighbor's boy and coming whimpering home, where my father told me to go out and thrash him, which I did with unforgettable satisfaction; seeing the stars for the first time on a clear night with two figures outlined there, each with a starry high silk hat upon his head, concerning which I made my first venture in theology, eagerly inquiring if one was God and the other Jesus. Most clearly of all, I recall the comet of 1884. My parents woke me up to see it, a glorious sight, hanging so low over our back roof that I asked my father to go out and get it.

The dark shadows of which I learned later, I personally do not recall. A sister, Ethel, was born, and early died of diphtheria. They expected me to die of it also, and my father held me in his arms watching the signs of death creep over me and looking for the end to come before he laid me down. My maternal grandfather and grandmother were divorced on grounds of incompatibility—a shocking affair in those days, even though there was no scandal. Finances were difficult. A small income and a growing family made a pincers movement against the peace of the home. For the first twenty years of his teaching my father's annual salary was twelve hundred dollars, and then it was raised to fourteen hundred dollars. Only in later years, as a high school principal, did he receive more than that.

Then in my seventh year a heavy blow fell on our home —my mother collapsed in nervous prostration. My father used to tell me how radiantly well she had been as a girl, what a stunning figure she made on horseback. There was trouble, however, in her background. Her brother and sister died of tuberculosis—"consumption" we called it then— and when I was born nobody knew its cause or cure. In all my recollections of my mother, while she was gay and gracious, a busy housekeeper and an endlessly careful and affectionate mother, she was never physically sturdy and strong. Ethel's death, the coming of the twins, three children to care for, and a financial debt to worry over were too much for her. That first nervous breakdown was serious. My mother was taken to Westfield where she could be relieved of all household cares and nursed back to health, and we children, divided between the Fosdick and the Weaver households there, accompanied her, while father taught in Buffalo, coming up to see us over week ends. So Westfield, one of the loveliest villages in the Chautauqua Hills, became for us a second home.

Our family's headquarters were there for only twelve months, but for many years—until I left home altogether— we regularly spent our summers there on the Fosdick farm, to which my grandfather had retired when his ten-year principalship of the Westfield Academy was over. As I glean my memories of the months spent there in the Weaver home when I was seven years old, they are for the most part, as Nanki-Poo sings, "a thing of shreds and patches." I knocked two birds out of a maple tree with a single stone from a slingshot; I had a fight in a ring of admiring spectators at the Academy which I attended, but the teacher stopped it before the outcome was decided; I picked up my first schoolboy smut, which I did not understand but have never forgotten. And once in a while I went up to my grandfather Fosdick's home to see my mother, who for many weeks could barely lift her head from her pillow.

An acquaintance of mine tells me that a few years ago, having friends in Westfield, he stopped for dinner with them while motoring through and, having recently heard me preach at the Riverside Church, he grew expansive in appreciation. An old lady present stood it as long as she could and then exploded. "What!" she said. "That little Harry Fosdick! Don't be ridiculous!"

That year in Westfield I made my first momentous religious decision. It is not easy for me to summarize the religious background of my life. My family, deeply Christian, believed in the church and were always active in its service. Moreover, my parents' faith was so persuasively transmitted by contagion rather than by coercion that I recall in my childhood no revolt against it, only a cordial acceptance and a sensitive response.

In these recollections I shall have ample opportunity to comment on the religious conditions of my time. I simply note here one factor of which, in my childhood, I was unaware: the tornado of revolt against the churches and against the religion for which they stood, which was gathering its threatening forces, making ready to strike. In the middle of the nineteenth century Auguste Comte, the French skeptic, had written that "God has gone unquestionably and forever," and that Jesus was "essentially a charlatan . . . whose long apotheosis will henceforth be greeted with irrevocable silence"; and while Comte's boast that "before the year 1860" he would be "preaching positivism in Notre Dame as the only real and complete religion" turned out to be ridiculous, still the revolt against Christianity and the church continued ominously to gather strength both in Europe and America.

Charles Darwin died when I was four years old. His *Origin of Species*, over twenty years before, had launched the controversy about evolution, and that same year, 1882, Herbert Spencer, who made agnosticism famous, visited the United States on a lecture tour and was greeted with distinguished acclaim. Along with Darwinism, Marxism aroused fear and indignation by identifying its radical social revolt with atheism, and off stage two other disturbing factors, the new Biblical criticism and the new study of comparative religion, were awaiting their cue to complicate the drama of revolt against the religious status quo. Sometimes the new skepticism was loudly lamented even by those who shared it; in 1879 George John Romanes, in his *Candid Examination of Theism*, sadly mourned his loss of faith in God. Sometimes the question of God or no-God was pushed to the side lines and a positive nontheistic humanism arose, as in the Society for Ethical Culture founded by Felix Adler in 1876. One way or another religious revolt was in the air. My sheltered boyhood little guessed what stormy days would soon befall the Faith.

To be sure, we knew about Robert G. Ingersoll. Born on
the western New York frontier in the family of a stern
Calvinistic minister, he had revolted, and by the time I
first heard of him his youthful rebellion had become for
him an absorbing crusade. He called himself an agnostic
but he proclaimed the logical results of atheism: nature
"produces man without purpose, and obliterates him without regret." I recall my father's quoting—not without appreciation of the measure of truth in it—Ingersoll's famous
saying: "An honest God is the noblest work of man." He
was not an important thinker but he was a powerful orator,
and his oft-repeated lecture, "Some Mistakes of Moses," attracted, perplexed and angered huge audiences across the
country. Moreover, he was a good man, fighting lustily for
humane causes. In that dreadful year, 1877, when the army
was crushing the revolt of the striking workers, he said: "I
sympathize with every honest effort made by the children
of labor to improve their condition. That is a poorly gov-
erned country in which those who do the most have the
least. There is something wrong when men are obliged to
beg for leave to toil. We are not yet a civilized people; when
we are, pauperism and crime will vanish from our land."
Ingersoll represents a tragedy, repeated innumerable times
in my day—a man with the makings of a good Christian,
in some of his attitudes and activities displaying a more
Christian spirit than the average run of churchmen, turned
into an atheist by the honest necessity of rebelling against a
crude, incredible orthodoxy. What a Christian Ingersoll
might have been if he had not in his boyhood faced such
dogmas as hopeless predestination and the damnation of

nonelect infants! The loss of Ingersoll to the Christian cause
on account of the reactionary orthodoxy of his early home
and church illustrates the remark of an experienced professor of theology, Borden P. Bowne: "Religion is a dangerous
drug, unless it is wisely administered." Through a long
lifetime I have watched this endlessly repeated tragedy: defenders of the faith, presenting the faith in indefensible
terms, and alienating the minds they might have won.

This problem which was so to concern my later life was,
of course, unknown to me as a boy of seven, and the outstanding event in my personal experience that year in Westfield was quite naturally my baptism into the membership
of the village Baptist Church. It was my first significant,
independent decision. My family were startled by it and
more than a little reluctant about it. I recall my mother's
anxious inquiries and protestations. At seven, how could I
know what it meant to join the church? There is no use now
trying to analyze the emotional basis of my decision, but it
was clear and determined. There was no revival afoot to
put pressure on me; my clearest recollection about my
motive is a sermon by Elder Tennant on foreign missions,
hearing which I secretly made up my mind to be a missionary. At any rate, I intended to be a Christian. That was
my business, I told my family, and not theirs to decide. So
on February 21, 1886, I was immersed. My mother had been
immersed in the creek in wintertime, when the ice had to
be broken to make it possible, but the ceremony in my
case was more merciful. I was so small that a stool was
sunk in the baptistry for me to stand upon, and thus I made
my confession of faith in an ancient ritual but with a genuine

assertion of individual self-committal that had the root of
the matter in it.

At that year's end the family's residence was changed
again. Mother was better. We moved to Lancaster, only
ten miles out from Buffalo. Grandmother Weaver came
with us and took charge of running the household, and once
more—with the addition of mother's sisters, Caroline and
Florence—our family was together and there began for me
about as happy a decade as any boy could have.

Chapter 2.

❦

Boyhood and Youth

GIRLS AND BOYS in this generation are much more
vividly aware of national and world events than we were in
my youth. In 1885 the United States, Great Britain and
Germany were in a tangle in Samoa, and by 1888 warships of
the three powers were there with conflict threatening. Today a boy of ten would hear about such a crisis over the
radio, would see it pictured in the movies, in television,
newspapers and magazines, and might even find it used
for background in the comics. In my boyhood I do not
recall hearing anything about it. The wide, wide world was
called to our attention mainly as a mission field. It grew
vivid to us when missionaries pictured it in all its heathen
need. When I graduated from high school in 1895 the
Turks had just been massacring the Armenians, and my
"oration" was an appeal for that decimated people. I suspect, however, that my impassioned interest had been
aroused because Armenian Christians were being slaugh-
tered by Muslims. Aside from missionary concern the world
at large seemed vague and far away.

The nation's affairs were closer at hand, especially its
politics. My family inherited Civil War Republicanism. I

recall vividly the pro-Blaine, anti-Cleveland discussions in
our household, and later we boys, with a wooden cannon
shooting firecrackers, paraded for Harrison against Cleveland in 1888. From eight to eighteen, however, my recollections have a fairly narrow horizon, and I suspect that
this was typical of American youth in those days. Then we
really were isolationists.

Of the economic situation in the nation our family was
sometimes poignantly conscious. In 1873 a devastating depression had struck the country. Long before I read about
it I heard my family's recollections of that fateful day when
Jay Cooke, the nation's leading financier, folded up, and
the economic collapse began which lasted for five dreadful
years. Its bloody climax was the railroad strike in 1877,
whose worst explosions were in Pittsburgh, but whose effect in Buffalo was so dangerous that the governor put the
entire military force of the state under arms. Indeed, we
have a letter from my father's half-brother, Charles Fosdick
—whose pseudonym, Harry Castlemon, was known to multitudes of youthful readers—in which he said: "When the
railroad troubles occurred in '77, I was a member of the
Seward Guard, the company that put down mob law in
Buffalo. We had a desperate fight with 3000 strikers who
had come out with the avowed intention of hanging us to
the telegraph poles, and we beat them in the end, although
we were badly cut up."

In general, however, our family's sympathies were with
the underdog. We had been underdogs ourselves. My grandfather wrote once: "My father came to western New York
in 1819, when it was the frontier, and we have all known

what such life was, but as a family we struggled against poverty and ignorance, until it is with some degree of pride that I review our record." As I recall our family's discussions, such "pride" was always tinctured with remembrance of the way the have-nots feel when they face the ruthlessness of the strong.

Indeed, far more radical protests against social wrong were brewing than the Fosdick family dreamed. Karl Marx had published the first volume of *Das Kapital* in 1867 and, while its reception in America was delayed, our worsening city slums, increasingly bitter industrial conflicts and deepening social resentments were preparing a hearing for it. I recollect nothing about Marxism in my youth, but echoes of economic unrest and of indignation at the luxury of the few and the poverty of the many were familiar in our home. Social rebellion was in the air. Henry George, who himself had known penury and hunger, wrote *Progress and Poverty* in 1879, and by 1905 it had sold two million copies.

Economic discontent exploded in this country in many forms, from the comparatively mild activities of the Knights of Labor, or the utopian hopes of Edward Bellamy's *Looking Backward*, which was published when I was ten years old, to the revolutionary strategy of the anarchists. To my boyhood all this was a vague and largely unknown background. Even in the church, I recall no serious echoes of it. Nevertheless, in the church the winds of concern about the social situation were rising. Washington Gladden, a well-known minister in Columbus, Ohio—born in 1836, he died in 1918—was one of the major pioneers in courageous insistence on the Christian social gospel. Maurice, Kingsley and Ruskin had spoken out in England, and they were to have many successors here.

Meanwhile, the crying need for social betterment was being answered by reform movements of varied kinds. In the seventies and early eighties the Women's Christian Temperance Union got under way; Clara Barton established the National Society of the Red Cross; the National Association for Woman Suffrage was organized. Strangely enough, long before any similar concern had been shown about the abuse of children, the Society for the Prevention of Cruelty to Animals had been founded in 1866. Then in 1874 a nine-year-old girl, starved and dreadfully bruised and beaten by a heartless foster mother in a New York slum, was brought into court, and on the ground that she was an animal was given the protection of the law. That day saw the birth of the New York Society for the Prevention of Cruelty to Children.

A native of Buffalo may note with pride that the first successful Charity Organization in any city of the nation was established there in 1877. By the close of the century one hundred and thirty-eight cities had followed suit. Across the nation the upsurge of voluntary philanthropic enterprise, widespread and varied, expressed America's concern about the problems of an industrialized society.

Meanwhile, these large affairs, which were to have so momentous an impact on my mature years, were mainly rumor to my boyish mind which was concerned with more intimate interests. Few things are so important in a boy's life as his first gang, and the crowd I fell in with in Lancaster was a supreme piece of good fortune. We went together to the village school until, graduating there, we began commuting to the high school in Buffalo. On Sundays we were a Bible class at the Presbyterian Church under the leadership of an engaging person whom we called "Father Bruce." What he taught us about the Bible memory does not record, but he himself won our loyal admiration. In early youth he had run away from a hard, intolerable home in Vermont and had carved his own fortunes. That gave him standing in our eyes. He was no milk-and-water saint. He knew life in the raw and he understood boys. The high point in his class came when we forced him off the formal lesson and he fell to talking to us about his own experiences in making his way against heavy odds. We stood by him without a break until, late in our decade together, we walked, a very sober group of young pallbearers, at his funeral.

As a gang we were a happy and often hilarious success. We fished Plumb Bottom and Cayuga creeks for miles around. We knew the woods by heart from the spring flower season to nutting in the fall. We swam in the village swimming hole, made life miserable for the townsfolk on Halloween, and rang the church bells furiously at midnight as July Fourth came in. When the tennis craze began, we built a court on which I recall winning one of the first distinctions I ever had—the second prize. As the early teens came on we built our first shanty, "Turks' Den," where under very primitive conditions we could cook and eat and sleep. No elaborate boys' club ever brought more satisfaction to its members than did that shanty, built by our own hands, alongside Plumb Bottom creek. And when we outgrew that we built a larger one which was the center of our life until one fateful day it burned.

Six of us made up that gang, a healthy group of boys then, and, I am glad to add, with good records since. Our moral sense in boyhood sometimes worked in strange ways. One Friday night we stole one of Old Man Watts' fat chickens. Then Saturday morning we volunteered to help him pick berries, and refused the proffered pay—two cents a quart. So Saturday noon we cooked the chicken for a feast, our consciences entirely satisfied. We were not the only gang in town, and once when a rival crew threatened to beat us to the ringing of the bells on July Fourth we forestalled them by stealing the clappers in advance. The Methodist Church bell's clapper was under my bed for a week before it was discovered.

When girls became interesting to us, our activities widened. There were parties in the old-fashioned country style, with all the attendant gallantries afterward, "seeing Nellie home." Sleigh rides and skating parties, hayrack rides and picnics—many an old-timer like myself must often wonder whether modern youths with their more sophisticated implements of pleasure have half so good a time. My own love life must have had an early start, for when I was ten years old my heart was disturbed and I wrote my first love lyric. I am glad it is no longer in circulation, for it began,

Fairer than the gardens that Babylon's princes kept,

and proceeding through a series of resounding historic comparisons came to a crashing climax,

> Fairer than a fuchsia—
> All this and more is Lucia!

Life was not without its boyish humiliations. When I graduated from the village school I made a hit with a recitation, and so many praised me that it went to my head. When next I was scheduled to appear, at a social event that packed the Presbyterian Church, I took it for granted I would "mow 'em down" again. I didn't. The poem I was supposed to recite began,

> The weaver's thoughts were wandering
> Afar on a distant track.

That was as far as I ever got. I repeated twice the information about the weaver's wandering thoughts and then ignominiously sat down, and afterward went home to weep bitterly.

The family's life in Lancaster was fundamentally happy, as it always was. Those were the days of Chautauqua Literary and Scientific Circles, and in the village group my father and mother were active participants. I can see my father yet, sitting on the floor preparing charts to illustrate his lecture on the development of the alphabet, and in our family archives we still have two essays which our mother presented, one on Charlemagne and the other on Madame de Staël. Those were the days when a community's music had to be self-created, and my father was a leader. I recall his presiding at an old folks' concert where, dressed in colonial costumes, the townspeople gave an exciting evening of early American music.

At home the basic security of love and loyalty was so taken for granted, that no other possibility was thought of, and whatever problems and tragedies came, the stability and happiness of the family were unquestionable. Problems and tragedies, however, did come. My mother's sister, Florence, at twenty-eight years of age, died in our home of tuberculosis, and her brother, Albert—thirty years old—returned from a vain search for health in California to die of the same disease four months later. I saw him die. I often wonder that that sight was permitted me, but I recall clearly the pathetic skeleton of that dying man, gasping for breath in his last hour and crying "Air!" My mother's health improved slowly. When I was ten my father took me into his sorrowful confidence, sharing with me the physician's prediction that she would probably not live another year. But live she did, seeing her children through the ups and downs of illness and the difficulties of our strenuous growing up with such successful care that in my memories she never appears as an invalid. At last she was well enough so that grandmother Weaver returned to Westfield, and in a smaller house Mother took over the family's management.

My father was a great schoolteacher. To thousands of boys and girls in Buffalo he was affectionately known as "Pop." One of them told me this typical story about him when he was principal of the Masten Park High School:

"Your father was one of the most powerful influences in my life. Once I represented the school in a public-speaking contest. I dreadfully wanted to win. I worked very hard, but lost. They gave me the second prize, and the first prize went to a rival school. When I came down from the platform that night I was one of the most brokenhearted boys you could have found on earth. I couldn't keep the tears back. Your father guessed how I was feeling, so he followed me out of the hall until he caught me alone before I left the building. 'Son,' he said, 'I want to see you smile.' So I forced a smile. 'Son,' he said, 'I want to see your shoulders back.' So I squared my shoulders. 'Son,' he said, 'chin up.' 'There,' said your father, 'that's better! Now you can go home.' And," added the man, "in all these years since, I never have been in a tight place without recalling that."

Thus understanding youth, my father understood his children. Many a time in later years, hearing expounded some new, progressive idea concerning the rearing of children, I have wondered why it was called new, because it was the familiar method of my childhood's home. We were a democratic family from the start. Among my earliest recollections are family conferences where all of us were called together to talk over some problem which concerned the whole household. We youngsters were invited to say what we thought. I never recall feeling that commands were handed down to me by a dictator. My father's typical method in getting something done he wanted done was to ask us what we really thought about it ourselves, and even when I asked him for counsel I was fairly certain to have the question thrown back at me—what did I think myself? So from the beginning we were trained for independence. That was the end and aim of our upbringing—to throw us on our own and enable us to handle ourselves.

Far from lessening paternal authority this method strengthened it. To feel that by unwise, wrong behavior we

had let down our parents who had trusted us to be wise
and right was in itself so severe a punishment that other
kinds were superfluous. I recall no corporal chastisement,
although tradition has it that when I was a mere toddler my
father spanked me for strewing a set of Shakespeare on the
floor after he had told me not to; and once I remember
being shut up in a closet until a spell of bad temper was
under control. Paternal authority, however, was uniformly
of another sort. Starting for school one morning my father
turned to my mother, who was waving him good-by, and
said: "Tell Harry he can cut the grass today, if he feels like
it." Then after a few steps he turned back and added: "Tell
Harry he had better feel like it!" In a recent article in *The
Reader's Digest* I called that the best advice ever given me.

The main source of unhappiness for me in early school
days was my religion. I took it desperately in earnest. I
judge that from the beginning I was predestined to religion
as my predominant interest and major vocation, for from
the time I overrode all objections and joined the church
when I was seven, I was always struggling with it. The
happy aspects of it I found in my family, where Christianity
was the natural, practical, livable spirit of the home. But
some of the most wretched hours of my boyhood were
caused by the pettiness and obscurantism, the miserable
legalism and terrifying appeals to fear that were associated
with the religion of the churches.

It may be that the fear of hell began earlier in my childhood than I now recall. Like many other children then, I
was introduced to the Bible through three books, *Line upon*

Line and *Precept upon Precept*, covering the Old Testament, and *The Peep of Day*, covering the New. As I remember my parents reading them to me before I could read myself, they were only exciting stories which thrilled me, but reading them now one runs upon reiterated appeals to terror intended to frighten naughty youngsters into being good: "God will bind them in chains and put them in a lake of fire. There they will gnash their teeth and weep and wail forever. . . . They shall not have one drop of water to cool their burning tongues." My guess is that my parents omitted passages like that. At any rate, it was in Lancaster that, so far as I now recall, the thought of God became a horror to me.

There being no Baptist church in Lancaster, we divided our allegiance between the Presbyterians and the Methodists. The Presbyterian Sunday School and the Methodist Young People's Meeting usually found me present, and on Sunday mornings the family attended one church or the other, as we chose. In general, my recollections of all this are happy. The Methodist minister whom I recall most clearly was Peter Thompson, father of Dorothy Thompson, the journalist, and he was kindness itself. Certainly, William Waith, who for over fifty years was minister of the Presbyterian Church in Lancaster, was an able and learned man, concerning whose sermons—especially a series on the ontological, teleological and cosmological proofs of God's existence—my chief memory is a sense of holy awe and a complete failure to understand anything he said. While I do not recall anything terrifying or unhappy in the ordinary ministrations of the village churches, I do recall that when

migrant evangelists came and heated up the town for a
revival, all hell opened its yawning mouth to receive us,
and among the major sins sure to land us there were
dancing, card playing and theatergoing. I hold it everlast-
ingly against them and all their kind that once, as a young
boy, because of their idiotic legalism, I refused my own
father's invitation to see Edwin Booth in *Hamlet*.

Not all the evangelistic campaigns then were terrifying.
I recall listening to Dwight L. Moody with boyish respect.
His preaching and Ira Sankey's singing are still vivid in my
recollection. They made a deep impression on western New
York. I remember one sermon in which Moody spent considerable time attacking the Sabbath-breaking wickedness
of Sunday newspapers, and I recall my father's acid comment afterward that, since Sunday newspapers are prepared
on Saturday, Moody would have been more logical had he
attacked Monday newspapers instead. That kind of legalism,
however, did not represent the real Moody, whom Henry
Drummond called "the biggest human I ever met." The
sermon of his which stands out most clearly in my recollection was a blazing attack upon the elder brother in the
parable of the prodigal son. A woman had written Moody a
letter defending that highly respectable gentleman, and
Moody in answer fell upon him with devastating censure—
"respectable," to be sure; in his own way, conscientious; but
mean-spirited, bad-tempered, narrow-minded and altogether
contemptible. I remember my father's enthusiasm about
that.

I was a sensitive boy, deeply religious, and, as I see it
now, morbidly conscientious, and the effect upon me of hell-

fire-and-brimstone preaching was deplorable. I vividly recall weeping at night for fear of going to hell, with my
mystified and baffled mother trying to comfort me. Once,
when I was nine years old, my father found me so pale that
he thought me ill. The fact was that I was in agony for
fear I had commited the unpardonable sin, and reading that
day in the book of Revelation about the horrors of hell, I
was sick with terror. I must not overemphasize this. Doubtless these onsets of morbidity were sporadic; to picture
them as overshadowing my childhood would be absurd; I
was too healthy and happy not to throw them off; but it
still is true that in those early days the iron entered my
soul and the scene was set for rebellion against the puerility
and debasement of a legalistic and terrifying religion.

In all this struggle my family was on the side of sanity.
Religion was a force in our family rather than a form, but it
was always there, vital and real, and I recall yet some
special occasions when family prayers made movingly explicit the unity and loyalty of the home. My father was
more than a father—he was a companion and chum. There
was a kind of fierce tribal loyalty in our home. We stood
together, and we children knew that through thick and thin
our parents were on our side. We read books and played
games together. I recall especially euchre, checkers, crib-
bage. Father enjoyed the swimming hole as much as we
did, and at last the great days came when he took me
fishing with him in a rowboat on Niagara River, where under
the spell of comradeship in sport he got over to me more
good sense than I would ever have taken in by way of
command.

Books were one of the most rememberable aspects of my

boyhood—all sorts of books from Oliver Optic to Scott, Dickens, Bulwer Lytton, Charles Reade; from Jane Porter's *Scottish Chiefs* and *Thaddeus of Warsaw*, to Anna Sewell's *Black Beauty*, Edward Eggleston's *The Hoosier Schoolmaster*, and Ingraham's *The Prince of the House of David*; from Lew Wallace's *Ben Hur* and R. D. Blackmore's *Lorna Doone*, to Artemus Ward and Mark Twain. As for poetry, I can hear my father yet quoting the then popular J. G. Holland:

> I've dreamed of sunsets where the sun supine
> Lay rocking on the ocean like a god,
> And threw his weary arms far up the sky,
> And with vermilion-tinted fingers toyed
> With the long tresses of the evening star.

Children have a rich feast of reading provided for them now, but we were not starved either.

The heaviest burden that rested on the household was lack of money. Out of my father's slender salary he had to support us and contribute as well to his own parents and to my mother's family. How he managed it I never have been able to guess. I recall my mother once in tears because, she said, she had lowered the cost of our food and clothing to what she thought was bottom level, and now she had to get it lower still. While such memories crop up, however, we children were unaware of lacking the necessities. I recall that we counted the pennies, but there always seemed to be enough to count and to satisfy our needs. I did not know until years afterward the often heartbreaking struggles through which my father and mother went in their endeavor to make both ends meet.

It seems strange, then, that in 1894 they bought a house of their own in Buffalo and we said good-by to Lancaster. The house was inexpensive and the financing of it was altogether mortgages. Still, it was our house, and my memories of moving into it light up the differences between the old world I had been living in and the world we have now. In Lancaster there had been no gas or electric lights, no indoor plumbing, no running water, no telephone. One winter day I boarded one of the first electric streetcars that ran in Buffalo, and seeing the old-fashioned cash register at the front of the car, mistook it for a thermometer and commented on how much colder it was than I had supposed. In Buffalo we moved into a house that seemed to me miraculous—we had gaslight fixtures, a bathtub and running water.

I know I must be an old man now when I note the sort of things I can remember. I recall the itinerant peddlers, some with wagons that were dry goods' stores carrying an amazing variety of household articles, some specializing in tinware, their vehicles hung all over with pots and pans, and some patent-medicine vendors who put on a slapstick vaudeville show to attract the crowd. I recall the last of the traveling cobblers, who went from house to house repairing the family's boots and shoes. I remember the days when tobacco chewing was a general custom, and cuspidors —"spittoons" to us—were a necessary article of furniture not only in every public place but commonly in private homes. I recall the beginning of bicycles. The first bicycle factory in the United States was organized when I was minus one year old—manufacturing, of course, the old monstrosities with a huge wheel in front and a small one behind. I learned to ride on one of them and vividly recollect the "headers" I took along with everyone else who rode them, and, as well, the excitement when the first "safeties" came in. I remember the days before hard-surfaced roads when in springtime even the main streets of the village were almost axle deep in mud. Illumination in my childhood was by oil lamps, and I recall when gas lighting came in, with necessary signs under the gas jets, "Do not blow out the gas. Turn it off!" Of course I remember pretelephone days— the first telephone exchange in the country, with twenty-one subscribers, was set up in New Haven, Connecticut, the year that I was born. Recalling the prebathroom days, I can almost believe the story that when in 1907 the Statler Hotel in Buffalo for the first time in history offered every guest a room and private bath at moderate cost, one rustic occupant wrote home: "The bathroom is so wonderful that I can hardly wait till Saturday night."

Strange recollections rise in memory, as I think of those old days—plank sidewalks; wooden Indians outside every tobacco store; iron hitching posts for horses and stone landing blocks for carriage passengers in front of houses and stores; mansard roofs, cupolas and porches screened with scrolls of ironwork as standard architecture; tomatoes called "love apples" and still regarded with suspicion by some as inedible; photographers propping our heads with a pair of metal prongs to keep them quiet long enough for the likeness to register; the parlors, used only on state occasions, with their horsehair furniture and whatnots in the corner; and even the old custom of carrying food to the mouth on a knife, which gave rise to the quatrain:

I eat my peas with honey;
I've done it all my life.
It makes the peas taste funny
But it keeps them on my knife.

Moving to Buffalo did not sever my association with the Lancaster gang. They, too, attended high school in the city, and all of us were members of the Cadet Corps of the National Guard. Pacifist though I long have been, I look back on that early military training with satisfaction. There were two companies of us, making a battalion, and in the Sixty-fifth Regiment Armory we conducted an interesting experiment in running a voluntary, democratic American militia. We did our own recruiting and elected our own officers. Obedience, orderliness, spick-and-span care of uniforms and equipment, and pride in the Corps are my chief recollections of the personal meaning of this "military" experience—plus the first exciting chance I can recall at leadership. I had been one of the youngest boys in the gang, a follower, not a leader. One day, however, having been promoted from private to corporal, the captain turned over a squad to me for drill. I can feel the thrill yet when I heard my voice snapping out orders and saw that squad doing what I told them to. Later I became adjutant of the battalion, and one proud day I brought the two companies into parade formation, and saluting the major, recited: "The battalion is formed, sir."

Marching with the National Guard in civic parades was one of the high spots in the experience of the Corps, but the most exciting days came with camping out. We began modestly, a few days at a stretch, and worked up to a

climax—two weeks in our tents on the shores of Lake
Chautauqua. In those days war seemed very far away from
the United States. I recall no association between all this
"military" drill and any thought of actual battle. We were
simply imitating peacefully some of the activities of our
elders, and I learned a lot.

My high school days began with a year under my father's
principalship in the "Annex"—the nucleus from which the
Masten Park High School later came—and went on to my
last three years in Old Central. The teaching was in the
classical tradition. My father himself taught Latin and
Greek and in that heritage I was reared at home and in
school. The most influential teacher I had in high school
was Arthur Detmers, who made the ancient classics live
so vitally that I gladly gave up Saturdays to the endeavor
to make Cicero's orations, when translated, sound like real
orations, and Vergil's *Aeneid* sound like real poetry. Beyond
his classroom work, however, Arthur Detmers brought a
group of us into his own home. How did he ever find the
time to do what he did for us! He introduced us to the
classics of English literature; he opened the doors to Browning and Wordsworth; he read the best of Walt Whitman to
us; and to my amazement I record that he and I read aloud
together the whole of Lecky's *History of European Morals*.
He was one of the best friends I ever had, and even yet
some of the great passages in the English poets carry my
recollection gratefully back to him.

In high school I began trying to speak in public, but I
was a shy, embarrassed youngster on my feet. Elected vice-
president of the debating society when the president-elect

was absent, I was petrified with stage fright, and taking the
chair, could not even say "Thank you." Those, however,
were the days of public speaking and debate and, like it or
not, we were supposed to be able to stand up and talk. That
debating society forced me into public speaking, and before
I was through with it, stage fright, while always present,
was not the whole of the experience. Once in a while I got
something across and liked it.

I was at first a socially awkward boy. A professor of mine
once said, in a theological seminary lecture, that an honest
man looking back on the things whose recollection makes
him cringe, must confess that it is not his real sins he feels
most ashamed of but his humiliating gaucheries. I agree. I
was clumsy and ill at ease, unsure of the proper thing to
do, embarrassed in conversation, sensitive and self-conscious
about my awkwardness, and unhappy at not being able to
put my best foot forward. Doubtless all youths go through
this stage; I suspect that I had more than my share of it.

I felt more at ease in the church. Always a large part of
the family's life centered there, and I took to it like a duck
to water. When I try to reconstruct in my imagination the
boy I then was, I cannot quite make myself out. Already I
was independent enough not to acquiesce in everything
I saw and heard in church. Certainly I saw some raw sides
of the church—one ecclesiastical trial, for example, that was
an outrage on ordinary decency, where the defendant,
charged with some misdemeanor, came in armed with a
heavy cane to protect himself in case of need. Still, I was
deeply loyal to the church, as I was a loyal patriot although
I knew the nation was not perfect. I was invincibly religious,

and yet, as I recall the pranks I enjoyed, the sports I loved, the books I read, the healthy living that filled my days, I was not "pious." Whenever anybody discussed religion, however, I wanted to be there. I still recall that awestruck hour when Munkácsy's painting, "Christ before Pilate," was exhibited in Buffalo and my father and I went to see it. Something indescribable and unforgettable happened inside of me that day.

No account of those boyhood years would be complete that left out the summers in Westfield. They were one of the healthiest experiences of my youth—fishing the creek, exploring the gorge up into the Chautauqua Hills, blackberrying on grandfather's hill farm, swimming in Lake Erie, camping, making friends with the village boys and girls, and finding one of my most attractive sweethearts there.

One of the interesting members of the family living in Westfield was my father's half-brother, famous then as a writer of boys' books under the pseudonym, Harry Castlemon. He was a startling character even to look at, a handsome man with far-flung mustachios, who wore a black sombrero hat racily tilted and could tell a story that would raise your hair. He had served in the Civil War on a "tinclad" on the lower Mississippi. He must have been in the thick of battle for he came out of the war with a bullet in his leg, a broken nose and a saber cut in his head. Returning to live quietly in Westfield, he wrote books for boys that, along with those of G. A. Henty and Horatio Alger, Jr., were read by my generation with breathless excitement. Grandfather Fosdick, I recall, did not altogether approve of him, partly no doubt because he drank too much, but also because his thrillers were not edifying. Nevertheless, in my younger boyhood I ransacked Harry Castlemon's library every summer for exciting tales, and welcomed each new book he wrote as a gift from the gods.

Such was my boyhood, confirming a remark by Henry S. Canby: "In our town, and I think in the American nineties generally, home was the most impressive experience in life."

Nevertheless, we were not left untouched by the critical economic and social problems of the nation. We knew about the Haymarket riot in Chicago in 1886 and the shocking Homestead battle between the steel workers and Pinkerton's men in Pittsburgh in 1892; and when the great depression in '93 landed on our people we felt the impact. Theodore Dreiser visited western New York in '94 and wrote that along the Buffalo water front he "could not help but see that, in spite of our boasted democracy and equality of opportunity, there was as much misery and squalor and as little decent balancing of opportunity against energy as anywhere else in the world."

I clearly remember those dreadful days when penury stalked the country, millions were unemployed, and the *Pittsburgh Dispatch* could say that the cause of the workers everywhere in America was hopeless. One section of Coxey's "army" marched through Westfield that summer and spent a night there, on its way to appeal in Washington that national relief be provided the unemployed millions and their destitute families. I can see yet the frayed and tired-out Coxeyites cooking their meal over open fires in the baseball field. All that Westfield desired was to be rid of them, and when they reached Washington Coxey was arrested and his "army" disintegrated.

One vivid recollection of those days is my father looking at his monthly pay check and commenting that, while a schoolteacher's salary was very meager, he at least could count on it, while millions had none at all. Nevertheless, despite all the calamity, no picture of the American background in my youth would be complete which stopped with that. Despite disaster and hardship, that generation was permeated with glorification of the rugged individual who began with everything against him and achieved success. Such a man was the national ideal. If one was a privileged aristocrat to start with, what credit did he deserve? But if one was born in penury and by dint of ability, industry and frugality attained wealth and station, he was a real man. The main point with Lincoln, my generation said, was not that he was born in a log cabin but that he got himself out of it. The American worship of "that bitch-goddess, success," as William James called it, has been bitterly condemned, but, in one form or another, it was inevitable. The pioneer virtues had been and were grit, gumption, daring, intrepidity in tackling forbidding situations; the individual had to depend pretty much upon his own self-reliant prowess; and if he proved that he had the stuff in him to meet the hazards, whip the difficulties and rise from indigence to plenty, he was a man. Ray Stannard Baker said that his father, who was a pioneer, had two mottoes: "Admit nothing to be a hardship," and "When in doubt, CHARGE!"

Moreover, until the western frontiers closed, about the

time I graduated from high school, the opportunities thus to prove oneself a man were exciting to multitudes, and even without pioneering westward, the hope of "striking it rich," the risky love of a gambler's chances, the faith that "there is always room at the top," that "you can't keep a good man down," that "every man has a goose that lays golden eggs, if he only knew it," was our characteristic national mood.

Horatio Alger, Jr.—who died while I was in college— wrote one hundred and nineteen books on this theme, and they sold at least twenty million copies. *Strive and Succeed*; *Bound to Rise*; *Luck and Pluck*; *Brave and Bold*—no one who did not live when these stories were being written about boys who started with nothing, faced all kinds of adversity and ended on top, can possibly imagine how aptly they fitted the mood of millions. Voltaire had said that "history is filled with the sound of silken slippers going downstairs and wooden shoes coming up," and while silken slippers going down were not obvious here, wooden shoes coming up were the nation's pride.

Moreover, the illustrations of such "rugged individualism" and its success were popularly intoxicating. Andrew Carnegie, child of a destitute immigrant family which landed in the United States in 1848, as a boy of eleven obtained a job in a cotton factory at one dollar and twenty cents a week, and by 1901 was the foremost steel manufacturer in the country. John D. Rockefeller, born on a central New York farm, was working ten hours a day digging potatoes when he was thirteen; twenty-seven years later, when I was born, he was a tycoon. Like it or not, this was America. One could not tell what unimaginable prizes awaited in-

dustry, determination and perseverance. James Truslow
Adams vouches for the fact that a woman in a far western
city, a social leader, had an assistant plumber fired because
he came to her house drunk. Ten years later he returned
from the mountains, sobered and worth millions, and, unaware that she had once ordered him out of her house, the
lady opened the city's most fashionable cotillion with him
as her partner. As Adams says: "That could happen only
in America."

Granted the malign perversions of such typical Ameri-
canism! Its potential dangers are obvious—money-madness,
crude and loutish standards of success, and all the evils of
a crass materialism. American culture escaped none of those
perils, and Americans have been mercilessly and justifiably
condemned for the sordid consequences. That, however, is
far from being the whole story. My family, like multitudes
of others, fought a frontier battle against "poverty and ignorance," but it was not for materialistic ends alone. Millions
of immigrants, fleeing the hopeless destitution of their European homes, found a land of promise where families could
rise from the bottom up. And in most cases, I suspect, even
when wealth was gained, it was not the wealth which
primarily counted, but the satisfaction of achievement, the
relish of starting nowhere and arriving somewhere, despite
hazard and handicap.

Nevertheless, the American background in my childhood
was becoming increasingly materialistic, and I thank God
that I was reared in a family where spiritual values were
cherished and conserved.

Chapter 3.

❦

Revolt Against Orthodoxy

M Y RETROSPECTIVE PICTURE of myself when I
entered college presents a very simple-minded boy—appreciative faculties wide awake, critical faculties asleep. I was
prepared to transform into romantic adventure almost anything that came along, and to make an adored idol of anyone
older and wiser than myself. My first letters home from
Colgate University were all agog with thrill and wonder. I
fell in love with the village of Hamilton and with the college
it enshrined. Everything about it seemed marvelous. I had
never been so far away from home before, had never seen
a larger college, had no disconcerting criteria by which to
judge the smallness of the school and the outward meager-
ness of its equipment.

At Colgate I found what I needed most—the impact of
some very stimulating personalities. Nevertheless, I look
back now with amusement at that simple-minded freshman
who marveled at the upperclassmen, stood in adoring awe of
the professors' learning, thought no other college could
house such teachers, desired nothing so much as to be like
some of the seniors, and in general saw opening before him

the most alluring opportunity for a college course that any boy could possibly enjoy.

My freshman year was largely spent in that mood. I joined the Delta Upsilon Fraternity, made fast friends, found a chum after my own heart, Clyde Sunderland, discovered that I could make the grade in the classroom competition, found nothing in the religious life of the village church or the campus to disturb the even tenor of my accustomed thinking. It was a good year. I recall no disquieting premonitions of the explosion that was to follow.

To be sure, I became a convinced believer in evolution, and I thought that that might shock the family. It may be that I wrote home about it, but my recollection is that on one of my vacations, at the dinner table on Sunday, when all were present and I thought that I could get the greatest possible effect, I announced as impressively as I could manage it: "I have made up my mind that I believe in evolution." There was dead silence for a moment and then a response that took the wind out of my sails. "Well," said my father, "I believed that before you were born."

The psychologists have a timetable of average ages when the critical faculties of boys and girls wake up and doubt begins. I was a little late, but the time inevitably came. I recall no special pulling of the trigger that brought on the explosion, but the setting is clear. At the end of my freshman year my father suffered a nervous breakdown, and in particular the family's finances were to him a burdensome anxiety. Thanks to a college scholarship, I had taken only three hundred dollars from the family exchequer for my freshman year, but I knew he was worrying about the repetition even of that expenditure. Family loyalty was too strong in all of us to let him stand that strain, and I volunteered to stay home and earn my keep until he should be on his feet again.

That year at home was a strange hodgepodge. I did not at all earn my keep, and it was a shock to discover how little I rated on the business market. To mend matters, I took a course in stenography and typewriting, but nobody wanted me. So I became a clerk in a bookstore at four dollars a week, and was overjoyed when I was raised to six. Meanwhile, father was enough better to return to his teaching and the family's anxieties smoothed out.

Whatever of importance happened to me that year at home took place behind the scenes. Something was waking up in me which I myself did not understand. I had hours of inner exaltation, with premonitions in them of truth to be seen and work to be done, that both excited and sobered me. I recall Saturday afternoons when, with a book of poetry, I slipped away to the lakeside in Delaware Park and had a high time in solitude. The content of these hours was vague, but Wordsworth's phrases concerning similar experiences in his boyhood—"Aeolian visitations," "Trances of thought and mountings of the mind"—describe them. They suggested no special vocation and called for no special action. They were self-sufficient, mystically complete in their own deep satisfactions, but their influence unwittingly was reorienting my life. I question whether even those closest to me noted any difference. What was happening to me was nothing I could talk about; I did not know its meaning. Outwardly I did the best I could in handling an awkward year—clerking at the bookstore, reading voraciously on the side, teaching a Sunday School class of younger boys, bicycling for exercise, and playing, where it would cost me nothing, with such of my old high school friends as were still in town.

Behind this outward façade of my very unimpressive nineteenth year, my first searching questions rose concerning the whole structure of religious thought in which I had been reared. The more I was aware of an inner center of spiritual satisfaction and resource, the more independent I became of the outward formulas of religion in which I had been trained. How I could have escaped this questioning so long I do not now understand. I had taken for granted the literal accuracy of the Bible as sound science and history, and while the Biblical days of creation had been rationalized into eras, and what could not be otherwise disposed of was read as poetry, still the inerrant inspiration of the Bible was assumed. Grandmother Fosdick once told me that if I did not believe in the whale's swallowing Jonah, I must in good logic surrender the whole Bible and all my religion. As for the church's major doctrines, I had not seriously questioned them. I recall, in high school days, talking with a boy who doubted the doctrine of immortality and who argued with me against its truth. I was horrified that such an attitude was possible. The fundamentalists in later years have hated me plentifully, but I started as one of them.

Just when the first crack in the old structure began I am not sure, but it concerned the stories of the Hebrew strong man, Samson. So childishly my religious doubts commenced. Why, I argued with myself, should I feel under duress to believe the Samson stories, while feeling under no similar coercion to believe tales about the Greek strong man, Hercules? Answering that naïve question—as after some inner tussling I did, by acknowledging that there was no more reason to believe Hebrew than Greek folklore—the conclusion was plain: I did not have to believe anything simply because it was in the Bible. How stunning that conclusion was, it is not easy now for an educated mind to understand. For me, as for many others in my time, it was revolutionary. The old basis of authority was gone. Truth was an open field to be explored. What one believed had to be discovered. Nothing could be settled by a text.

I suspect that this Samson-Hercules question had first arisen in high school days, but it was after my freshman year in college that I faced the full effect of an honest answer to it. What finally smashed the whole idea of Biblical inerrancy for me was a book by Andrew D. White, president of Cornell University, entitled *History of the Warfare of Science with Theology in Christendom*. It was a ponderous two-volume work, but I devoured it. It seemed to me unanswerable. Here were the facts, shocking facts about the way the assumed infallibility of the Scriptures had impeded research, deepened and prolonged obscurantism, fed the mania of persecution, and held up the progress of mankind. I no longer believed the old stuff I had been taught. Moreover, I no longer merely doubted it. I rose in indignant revolt against it.

When I returned to college for my sophomore year, my friends who had known me as a devout Christian were astonished. Wild horses could not have dragged me into church; I would have none of it. The old class prayer meetings saw me no more. In bull sessions I was a disturbing upsetter of the saints. One group of pious souls—a prayer circle of the Y.M.C.A.—used to pray for my return to the faith, but I was a long way from returning. Religion had been to me the center of my personal life; the church had had my devoted loyalty; and in the family religion had been real and vital. When my religion was disturbed, I was disturbed from the ground up. Others might pass through this phase of questioning and doubt and take it easily. I took it hard. All my sophomore year I thought fast and furiously.

I do not mean that I did nothing else except struggle over religion. I had a good time. I was in on all the fun the campus afforded. But behind the scenes I was vehemently rebelling against the kind of bibliolatry and theology I had been taught. This struggle was mental rather than moral. I had the normal moral difficulties of a healthy growing youth, but as I see it now they never very seriously threatened me. I cannot recall that a loose woman ever attracted me, and when relationships with a girl approached the point of danger, either in loss of self-control or in a greater self-committal than I cared to make, there was something in me that waved a red flag in ample time.

My real struggle concerned the intellectual credibility of Christian faith. Morally I went on trying to grow up, experimenting as youth must do, and learning by making a fool of myself as human beings always will. Intellectually, however, I faced a disturbing fight, from which, as easily as not, I might have emerged minus religion. The story of that

struggle, while I tell it as intimately mine, is not alone autobiography but history, for through that same kind of conflict went multitudes of youths in my generation, some
emerging as fundamentalists, others as liberals, and others
as agnostics and unbelievers. That was the choice in those
days.

At any rate, when I left for college at the beginning of
my junior year I said to my mother: "I'll behave as though
there were a God, but mentally I'm going to clear God out
of the universe and start all over to see what I can find."
That was a large order and I feel now mingled amusement
and admiration as I recall the lad who tackled it. No one
watching me during my junior year, however, would have
supposed that I was tackling it very hard. It was my gayest
year in college. To be sure, gaiety in that community was
simple and uncostly, but there was plenty of fun afoot and
I played the traditional junior, having my fling. Behind
closed doors, however, I was beginning to doubt some of
my doubts. My rebellion came full circle and I started questioning my questions. There was no thought of returning
to old positions, but I began seeing the possibility of new
positions—old spiritual values in new mental categories.
Books, like those of John Fiske of Harvard, helped, and
I was encouraged to hope for a solution by the fact that
men of first-rate intellectual eminence had evidently found
one.

Personalities on the Colgate campus helped. The strength
of Colgate in my student days was the quality of its professors and their personal accessibility to the students. There
were less than forty men in my class when we graduated.
The college community was small enough so that a professor

became a friend as well as a teacher. "Prof. Jim"—James M. Taylor, the mathematician; "Kai Gar"—Newton Lloyd Andrews, the Grecian; "Craw"—William Henry Crawshaw, in English literature; "Tommie"—Ralph Thomas, in public speaking; "Johnny"—John Greene, the Latinist; "Brig"— Albert Perry Brigham, the geologist; "Bobbie"—Robert Moore, in German; these men were my friends and I was at home with them and their families. I took a course in Modern Greek alone with "Kai Gar" and we met in his home study. All these men were first-rate in their departments; they were intellectually respectable and in one or two cases eminent; and they all were men of Christian faith. This fact had an incalculable influence in maintaining my confidence that there must be some way of being both intelligent and Christian, and that at any rate the attempt was worth making.

Most of all Professor William Newton Clarke, of the Theological Seminary, helped me. He was a religious liberal. His new book, *An Outline of Christian Theology*, had already brought down upon him the invectives of the orthodox. We heard the echoes of the controversy and admired him as a heretic. Other universities gave him honorary degrees, and news of British admiration for his work fanned the flames of our pride. Long before I knew him as a loyal personal friend, he was a powerful influence in my life. Here was an honest man, saying what he really thought, defying the obscurantism of old opinions and daring to phrase the Christian faith in the categories of modern thinking. Every time he walked across the campus he was a living argument that it could be done.

I remember once, as an undergraduate, falling in with

him by chance and walking in his company. He soon had me talking about my problems. Troubled about the virgin birth of Jesus, I remarked that I could believe that Jesus was spiritually but not that he was physically divine. "Physically divine?" said Dr. Clarke with a quizzical inflection. There was dead silence for a moment and then I said: "That is nonsense, isn't it?" "Of course it is nonsense," he answered; and then added in effect that if I would start by seeing that any divinity in Jesus must consist in his spiritual quality, I might get somewhere. Looking back on the conventional orthodoxy of those days, I can understand now why the die-hards hated him, and why we youngsters turned to him for help.

So I came to the end of my junior year, not believing much but at least believing in the possibility of finding something to believe, and, with that much of a solution in hand, I came to the choice of my vocation. Although at first I had intended to be a teacher, like my father and grand-father, I had played with other ideas—the law and medicine —but they had no attraction for me. I really wanted to teach. Along with that desire, however, had always gone my overmastering concern about religion, and that concern was only deepened by my struggle for a credible faith. The ministry began to loom as a possibility. Not preaching —I did not at first picture my ministry as centered in the pulpit—but teaching. If I could only teach some subject associated with religion! When I went home at the end of my junior year, my mind was seething with that idea, and it was my father who precipitated the decision. We were taking a walk one evening, talking about my problem when, turning to me, he said: "Harry, you know that you will never be satisfied outside the Christian ministry." That brought me to jell.

When I returned to college as a senior and the rumor spread that I was headed for the ministry, the college community was surprised and amused. I was not the sort to be taken for a theologue. I pride myself that I was one of the best dancers in college. When any social hilarity was afoot I was generally in on it. I had not, since I was a freshman, worn my heart upon my sleeve so far as religion was concerned. Professor Thomas, I suspect, summed up the general impression among my friends. "Fosdick," he said, "I hear that you are thinking of entering the ministry." "Yes," I answered, "that is true." "Well," he said, "I have just one question to ask you. Has it ever occurred to you that a minister is supposed to be an exponent of the spiritual life?"

Thus I headed for the ministry with very little that could presage a welcome by the church. I was through with orthodox dogma. I had not the faintest interest in any sect or denomination. I could not have told clearly what I believed about any major Christian doctrine. I did not see how any denomination could ever accept me as its minister. But I did not care. I wanted to make a contribution to the spiritual life of my generation. I said that to myself again and again. That was all I felt sure about. If I prepared myself to make a spiritual contribution to my generation, somewhere a door would open—with that faith I headed toward the ministry.

Courses in philosophy at Colgate were very useful. Pro-

fessor Melbourne Stuart Reed was a young teacher then,
shy and self-effacing, but he taught us painstakingly the
history of philosophy and then gave us a constructive course
in metaphysics which I recall with respect and gratitude.
Six of us took it. One has since become a leading New York
lawyer; another at the Rockefeller Institute became one of
our foremost biologists; another at Cornell became an ento-
mologist; two others became important figures in public
education in New York State and Pennsylvania. We were
an earnest group, and one day, as we stood after class on
the steps of Alumni Hall, the future biologist exclaimed:
"Fellows, you know there really is a God."

This not untypical struggle for a credible Christian faith
in the last decade of the nineteenth century strongly empha-
sizes one contrast between then and now. The tragic state
of the world at large played no conspicuous part in my problem. We denounced the new monopolists, sympathized with
the rising trades unions, took the Spanish War in our stride,
welcomed the new American imperialism which followed it,
debated the iniquities of the Boer War, but that the world as
a whole was gradually growing better was the pretty much
unquestioned assumption of that generation. Such optimism
was primarily a matter not of religious faith but of current
secular philosophy, with irreligious thinkers among its main
supporters.

Today, under the impact of two world wars, such sentimental optimism has collapsed and Christian faith confronts
social despair over abysmal human tragedy, the like of which
the eighteen-nineties did not face. "It is a bad world,"
wrote Cyprian many centuries ago, "an incredibly bad
world, with its philosophy of materialism and force, deter-

minism and world despair." That grim fact I was to confront later, and I have often wondered how my struggle for faith in college would have issued if its problems, serious enough, had been complicated then by the tragic truth about human life and history which current optimism was concealing. As it was, to us sheltered collegians the conflict between faith and no-faith seemed primarily philosophical, and on that basis we argued it out with zest.

Nevertheless, important as it was to me, senior year was the least satisfying of my college course. I was bored with it long before the end. I wanted to get on with my main business. Moreover, my rebelliousness could not be kept within the compartment of religion. I fear that I made a fetish of independence, reveling in discontent, and liking to say things that would make people open their eyes. As editor of the college annual, *The Salmagundi*, in my junior year, I had carried the accustomed slams on individuals to unaccustomed lengths; and, elected editor-in-chief of the college paper, *The Madisonenses*, in my senior year, I resigned the administrative office on condition that I should still write the editorials, which I sometimes did with more pertness than good taste.

My success in college competitions did not help to curb this youthful cockiness. I was no athlete, and cheering on the side lines was my only useful participation in college sports, but elsewhere I had things too much my own way. I had taken declamation and essay prizes as a freshman and sophomore, and in my junior year I won the oratorical contest with a shamelessly militaristic piece on "Roosevelt's Rough Riders," which was widely used in school declamations across the country for years afterward. All this was not good for what ailed me. Fewer winnings and more defeats would have been salutary. I may have been heading for the ministry, but I was not distinguished for meekness.

This was a matter of concern to my wise and thoughtful parents. They were not fooled by my superficial collegiate successes. I clearly recall coming home with college laurels fresh upon me, and feeling my mother's eyes assaying my real condition with an objective, unflattering realism that made me distinctly uncomfortable. She did not like my cockiness, and my father, who had been cocky before me and understood it better, did not like it either. In later years, with appreciative affection, they used to say that none of us children had ever caused them a moment's anxiety— but I know better. Once on a vacation from college, my father took me fishing down the Niagara River, and in the course of the day got across to me just what my mother and he were thinking about me. It differed at some very important points from what I had been thinking about myself.

Nevertheless, despite my cockiness, there was another side to me. Underneath my rebelliousness my appreciations were warm and lively—the love of nature, of music, of great books, and especially of poetry. I knew well what Walt Whitman meant by the "mystical, moist night air" where one could "look up in perfect silence at the stars." I even wrote "poetry" myself, very mid-Victorian and lush—

> Now soft and drowsy melodies come
> humming from the bees,
> Now orioles sing canticles from
> choirlofts in the trees,

>   And branches shake their castinets,
>   a-dancing on the breeze—

but happily I soon grew wise enough to stick to prose. And
most stabilizing and heart warming of all there was always
my home.

While college days meant absence from the household, the
home was always the center of my life. It was in my later
college years, indeed, that I began to appreciate my brother
and sister. The difference in our ages had in boyhood made
common interests few and far between. Then they had endured from me the hardships of oversight and condescen-
sion that an older brother commonly practices. Now,
however, they were coming on. The Masten Park High
School was built; father's principalship was something to
be proud about; Raymond and Edith were making an outstanding record in the school. If it had not been for financial
difficulties, there would have been no fly in the ointment.

When I graduated from college the financing of a postgraduate course in theology presented a critical problem.
I had no right to take any more money from the family. The
seminary at Colgate offered me a generous scholarship, and
I wanted to spend a year there studying under William
Newton Clarke. The decision to do this, however, left a
margin of financing unprovided for, about which we all were
worried. I often wonder what would have happened if I
had given up the fight. I had already passed the teachers'
examinations in Buffalo and could have stepped into the
Latin department of the high school. It would have been an
easy move to make—and what a financial relief to the family!

Instead, I wrote an essay against vivisection in a state competition and, venturing back to Colgate before the results
were announced, waited with more anxiety than I care to
recall to see whether or not I was going to get through the
year. I won third prize. It meant two hundred and fifty dollars. I have always felt guilty about my specious arguments
against vivisection, concerning which I knew nothing, but
at least I believed them when I wrote them, and that check
launched me on my preparation for the ministry.

Chapter 4.

❦

Preparation for the Ministry

WHEN I ENTERED divinity school in 1900, the development of a "new theology" was well under way. The earliest discussions about it which I recall in our family were aroused by two novels, Margaret Deland's *John Ward, Preacher*, and Mrs. Humphry Ward's *Robert Elsmere*, both published when I was ten years old. They demanded, by implication, a revolt against the current thinking in the churches, and the latter especially stirred up a hornets' nest. In England Gladstone exploded in wrath against it, while Oliver Wendell Holmes in Boston said: "It is, I think, beyond question, the most effective and popular novel we have had since *Uncle Tom's Cabin*." Such a novel—selling half a million copies in the United States within a year—plainly indicated that the theological revolt was not simply theological, but came from the bottom up out of popular unrest, as well as from the professional top down.

The old Calvinism was clearly giving way during the nineties, even in the theological seminaries. There had been heresy trials aplenty, but they were becoming increasingly futile and unpopular. Preachers like Washington Gladden in Columbus, Ohio, Theodore Munger in New Haven, Connec-

ticut, Lyman Abbott in Plymouth Church, Brooklyn, George
A. Gordon in Boston, were gaining the public ear. The results of Biblical criticism, already influential in Germany
and Britain, were being taken in earnest by American scholars and, as one result, much of the church's dogmatic theology was seen to be not Biblical at all. The metaphysical
theories used to explain three persons constituting one Deity,
for example, were not in the Bible. A trinitarian *experience*
was there—"the grace of our Lord Jesus Christ, the love of
God, and the fellowship of the Holy Spirit"—but not the
church's theoretical dogma. This fact, illustrated in one theological area after another, that Christian doctrine had far
exceeded its Biblical support, was disconcerting, and theologians were forced to seek some broader base for doctrine
than the Bible only. The trouble was not simply that historical scholarship did find in the Bible ideas no longer scien-
tifically credible, but that it did not find in the Bible certain
ideas which had become Christian orthodoxy.

Under the influence of such thinkers as Hegel, Lotze and
Schleiermacher philosophical idealism powerfully affected
American theology in the late nineteenth century. In my
early ministry, for example, like many of my generation, I
was strongly attracted by Borden P. Bowne's *Personalism*.
At the same time Ritschl's emphasis on the historical revelation brought to man in Christ was very appealing, and we
were influenced by this "back to Christ" movement, which
seemed to promise a middle way between literal Biblicism
and metaphysical speculation. Either way, however, the old
foundations of Biblical authority were shaken and, consciously or not, a direct appeal to Christian experience became more and more the factual basis for theology.

When I began my year at the divinity school at Colgate all these influences were playing on me, but far from being mainly theoretical my problem was intimately personal.

The major effect which William Newton Clarke had upon me at first was to outflank my intellectual difficulties. He went back behind the forms of doctrine to the basic and abiding experiences of which they were the attempted expression and interpretation. He made essential religion live again for me, real and vital, and let the mental formulations trail along afterward as a matter to be taken up at the mind's leisure. To use his own comparison, he was sure the stars were there, though we had to change our astronomy, and the flowers real, though botany might alter its explanations. He himself was one of the most inspiring teachers I ever sat under. I recall more than once leaving his classroom to seek solitude, that I might gradually come down from the heights to the mundane earth again.

Not all his students were so affected by him. Some were utterly critical of his doctrinal reinterpretations and even contemptuous of what they deemed his intellectual vagueness. Moreover, outside the seminary angry voices in the churches rose against his retention of the professorship, and he once said to me, "They will get me yet." They never did, however. He went from strength to strength. Had it not been for him, I suspect that I should never have been a Christian minister.

I do not mean that I swallowed his opinions whole. He never asked that. Once some of us took him to task for what seemed to us his too labored endeavor, in his book on theology, to save incredible ideas associated with the Trinity. "Well, gentlemen," he said, "sometimes when I read that passage over I think I have said something—and sometimes I don't."

Much that was said in his classroom would now seem out-moded, much of it matter-of-course, some of it strangely conservative, but to me then it was the water of life. All the best meanings of personal religion could be mine again with-out the crucifixion of the intellect—this assurance he brought me and it was music in my ears. I was sure at last that I would be a minister, not a preacher but a teacher, perhaps of comparative religion.

Some theologians today vehemently condemn the faults of liberal theology, and often they are right about its flaws and failings. There were distortion of perspective, lack of depth, oversimplification, too complaisant optimism, too easy surrender to current categories of modern thought; but such defects, which characterized liberal theology at the turning of the century, were not unperceived by liberals themselves, and always voices from within the liberal camp called for amendment and correction. What present-day critics of lib-eralism often fail to see is its absolute necessity to multi-tudes of us who would not have been Christians at all unless we could thus have escaped the bondage of the then reigning orthodoxy. Of course the revolt was not the whole answer! Of course it left out dimensions in Christian faith which would need to be rediscovered! Despite that, however, it offered to a generation of earnest youth the only chance they had to be honest while being Christian.

As for men such as Dr. Clarke, their revolt, like that of Jesus against the orthodoxy of his time, was in the interest of a deeper, more vital, more transforming Christian experience than literalism, legalism and authoritarianism could supply. The result for many of us was not alone a new theology but a new spiritual life.

Nevertheless, I did not intend to stay at Colgate longer. In the books I read I discerned a wider world than the seminary at Hamilton could offer. A kind of scholarship was available which I wanted to meet at firsthand and which only a great university could offer. I caught a glimpse of it when James Rendel Harris, an English scholar, then a professor at Cambridge University, lectured at Colgate on the *Diatessaron of Tatian*. My excitement that evening I still remember. It was my first encounter with a scholar of that type. He opened windows on a new world. I walked the campus afterward with my head in the clouds. Here was a dream that must come true; it was too good not to come true: a chance to watch at firsthand such scholarly research as Rendel Harris represented. As I sought the implementation of this dream, I centered my hopes on Union Theological Seminary in New York. I wanted to study there and at Columbia University. How to manage it was a problem. At first it seemed to me an incredible hope and to my family a matter of anxious foreboding.

When I went back to Buffalo, however, at the end of that seminary year at Colgate, it was only for a fleeting visit. I had been admitted, with a scholarship, to the Union Theological Seminary, and was granted the privilege of the dormitory during the summer. Thanks to a fraternity brother, Charles Hatch Sears, who had graduated from college two years ahead of me, I had a summer job in New York, working in the Vacation Daily Bible Schools and, as well, the promise of a winter job, helping in a mission on the Bowery under the Baptist City Mission. It looked as though financially I could make the grade.

When, early in July, I left Buffalo for New York I took a roundabout route by way of Massachusetts. I had some business to settle with a girl named Florence Whitney. I sold for forty dollars the gold medal which I had won as valedictorian of my class in high school, and fared forth to offer the hand of an impecunious theologue to the girl I loved.

While I was in the seminary at Colgate, Florence Whitney, just graduated from Smith College, had come to Hamilton on a visit to her relatives, Professor and Mrs. Frank L. Shepardson. One Friday evening I met her and on Sunday I wrote my mother that I had found the girl I was going to marry. The girl herself did not know about this precipitant passion as soon as my mother did, but if she did not soon suspect it she must have been blind. I rushed her with headlong determination. Other swains presented themselves but I gave them small chance. Our Victorian courtship would doubtless amuse the current generation. We took books, especially poetry, and driving a horse and buggy into the countryside read together in some comfortable nook. My preliminary collapse at the first sight of her turned into utter rout. I was my own man no longer and never have been since. I persuaded the Shepardsons to invite her back again before the year was over, and when she accepted the invitation my first clear gleam of hope came.

I am trying—with difficulty!—to make these memoirs as unself-centered as possible in portraying my generation as I

have experienced it, but if this is to be an autobiography at
all it must be intimately personal now. The story runs that
when Frederick C. Howe finished the first draft of his autobiography he submitted it to his wife's criticism and, having
read it, she exclaimed, laughing: "But, Fred, weren't you
ever married?" To which his stammered answer was: "Oh,
yes! I forgot that. I'll put it in." In my case it certainly
cannot be left out. There was a little summerhouse close
to the Whitney home in Westminster, Massachusetts, where
one night, though my self-confidence collapsed and my
speech was tongue-tied, I managed to make my hopes
known, and received the answer that was one of the most
significant factors in my preparation for the ministry.

So with a high heart I reached New York. My best hopes
were coming true. I was superlatively happy. I did not guess
what perdition lay immediately ahead on the road that began
with such alluring prospects.

I worked hard that summer, dealing as best I could with
the boys and girls off the streets. Fifty years afterward, when
the Vacation Church Schools celebrated their golden anniversary, I was awarded a "Certificate of Gratitude" as a
"pioneer" in the movement. I accepted the honor with appreciation but I was thankful that no one there could visualize
what went on that first summer. The experience probably
taught me more than it did the children; I am sure that it
did not do them the harm it did me. For I was over-
stimulated, keyed-up, kindled by the marvel of a successful
love, the excitement of the city, and the almost unbelievable
fruition of my hopes for a chance at a great university.

More than once in later years I have seen sensitive boys from simple surroundings thus overwrought by their first invasion of New York—sometimes with tragic results—and dealing with them has been dealing with my own autobiography. I did not take care of myself. A twenty-five-cent Sunday dinner in a little restaurant under the Third Avenue elevated was the best meal of the week. The humid heat of the city got me down. I worked without respite, took no exercise, and in general fulfilled all the conditions of unhealthy living. If I had been nervously tougher I might have stood it, but I never had been nervously tough. I understood too late why my wise mother had been so concerned about that summer in New York.

Still, when the academic year began in September, I was on my toes with excitement. I was going to face alike the greatest opportunity and the stiffest competition I had ever met. I passed a special examination for advanced standing in Greek, and that encouraged me and whetted my appetite for more. I took theology at the seminary, philosophy at Columbia under Nicholas Murray Butler, and helped run the Mission at Mariners' Temple on the Bowery. It was a devastating schedule. I helped conduct as many as nine meetings in Bowery lodging houses on a single Sunday. As for Mariners' Temple, I met there at firsthand the down-and-out riffraff of the city, from constitutional ne'er-do-wells to a Yale Phi Beta Kappa, done in by drink. Dealing with the crowd that gathered there, one had to be wise as a serpent if one were not every day to have the wool pulled over one's eyes by some clever panhandler, and when one talked about religion one had to be as simple as A B C. In the public meetings one could expect almost anything. Once "News-paper Mary" wandered in from her huckstering, very much lighted up with liquor, and at an impressive pause in the meeting arose, thrust a plug of tobacco into her mouth, and proceeded to nominate Mr. Love, the head minister, for President of the United States on the Democratic ticket. One never could predict what response might come from a sermon. I can readily credit a neighboring missioner who said that after as moving a presentation of the prodigal son's return as he could make, a cynical voice said: "So! He put it over on the old man again!"

This experience also was a significant part of my prepara-tion for the ministry. I was seeing America's slums at first-hand. My name is now associated with the Riverside Church, but my ministry began in the raw filth, poverty and degra-dation of the Bowery, worse then than is easily imaginable now. Ten years before, Jacob Riis had written *How the Other Half Lives,* and I was now seeing it for myself. Some five years before I got there Theodore Dreiser had taken "end-less walks" along the Bowery, and had written: "I was never able to get the spectacle out of my mind. It caused me to fear for myself—that in due course I might land here, in this region of forgotten men." I had heard, of course, about Theodore Roosevelt, appointed to New York's police board in 1892, and facing every kind of frustrating opposition in his endeavors to clean up the city, but now I saw day after day the rotten mess beneath the city's glamour.

Charles H. Parkhurst, minister of the Madison Square Presbyterian Church, had launched in the early eighteen-nineties his campaign to arouse New York to its shocking need of reform. He became famous across the continent almost overnight. I vividly recall hearing him preach in later years—his full gray beard, his bespectacled but piercing eyes, his close reading of his manuscript, the utter absence in his delivery of any trick of the orator, and yet his strange fascination which kept his audience fairly on the edge of their pews. I had heard about his personal, firsthand investigation of the town's worst sinks of iniquity and of his unflinching exposure of them, but now I was seeing for myself why he had called the city "a very hotbed of knavery, debauchery and bestiality."

I learned a lot about the social situation during those months in the slums, but my work there, plus philosophy at Columbia and theology at Union, proved too much. One night in late November I could not sleep. It was the beginning of the most hideous experience of my life.

I have no intention of shadowing those recollections with a full account of that dreadful time. I suppose I had a nervous breakdown coming to me. High-strung and sensitive, I was built for one, and the experience was not unfamiliar to my family. It was not trouble that slew me but happiness—the excitement of the most exhilarating opportunity I had ever had. After a few days and nights of sleepless, agonizing tension, I fled to Worcester, hoping that a brief respite in my fiancée's company would set me to rights. Instead, I went from bad to worse. Then I fled to Buffalo, a humiliated nervous wreck, returning to be an emotional and financial burden on a home from which so recently I had gone forth with flags flying.

Many times in later years I have faced people who started in to tell me the inner hell of their neurotic agony—the waves of melancholia, the obsessive anxieties, the desire for suicide and all the rest—and I have stopped them, saying: "Don't you tell me, let me tell you how you feel." One typical man, with wide eyes, exclaimed when I was through: "My God! how did you know that?"

In one of my later sermons I note a passage telling how young Tolstoi, utterly disheartened, decided to kill himself; how Mark Twain, thirty years old, put a loaded pistol to his head but lacked the courage to pull the trigger; how William James, who inspired my generation as few men did, in his dispirited youth almost committed suicide. My congregation at Riverside did not recognize, I am sure, that those references were autobiographical. One dreadful day I reached the pit of utter despair, sure that all my hopes were vain and that I was finished. I have often wondered whether, if my father had not been there saying, "Harry! Harry!" I would really have cut my throat with that razor.

After months of perdition, my physician insisted that I be sent to some rest cure, and so I found myself in a sanitarium in Elmira, New York. I shrink yet at the thought of what that meant to my family. Raymond and Edith were in college, and I, who should have been on my own, was eating deeper and deeper into the family's capacity to borrow money at the bank. After a few weeks in the sanitarium, however, the head physician began canceling all bills in return for my tutoring of his son in Latin, and that eased my mind. Slowly but surely recovery progressed, and after four months I was set free and hurried to Worcester

to see my long-suffering and worried fiancée. I was a poor
risk to be engaged to at that stage of the game. With casual
acquaintances I passed as normal, but anyone under the
same roof with me could see that I was nervously ragged
still. Then my father-in-law to be—one of the best men I
ever knew—sent me to Europe.

It was a six weeks' trip—long days each way on cattle
steamers and three weeks in England—and it marked the
turning of the tide. Stratford-on-Avon is chiefly notable to
me not as Shakespeare's birthplace but because for two
nights running I got there long nights of natural sleep. I
began to see hope ahead. I even recall with satisfaction my
first glimpses of England and its historic sites. I managed
to be in London for the coronation of Edward VII, and
cheered lustily when the Horse Guards' band, followed by
the king, swept down toward the Abbey, playing Sousa's
"Stars and Stripes Forever."

Even when I returned home, however, I was far from well.
My fiancée questioned the wisdom of my tackling the New
York proposition again, and my family advised it only on
condition that I undertake nothing beside my studies. So, for
the first time, I borrowed money on my own—a friend
wagered three hundred dollars on my ability sometime to
repay him—and in September I came back to Union. It was
hard going. I used to study a half hour, and then walk a
half hour, and so inched along, but the fact that I could
take up my work on any terms helped immensely. Gradually the clouds lifted as it became clear that I could carry on.

This whole horrid experience was one of the most important factors in my preparation for the ministry. For the

first time in my life, I faced, at my wit's end, a situation too much for me to handle. I went down into the depths where self-confidence becomes ludicrous. There the technique I had habitually relied upon—marshaling my wit and my volition and going strenuously after what I wanted—petered completely out. The harder I struggled, the worse I was. It was what I did the struggling with that was sick. I, who had thought myself strong, found myself beaten, unable to cope not only with outward circumstances but even with myself. In that experience I learned some things about religion that theological seminaries do not teach. I learned to pray, not because I had adequately argued out prayer's rationality, but because I desperately needed help from a Power greater than my own. I learned that God, much more than a theological proposition, is an immediately available Resource; that just as around our bodies is a physical universe from which we draw all our physical energy, so around our spirits is a spiritual Presence in living communion with whom we can find sustaining strength. Without that experience I do not think I would have written one of my early books, *The Meaning of Prayer*. And I learned as well much about human nature that academic courses in psychology leave out.

I struggled through my year at Union and the following summer took my first pastoral charge—a parish on the northwest fringes of the Adirondacks. It was a tiny church, closed during the winter. Many of the people still lived in log cabins. I had seen one kind of human problem on the Bowery; now I saw another on the rural frontiers. It was a healthy summer in the out-of-doors, where trout were to be found in neighboring streams, deer frequented the woods and fields, and venison was to be had in season and out. My family came from Buffalo and spent a large part of the summer with me, and my fiancée made us a visit too. I had a good time preaching. I liked the people and they were endlessly kind. Long afterward, when I was minister at the Riverside Church, a student of mine was serving this same parish when, in his presence, an old-timer chanced upon a picture of me taken when I was there. "That was a nice young man," she remarked. "I wonder what ever has become of him."

When I returned for my senior year things looked better. To be sure, it took years to surmount the effects of my breakdown and some scars have never left me, but still I could handle the situation now. Toward the previous year's end I had made a ten-minute speech at a Colgate banquet in New York and had put into it everything I had. James C. Colgate, patron of the college, who had known me as a student there, put his arm around me afterward, and leading me up to George C. Lorimer, minister of the Madison Avenue Baptist Church, said: "Keep your eye on this young man." More hung on that recommendation than I could have foreseen. Soon afterward Dr. Lorimer called me down to his office and offered me the student assistantship at his church during my senior year.

That senior year was a rich experience in the seminary and the church. It would be useless here to undertake an adequate appraisal of what Union Seminary meant to me. It offered a kind of intellectual liberty in the study of religion of which I had dreamed. To be sure, theological emphases have changed since then, even in Union Seminary; theological emphases are transient and are meant to change; but, when some members of the new generation now discount the necessity and underrate the importance of what Union was doing at the turn of the century, they do not know what they are talking about. My generation desperately needed emancipation from the old, hidebound orthodoxies, and Union made this possible for us, without loss of Christian vitality and devotion. In classrooms presided over by men like Francis Brown in Old Testament Hebrew, Arthur Cushman McGiffert in church history, George William Knox in the philosophy of religion, and James Everett Frame in New Testament Greek, one's mind was stretched. Under the stimulus of the president, Charles Cuthbert Hall, Christianity was made vivid to us, both as a profound personal experience and as an affair of world-wide concern. William Adams Brown's courses in systematic theology that I approached with initial doubt and reluctance turned out to be among the most thought provoking that I took. Men who came from ampler university backgrounds and freer church associations might take Union's attitude for granted; to me it meant the liberation of my mind and at the same time the retention of my Christianity.

It stirred me up not only on theological issues but on social and economic questions too. And while in its interdenominational fellowship my impatience with sectarian distinctions was confirmed and deepened, it made real to me the historic continuum of the Christian tradition in the church, and the basic importance of the institutional vehicle that had carried it across the centuries. In my early life I had been taught that converted individuals, pooling their convictions and their efforts, made the churches. Now I saw also that the church, catholic and universal, carrying the faith from one generation to another, is the mother of all Christians and makes us. I began to want to preach.

This shift of center from a teaching to a preaching ministry began during my breakdown. That was an experience fit to shake a man out of any intellectual conceit he may have had and make him face up to human problems of another kind. One effect of it on me was to make me want to get at folks —ordinary, everyday folks—and try to help them. It was a wise shift of emphasis. I never would have been an important scholar. Although I had an acquisitive mind and plenty of mental curiosity, creative scholarship would not have been my forte. My vocation was to be an interpreter in modern, popular, understandable terms, of the best that I could find in the Christian tradition. Humbled and chastened by a harrowing experience, and enlightened by study at a great seminary, I turned with increasing eagerness toward that calling.

Alongside the classroom my assistantship with Dr. Lorimer offered stimulating opportunity. He was a preacher of the old school, an orator, insisting on an open platform with no impediment to his dramatic use of everything he had, who told me once, whimsically to be sure, that the most eloquent part of a preacher was his legs. From the standpoint of our more chastened habits now, he certainly put on a show. He himself, however, was a rare and charming person, genuine, and deeply in earnest, and what he said was never cheap nor merely sensational. Twice a Sunday, throughout my senior year, I was in the pulpit with him, helping in the service, and once or twice was trusted with the sermon.

To be sure, the church as a whole was run on an inadequate plan—one minister, with a few assistants for minor tasks, very little going on throughout the week except the Wednesday evening prayer meeting, and everything centered and focused in the two sermons on Sunday. It represented Protestantism's sorry failure in dealing with the metropolitan problem, carrying over into the thick of a great city a church organization and program fitted to a primitive rural area. I saw that that setup did not work. The only thing that could make it even seem to work was a preacher able to make noise enough to be heard above the city's din, and Dr. Lorimer met that specification. He preached habitually to packed congregations, but while I was devoted to him, I knew that there was something radically wrong with the way the church was run.

He wanted his student assistant to be an ordained minister. After some spirited opposition the examining council passed me, more, I fear, because of Dr. Lorimer's influence than from any cheerful disposition to do so. On November 18, 1903, I was ordained in the Madison Avenue Baptist Church. William Newton Clarke came down from Colgate to preach the sermon. My mother came from Buffalo to be present at the ceremony. It was the last time I ever saw her alive.

Mother's death was the dark shadow on what was else a happy year. One day in the spring the ominous news came from home that she had pneumonia. I was not to be too alarmed, the letter said; it was not necessary for me to come

home—not yet—but the situation was serious. I did not
wait, but although I took a train within a few hours, I was
too late. When I walked up the steps at home I was met with
the heavy news that she had gone.

mother

When a man has had a mother like mine, it is useless to
try to tell what he feels about her. The old saying of the
Talmud that God could not be everywhere, so he made
mothers, is real to me. One of the most poignant regrets of
my life—as I recall the years of struggle she invested in us
children—is that she did not live until we were able to make
life easy for her, and compensate her a little for the sacrifices
she endured to give us our chance. She would laugh at that
and say that what she did for us is what mothers are made
for, but that does not take the poignant regret away. I am
writing this over fifty years after she died, but neither death
nor passing time can put an end to an inward fellowship.

So through sunshine and shadow, my ministerial preparation drew toward its close. It had certainly been various—
a great seminary course, a triumphant love, a catastrophic
breakdown, and parish experiences in a city's slums, on the
rural frontier, and in a metropolitan church. Nor should I
omit the student friendships formed at Union. They have
lasted all my life. Four of us from the class of 1904 were
later called back to professorships. The thing I am proudest
about in my scholastic record is that despite the handicap
of my nervous collapse, the seminary gave me a *summa
cum laude* at the end.

Toward the close of that senior year Dr. Lorimer's health
broke and my responsibilities increased. The church asked
me to stay on until he could return or his successor be

found, but I wanted a parish of my own. When, therefore, the First Baptist Church of Montclair, New Jersey, called me, I accepted. During July I took my first plunge into an independent pastorate; during the August vacation Florence Whitney and I were married, and after a honeymoon in Nova Scotia we settled down in our first home in Montclair and went to work together.

That word "together" needs emphasizing. In no vocation is a man's wife more vitally important to his work than in the ministry. It was over fifty years ago that my wife and I started out as a team, and she has been so effective a part of it that, while of necessity in this autobiography I use the pronoun "I," in every important part of the story the word should be "we." On the fiftieth anniversary of her graduation Smith College gave her an honorary doctorate, and for once at least I heard a citation concerning which I could personally vouch that it was richly deserved. For the president said: "Her career is one that is basic to our society. As wife and as mother she has been many things—teacher, nurse, business woman, philosopher and spiritual comforter. Her talents have been used to help build the lives of her husband and her children, and through them, as well as through her own participation, she has served her church, her community, her country, her world. We salute her as one who superbly exemplifies, and who represents, that great number of Smith alumnae of whom this college is deeply proud."

Certainly our golden wedding anniversary found me a very grateful man. What home life with my wife has meant to me since we started our work together in Montclair I cannot even try to express, but I cannot imagine my life without it. The author of the book of Proverbs wrote with deep feeling about "a good wife," but even so his glowing words are an understatement:

> She is far more precious than jewels.
> The heart of her husband trusts in her.

Chapter 5.

Learning to Preach

I WAS TOSSED into my first parish over fifty years ago, like a boy thrown into deep water and told to swim when he does not know how. At the beginning I was an ignoramus about the effective preparation of a sermon. The seminary's courses in homiletics had been of slight use to me. We listened to lectures on preaching, full of good advice, I do not doubt, but lacking relevance to any actual experience of our own, and soon forgotten because not implemented in practice. You cannot teach an art simply by talking about it. Years afterward, along with Henry Sloane Coffin and others, I played a small part in helping to make the teaching of homiletics at the seminary an affair of practical drill. We brought groups of students into the chapel, heard them preach, and then fell upon them with approval where they deserved it and with rigorous criticism of their faults. That kind of training would have saved me a protracted struggle in my first pastorate, but in those old days theologues had little or nothing of such discipline. What saved me was my earlier training in public speaking so that, however little I had to say, I could somehow manage to say it.

I recall vividly the tormented weeks I spent during the

first year and more in Montclair, often distraught myself and fairly driving my wife to distraction, trying to prepare sermons that would be worth preaching. Probably my memory exaggerates the occasion when improvement began. One Sunday morning, quite unexpectedly, in the midst of my sermon, the idea I was dealing with caught fire. I had a flaming few minutes when I could feel the congregation's kindling response. I am sure that they were as much surprised as I was. I had never preached like that before, and I went home sure that preaching could mean that kind of moving and effective communication of truth.

Nevertheless, it was a struggle. Preaching for me has never been easy, and at the start it was often exceedingly painful. In later years I used to envy some of my students at the seminary who from the start seemed to know instinctively how to prepare a sermon and deliver it. Ralph Sockman, for example, in his first student sermon, exhibited such mature ability and skill that I told the class he acted as though he had had twenty years of experience behind him and I doubted whether even a homiletical professor could spoil him. My road as a preacher was very rough at the beginning, but little by little I saw more clearly what I verily believed and wanted most to say and, as clairvoyance into the needs of those to whom I spoke increased, I discovered, at least occasionally, the satisfaction of preaching so that something creative happened in the listener.

Because Montclair had been religiously well taken care of already, before the Baptist congregation was organized, denominational peculiarities were stressed in the new church as a justification for its founding, and at the heart of it were some reactionary sectarians. Dr. Lorimer, hearing rumors of cantankerous elements in the congregation to which I was going, said to me in our last conversation: "Young man, never you fear the face of mortal clay!" I needed that admonition. There were, however, saving factors in the situation. The church, having already had some unpleasant experiences in its eighteen years of existence, sincerely wanted to get on with me, and were willing to put up with a good deal to do it. Moreover, on the fringes of the congregation were new people, waiting to be members if things went well. This new group was, on the whole, liberal in spirit, and the church, for every sort of reason, needed its support. So, while skating at times on thin ice, I got along. Even close communion had been the accepted custom before I arrived; no general invitation was extended to non-Baptist Christians to partake of the Lord's Supper. On that point, taking matters into my own hands, I extended an open invitation to all Christians to join in celebrating the first Lord's Supper at which I officiated. No one cared to start a fight about that with the new minister, but there was grumbling over my irregular assumption of authority.

The only crisis I had on matters of orthodoxy came after more than a year had passed. I had painfully felt my way at first, having plenty of inward troubles of my own, and my preaching, which was as much an endeavor to discover what I thought myself as it was to help anyone else, was, I suspect, not particularly disturbing. The issue between old and new theology, however, could not remain hidden, and at a meeting of the official board, when I was absent, two deacons complained about the liberal drift of my sermons. Having in hand at that time what amounted to two calls from other churches, one of them offering greater opportunity than was conceivable in Montclair, I invited those two deacons to a private conference. Not disposed to stay where I was not wanted, I told them, I put it up to them to say whether I should stay in liberty and peace or leave at once. They capitulated and, while they never agreed with me about theology, they stood by me, albeit with some pain, until the end.

The auditorium in which my pastorate began was the chapel of what was intended to be later a larger structure. As I recall the growing congregation that at last crowded us to the doors—it took less than three hundred to do it— I am reminded of the relative nature of all satisfactions. No preacher ever found more encouragement from vast assemblages of auditors than I found as I watched the growing numbers of those to whom my message was welcome in that little chapel. When the time came to venture on a building enterprise the church was ready for a fresh start altogether. In 1911, seven years after my pastorate began, a new building on a new site was dedicated.

From then on my memories of the Montclair ministry are very satisfying, save for regret at my own shortcomings and mistakes. The people were overwhelmingly kind, and lifelong friendships have their roots in those happy days. The church flourished and grew steadily in numbers. An associate membership was established so that Christians of all denominational backgrounds could become actively incorporated into the congregation, and while this compromise was far short of what was later done at Riverside Church, it was a start.

To be sure, I found preaching two sermons on Sunday difficult. I used to burn the logwood in the morning and the chips at night, and the first sometimes made a slow blaze and the latter a thin one. Still, my congregation was merciful and sustained me with a friendliness for which I am endlessly grateful. I have seen many a young minister so maltreated by his first parish, so twisted by criticism and disheartened by meanness and coldness, that irreparable damage was done him. I was fortunate.

One member of the church, Clayton Cooper, was a leader in the student work of the Y.M.C.A., and one June he invited me to share in the Northfield student conference. In those days John R. Mott, Robert E. Speer and others like them stirred great audiences of students gathered at Northfield from the colleges of the east. I went there first as a teacher of a daily Bible class, and for many years, beginning at Northfield and going on to Silver Bay, New York, I shared in those student gatherings and in other similar conferences across the country.

I do not recall that I ever cherished any ambition to be an author. I wanted to teach and preach, but I remember no aspiration to write. One summer at Northfield, however, I delivered a message on Jesus' saying about going the second mile, and when my friends in the Association Press—especially Frederick Harris, to whose encouragement I owe a great debt—asked for the publication of it in expanded form, I tried my hand at writing it out. The result looked satisfactory to me until I showed it to my wife. She definitely thought otherwise. She fell upon it tooth and talon. Its loose sentences, redundancies, circumlocutions and verbosities were a trouble to her. So I discovered that, along with other blessings, I had married my best literary critic. She insisted on conciseness, succinctness, directness and simplicity. When we finished the manuscript, a brief booklet of fifty-two pages was the result, and under the title, *The Second Mile*, it is in circulation yet.

As a result of these student conferences, invitations to preach in college chapels began coming in. I still remember my amazement when the first invitation came from Harvard and my trepidation in accepting it. I was too immature to handle adequately that challenge. When the time came I spent a sleepless Saturday night, and the next day in Appleton Chapel, very ill at ease, I faced an audience which later I learned to love, but which on that first occasion petrified me. It was several years before Harvard asked me back again!

College preaching in those days was an adventure. Compulsory chapel was the practice in many institutions, and the students, often resenting it, treated it with neither reverence nor attention unless the preacher made it impossible to do otherwise. The first time I preached at Princeton I faced a sea of Sunday newspapers spread wide open when I began the sermon, and in the middle of the first sentence a huge six-footer on the center aisle heaved himself up with extended arms in a mighty yawn. For five minutes it was a tussle to see whether they would sleep, or read their papers, or listen to this cub preacher they had never heard of. I hope I may be forgiven some reminiscent satisfaction in the fact that I won.

An itinerant ministry, speaking ever to new audiences,

with only a chance to strike a glancing blow, has never been my first love. I have cherished more the opportunity of dealing steadily with a congregation on whom a sustained ministry might have cumulative effect. Life would have been much poorer, however, had it not been for enriching experiences with many varied audiences in this and other lands. Especially at the beginning it was an encouragement to see the doors open. And I am indebted also to college preaching for personal friendships with men like Andrew D. White and Jacob Gould Schurman, presidents of Cornell, President Lawrence Lowell of Harvard, President Woodrow Wilson of Princeton, and many others.

I do not see how a man can preach without writing. I always have thought with my pen in hand. My preaching naturally began to turn into books. Wanting to know what I really thought about immortality, I broke up my questions into as orderly an arrangement as I could manage, and announced a series of Sunday evening sermons on the subject. Then I was in for it. I read everything pro and con that I could lay my hands on, and under the coercion of teaching others, taught myself everything I could learn from books, and searched my own mind for what I honestly thought. Those Sunday evening sermons were a rough-and-ready product, but they at least surveyed the field, and whatever they did for others, they did much for me. Afterward I wrote the book, *The Assurance of Immortality*, not really expecting that any publisher would accept it. To my surprise, it was welcomed.

The greatest single satisfaction I ever had from an accepted manuscript, however, had come before any of my books were written. I submitted to the *Atlantic Monthly* an article on "Heckling the Church," and it was given a warm greeting. Ellery Sedgwick's letter accepting the manuscript was a notable event in my life. His graciousness about the article, his apology—very humorous to me—because he had not the faintest idea who I was, and his friendly hopefulness about my work, were an encouragement I have never forgotten.

The Manhood of the Master was written by request of the Association Press. The basic material in it was first presented in addresses at the church, and then reworked into a book. Its gratifying reception is, I suppose, one of the major reasons why I have gone on writing books. It was even translated into Coptic in Egypt, although under unique conditions, so far as my experience goes. My name was not in any way associated with the Coptic version, and the anonymous manuscript was altered to suit the opinions of the translators, with omissions where they disagreed and additions where they thought some doctrine of the Coptic Church should be introduced. Moreover, so my friends in Egypt told me, this was done without the slightest conscious dishonesty, the procedure illustrating the free, anonymous way writings were handled in preprinting and precopyright days. The only way I have ever succeeded in fulfilling my childhood's desire to be a foreign missionary has been through my books. *The Manhood of the Master,* written forty years ago, has been many times translated on the mission fields, and recently I received from India a new rendition of it into Tamil. My greatest single source of satisfaction, so far as this early book of mine is concerned, is that during one of his imprisonments Mahatma Gandhi read it. A friend of his saw his copy, well underlined and annotated, and wrote me about it. Gandhi has been one of my heroes; he will remain an unforgettable character in man's spiritual history; I wish more than I can say that I could have had the privilege of meeting him. Imagining him in prison reading that book of mine about the Master, I have been both humbled and encouraged.

The Meaning of Prayer, which has been translated into at least seventeen foreign languages, sprang originally from my desire to clarify my own thinking. It started with a series of sermons, went on to a series of midweek discussions where I could get the questions, objections and difficulties of the people, and then in an abandoned cottage on the Maine coast, near our summer home, I sat down daily for two months at a rickety kitchen table in a bare room and wrote the book. When I sent the manuscript to the publishers, I told them that a book on prayer could not expect a large sale and that I thought two thousand copies would be adequate. I guessed wrong that time. I never met Luther Gulick—uncle of the present well-known bearer of that name —without remembering the first time I saw him, more than forty years ago, in the office of our publishers, the Association Press. When Fred Harris introduced us, Gulick looked at me with my nonmonastic, nonascetic, "prosperous butcher-boy" appearance—as one newspaper reporter once described me—and said: "You certainly do not look like the author of *The Meaning of Prayer.*" And I looked at him—lean, spare and gaunt—and answered: "You certainly do not look like the author of *The Dynamic of Manhood.*"

Meanwhile, my struggle to discover how to preach went on with no little perplexity. The stereotyped routine into which old-fashioned expository preaching had fallen was impossible to me. First, elucidation of a Scriptural text, its historic occasion, its logical meaning in the context, its setting in the theology and ethic of the ancient writer; second, application to the auditors of the truth involved; third, exhortation to decide about the truth and act on it—such was the pattern in accordance with which every week multitudes of sermons were manufactured. That a vital preacher could use that model to good effect goes without saying, but there was something the matter with the model. To start with a passage from Moses, Jeremiah, Paul or John and spend the first half of the sermon or more on its historic explanation and exposition, presupposed the assumption that the congregation came to church that morning primarily concerned about the meaning of those ancient texts. That certainly was not what my congregation in Montclair was bothered about.

It was easier, however, to be impatient with the prevailing stereotype than constructively to replace it with a better method. I spent some vexatious years, impatient and floundering. "Only the preacher," I petulantly wrote, "proceeds still upon the idea that folk come to church desperately anxious to discover what happened to the Jebusites."

One difficulty was that rebels against this prevailing pattern of expository preaching commonly became topical preachers. They searched contemporary life in general and the newspapers in particular for subjects. Instead of concentrating on textual analysis, they dealt with present-day themes about which everyone was thinking. I watched those

topical preachers with a dubious mind. Week after week
turning their pulpits into platforms and their sermons into
lectures, they strained after new intriguing subjects, and one
knew that in private they were straining even more strenuously after new intriguing ideas about them. Instead of
launching out from a great text they started with their own
opinions on some matter of current interest, often much
farther away than a good Biblical text would be from the
congregation's vital concerns and needs. Indeed, the fact
that history had thought it worth while to preserve the text
for centuries would cause a wise gambler to venture confidently on the text's superior vitality.

Across the years since then I have seen those topical
preachers petering out and leaving the ministry. If people
do not come to church anxious about what happened to the
Jebusites, neither do they come yearning to hear a lecturer
express his personal opinion on themes which editors, col-
umnists and radio commentators have been dealing with
throughout the week. So I floundered until personal counseling gradually led me into an approach to preaching which
made it an exciting adventure.

Personal counseling does not begin full force in the experience of a young minister, fresh from the seminary. He is
too callow, inexperienced, immature. Children may flock
around him but adults do not naturally seek his advice. I
vividly recall the first serious case of personal need presented
to me—a youth from one of the church's finest families, con-
quered by alcohol and in utter despair. "I don't believe in
God," he said to me, "but if *you* do, for God's sake pray for
me, for I need him!" That was a challenge to everything I

believed and preached. Few experiences in my first pastorate
had so deep an effect on me as the battle in which that youth
and I for long months engaged. That it ended in victory is
one of the satisfying memories of my early ministry. "If you
ever find anyone who does not believe in God," the youth
said at last, "send him to me. I know."

In retrospect the relevance of such an experience to
preaching seems obvious but only gradually did I stumble
up the road until I saw it. Many other young preachers in
those days were stumbling up that same road, discontented
with both the prevalent expository and topical sermon pat-
terns, but not sure how to replace them. Little by little, however, the vision grew clearer. People come to church on
Sunday with every kind of personal difficulty and problem
flesh is heir to. A sermon was meant to meet such needs; it
should be personal counseling on a group scale. If one had
clairvoyance, one would know the sins and shames, the
anxieties and doubts, the griefs and disillusionments, that
filled the pews, and could by God's grace bring the saving
truths of the gospel to bear on them as creatively as though
he were speaking to a single person. That was the place to
start—with the real problems of the people. That was a sermon's specialty, which made it a sermon, not an essay or a
lecture. Every sermon should have for its main business the
head-on constructive meeting of some problem which was
puzzling minds, burdening consciences, distracting lives, and
no sermon which so met a real human difficulty, with light
to throw on it and help to win a victory over it, could possibly be futile.

As I experimented with this approach I found that within

a paragraph or two after a sermon started first one listener
and then another would discover that the preacher was bowling down his alley, and sometimes the whole congregation
would grow tense and quiet, seeing that the sermon concerned a matter of vital import to every one of them. The
preacher was handling a subject they were puzzled about,
or a way of living they were dangerously experimenting with,
or an experience which had bewildered them, or an ideal
they were striving for, or a need they had not known how to
meet.

Any preacher who, with even moderate skill, is thus helping folk to solve their real problems is functioning. He never
will lack an audience. He may have little learning or eloquence but he is doing the one thing which is a preacher's
special business. He is delivering the goods which the community has a right to expect from the pulpit.

This did not mean that the Bible's importance in preaching diminished. Upon the contrary, I had been suckled on
the Bible, knew it and loved it, and I could not deal with
any crucial problem in thought and life without seeing text
after text lift up its hands begging to be used. The Bible
came alive to me—an amazing compendium of every kind
of situation in human experience with the garnered wisdom
of the ages to help in meeting them.

Nor did this "project method" shut out the best values in
topical preaching. The problems that came to church on
Sunday in the minds and hearts of the worshipers were not
simply individual but social, economic, international. The
preacher, however, did not need to deliver a lecture on them,
as though he were a trained specialist in these diverse fields.

He could not possibly know enough for *that*, but he could know the inner impact of those problems on his people in their defeatism and disillusionment, their agnosticism and despair, their surrender of Christian principles in the face of life's terrific realism, their reactionary clinging to old prejudices despite new light, and their class-bound loyalties to the wrong side of great issues. Let him start with the people confronting him in the pews and speak as wisely and Christianly as he could to their "business and bosoms," and he might help at least one individual that Sunday.

I have often been asked to deliver lectures on the art of preaching with a view to their subsequent publication in a book, but I have always declined. Many years ago I wrote an article for *Harper's Magazine* on "What Is the Matter with Preaching?" in which I said in gist what I am saying now, but I never expect to write a book about it. This thing that I am saying here is all I have to offer—this and a few corollaries which can be briefly noted.

I found my sermons becoming more and more co-operative enterprises between the preacher and the congregation. When a man takes hold of a real difficulty in the life and thought of his people and is trying to meet it, he finds himself not so much dogmatically thinking for them as co-operatively thinking with them. A preacher can easily play "Sir Oracle," assertive, dogmatic, flinging out his dictum as though to say "Take it or leave it," and such preaching has its appeal to credulous and emotionally impressionable minds. It has lost its influence on intelligent folk, however, and the future does not belong to it.

Later, in my classes at the seminary, I repeatedly used the

story of a headmaster in his school chapel who had plunged
into the first statement of his sermon theme, when a professor
arose from the congregation, mounted the pulpit beside the
preacher and offered a criticism of what he just had said.
Excitement reigned. The headmaster answered the objection
but the professor remained in the pulpit, and the sermon
that day was a dialogue on a great theme of religion. The
boys had never before been so entranced by a sermon. It
was, of course, a prearranged affair, an experiment in having
the congregation represented in the pulpit.

It certainly takes more than a preacher alone in the pulpit
to make an effective sermon. If, however, the people can be
there too, so that the sermon is not a dogmatic monologue
but a co-operative dialogue in which the congregation's
objections, questions, doubts and confirmations are fairly
stated and dealt with, something worth while is likely to
happen. Sometimes this can be done implicitly through the
preacher's evident sympathy and understanding; sometimes
it can be made explicit in paragraphs beginning "But some
of you will say." Of course this style of preaching requires
clairvoyance on the preacher's part into the people's thinking, but any man who lacks this has no business to preach
anyway. And of course this method can be exaggerated and
become a mannerism, but so can any other. We have plenty
of sermons that are sheer propaganda, where preachers set
out by hook or crook to put something over on the congregation. We have pugnacious sermons, where preachers wage
campaigns, attack enemies, assail the citadels of those who
disagree, and are in general warlike and vehement. We need
more sermons that try to face people's real problems with

them, meet their difficulties, answer their questions, confirm their noblest faiths and interpret their experiences in sympathetic, wise and understanding co-operation. This is the only way I could find to achieve excitement without sensationalism. Constructively to help people to meet trouble triumphantly, or to live above the mediocre moral level of a modern city, or to believe in God despite the world's evil, or to make Christ's principles standard in the face of our disordered world, is really not sensationalism. If it is well done, however, with no dodging of the difficulties, it can be vitally stimulating and can spoil all somnolent use of sermon time. An auditor, after one Sunday morning service, exclaimed: "I nearly passed out with excitement, for I did not see how you could possibly answer that objection which you raised against your own thought. I supposed you would do it somehow but I could not see how until you did it." At any rate, it was toward this style of preaching that I set my sights.

No homiletic method is without its dangers, and this one which I espoused has perils aplenty. I presented it once to a group of experienced ministers and collected a galaxy of warnings about its possible perversions. They had endeavored so precisely to deal with a real problem that Mr. Smith had vexatiously waked up to the fact that they were talking about him; or they had tried to be so fair about objections that, overstating the opposing side, they had found neither time nor ability to answer it; or they had been so practical in dealing with some definite problems that they had become trivial, failing to bring the eternal gospel to bear on the issue; or they had been so anxious to deal with felt needs in the congregation that they had forgotten still deeper needs, unfelt but real; or they had so limited the difficulties they preached about to private, psychological maladjustment that they became merely amateur pulpit psychiatrists, neglecting the public concerns of the Kingdom of God. These dangers are real, but such perversions are the fault of unskilled handling the like of which would wreck any method whatsoever.

My own major difficulty sprang from the fact that starting a sermon with a problem, however vital and urgent, suggests a discussion, a dissertation, a treatise. A sermon, however, is more than that. The preacher's business is not merely to discuss repentance but to persuade people to repent; not merely to debate the meaning and possibility of Christian faith, but to produce Christian faith in the lives of his listeners; not merely to talk about the available power of God to bring victory over trouble and temptation, but to send people out from their worship on Sunday with victory in their possession. A preacher's task is to create in his congregation the thing he is talking about.

I learned that such direct results could be achieved through personal counseling. It was a great day when I began to feel sure that a sermon could be thus immediately creative and transforming. A good sermon is an engineering operation by which a chasm is bridged so that spiritual goods on one side—the "unsearchable riches of Christ"—are actually transported into personal lives upon the other.

Here lies the difference between a sermon and a lecture. A lecture is chiefly concerned with a *subject* to be elucidated; a sermon is chiefly concerned with an *object* to be achieved. A justifiable criticism of much modern, liberal preaching is that, though it consists of neat, analytical discourses, pertinent to real problems, and often well conceived and happily phrased, it does nothing to anyone. Such sermons are not sermons, but essays, treatises, lectures. It is lamentably easy to preach about moral courage without making anyone more courageous; to deliver a discourse on faith without creating any of that valuable article in a single life; to argue that man has power to decide and choose without causing anyone then and there to make a momentous decision.

So I went through project preaching and beyond it, and began to see how much the old preachers had to teach us. At their best they did achieve results. Their sermons were appeals to the jury and they got decisions. They knew where the great motives were and appealed to them with conclusive power. I began studying sermons of men like Phillips Brooks —not merely reading them, but analyzing sentence by sentence the steps they took toward working in their auditors the miracles they often did achieve—and I concluded that while we modern preachers talk about psychology much more than our predecessors, we commonly use it a good deal less.

After that preaching became exhilarating. It need never fail to make a transforming difference in some lives. One is not merely making a speech about religion; one is dealing with the profoundest concerns of personality, with incalculable possibilities dependent on what is said that day. My silent prayer rose each Sunday before the sermon started: "O God, some one person here needs what I am going to say. Help me to reach him!" Nothing can make preaching easy, but seen as a creative process which can transform lives, it becomes so stimulating that it reproduces in the preacher the strength it takes from him, as good agriculture replaces the soil it uses.

The supreme reward of the preacher is nothing that the public knows about. It comes in letters like this:

More than twenty-five years ago a dirty and wretched young man crept into a church one evening and listened to your talk. . . . The drunk young man went out into the night and the words stayed with him. And things happened. He heeded the words, straightened up, went to night school for years and years until at last he graduated from ——— University, from postgraduate work at ——— University, became nationally and internationally known in his chosen field, and only recently ——— University asked him to write a new book. . . . I am that man.

The early nineteen hundreds saw a stormy upsurge of social reform in the nation and, while our suburban church with a juvenile preacher did little about it, we felt its impact. In 1905 Charles Evans Hughes made his famous investigation of the insurance companies. Later, in the Riverside Church, I had his warm friendship and his family's, but in my memory he appears first as the intrepid investigator who converted the insurance business "from a public swindle to a public trust." The earliest "muckraking" articles appeared in *McClure's Magazine* in 1902, and such was the popular reception of these exposés of public corruption that soon *Munsey's*, *Everybody's*, the *Cosmopolitan* and others plunged into the fray. I used to play golf with E. J. Ridgeway, editor of *Everybody's*, thereby hearing some of the inside story, and as a spectator I applauded what Lincoln Steffens, Ray Stannard Baker and Ida Tarbell, the star "muckrakers," were trying to do.

I was not at home in economics, however, and I was troubled by my unschooled ineptness in an area where there was so much uproar. So I took courses at Columbia in sociology and economics, under Franklin H. Giddings and John Bates Clark, getting an M.A. in 1908. My thesis was a first-hand study of the organized labor movement as it had developed in Montclair, from the old Knights of Labor to the new craft unions. The latter—masons, carpenters, plumbers, painters, sheet metal workers, electricians and hod carriers— were well organized when I came to town, and beginning that year there was a labor war, a combined strike and lock-out, which lasted fourteen months. Rereading my Columbia thesis reveals that I made the acquaintance of the major labor leaders in town, attended meetings of the locals, and helped in founding a social headquarters for union men where it was vainly hoped that friendly intercourse might issue in more efficient co-operation. Resentment was seething among the laborers, much of which, in my judgment, was justified. I saw, however, that human nature on the unions' side could be quite as selfish as the human nature exhibited by ornery operators, and as for bringing the union men into the church's fellowship, I made no gains which I recall, save in the case of the head of the carpenters' union.

I note this frustration in trying to save a Protestant congregation from being a class church because it has haunted all my ministry. It constitutes today one of Protestantism's major problems.

In 1912 the *Outlook*, then one of our leading weeklies, sent me to cover the famous textile strike at Lawrence, Massachusetts. I saw there the raw side of the labor situation in our nation. Twenty thousand men and women had been on strike for ten weeks. Forty different languages and dialects were spoken by those workers; in one of the largest mills 67 per cent were wholly ignorant of English. Save for a few in the upper brackets, the wages were pitiful, and when a new state law reduced the hours of labor from fifty-six to fifty-four per week and the next pay checks showed that wages were to be reduced accordingly, the workers rebelled. Five hundred Italians broke loose in the Washington Mills, and in one of the worst riots of the strike stampeded one factory after another.

At the beginning the laborers were unorganized. The Industrial Workers of the World, a radical left-wing syndicalist group—we should call them communists now—had barely three hundred members among the workers at the start, but they saw their chance, took over, and before the strike was finished, more than ten thousand members were in their ranks. Like the communists now they found their best opportunity in the worst social conditions.

In my report for the *Outlook* I tried to play fair with both sides of the angry struggle. Concerning much of the writing that had been done about the situation, which was attracting nation-wide attention, I said: "The main endeavor has been to find someone to blame." I did my best to avoid that attitude. One could easily understand the position of the mill owners. "As a class," I wrote, "they are not less kindly and conscientious than other men, nor are they so blind to their own interests as to desire a body of discontented workmen."

They did face competition with factories in other states where working hours were longer and wages lower. They could produce figures to show that some of their mills were losing money and that others were paying wages out of capital surplus. And while, after the strike, the factories were humming again with wages raised from 5 to 15 per cent, they could argue that this was made possible by an upswing in the market.

This ability of each side to defend itself, however, did not lessen the total tragedy.

Two of the strike leaders, Ettor and Giovanitti, were thrown into prison. I visited Ettor there. He was held on a phony charge of homicide, although the evidence was conclusive that when the crime was committed he was two miles away. The authorities jailed him, however, for he was too flaming a personality to be left at large. A genial, magnetic young fellow, twenty-seven years old, born in New York City and educated in the public schools, he was what we would call a left-wing radical. As we sat together in the Lawrence jail, he said to me: "They tell us to get what we want by the ballot. They want us to play the game according to the established rules. But the rules were made by the capitalists. *They* have laid down the laws of the game. *They* hold the pick of the cards. We never can win by political methods. The right of suffrage is the greatest hoax of history. Direct action is the only way. . . . No class of people ever gave up the chair of privilege until somebody tipped the chair over." So in 1912, in the United States, a young American was proclaiming what we now think of as Russian communism. After the police, on a freezing January day, had played their fire hoses on a crowd of strikers, Ettor said: "There is being kindled in the heart of the workers a flame of proletarian revolt which no fire hose in the world can ever extinguish."

The great majority of the workers—even those who joined the I.W.W.—did not agree with Ettor's theories and commonly did not know what they were. I talked with many of the strikers. All they wanted was enough income to live on, and all they welcomed in the I.W.W. was organized leadership in winning their strike. Because of what I saw in Lawrence I understand much more clearly than I otherwise could have understood what it is that even in America gives communists their chance—the desperate plight of some of the underprivileged on one side and, on the other, the starry-eyed, idealistic sympathy of some of the intelligentsia, who think that Ettor's road is the only way out.

While, however, there were dangerous extremes on the left wing of the strikers, there were dangerous extremes also on the right wing of the stockowners and operators. Said one lady on Commonwealth Avenue in Boston: "The strikers should be starved back to work." Cried one Boston lawyer: "The militia should have been instructed to shoot. That is the way Napoleon did it. The strikers should have been shot down. *I stand for law and order!*" This persuasion that any means was justified in crushing the laborers came to its most outrageous exhibition in the action of John J. Breen, son of an ex-mayor of Lawrence, who, so his conviction ran, secretly planted dynamite in the Syrian colony of the town in order to bring discredit on the strikers. The court only fined him five hundred dollars. Who paid Breen to plant the dynamite? the strikers wondered. What would the sentence of a striker have been, if he had done it? As a matter of fact, surprisingly little violence was used by the strikers.

The more I talked with the aggrieved laborers the more apparent it became that while higher wages were a major issue, a deeper problem in human relationships lay underneath the economic issue. "They treated us like dumb cattle," said one of the men. The evidence backed up that charge. A friend of mine who knew the mills thoroughly— his interests all on the side of the employers, not of the workers—said to me: "I myself have seen a foreman go cursing and blaspheming through a department to fire a workman without explaining why, until my blood boiled."

One of the workers, a trusted and highly paid man, told me that in his department there were only English-speaking girls—decent, self-respecting young women from American-trained families—but that the overseer habitually addressed them with oaths that would not bear repeating. I asked one of the most highly paid women in the mills to tell me the names, which she herself had heard, with which the foremen commonly addressed the workers. She started in but I asked her to stop. Nothing much more brutal and obscene could be imagined. One of the well-paid women operatives —twenty dollars a week—who became the foremost woman leader of the strikers explained to me why she, who had nothing to complain of for herself, had joined the strike: "I have been getting madder and madder for years at the way they talked to those poor Italians and Lithuanians." And one man, not a laborer but altogether on the owner's side of the issue, said to me: "The manufacturers had it coming to them, and they got it!"

At any rate, I came home sympathizing in a way with all the parties in the tragedy, but boiling with indignation at the gross betrayal of all that democracy stands for which the factories in Lawrence illustrated. That was *not* America! In the four decades and more since then admirable progress has been made throughout the nation in the relationships between employers and employees, but anyone who supposes that organized labor was not indispensable in achieving it does not know what he it talking about.

Twenty-five years after the Lawrence incident I said this:

Whatever may be the details of the struggle of the American laboring man for a larger share in the products of industry, and whatever the rights and wrongs of the present troubled scene, it is a safe affirmation, backed by long history, that a century from now it will be clear that the laboring man was right about the main matters. That is, he was not receiving a just share of the products of industry, and he had a right to collective bargaining on a scale that was denied him. Again, the truth is not that the privileged fail in estimating the situation because they are bad, and the laboring men see it more truly because they are good. The truth is that it is the man who is being hurt who feels where the shoe pinches.

I said *that,* however, in the Riverside Church to a congregation made up of professional and business people, with very few if any manual laborers present. I have often dreamed of two other opportunities—one in which I might be minister in a country church, seeing what I could do with the rural problems, and the other in which I might be pastor of a congregation of workers in a factory town. Vice-Admiral Woods of the British Navy, who received the Distinguished Service Order for his conduct in World War I, later retired from the Navy, took a theological course, became a priest in the Church of England, and was sent at his own request to a parish in the dockyard section of London's East End. At the beginning his congregation numbered seven; at the end the crowds could not get in. I take off my hat to him!

Meanwhile in Montclair I watched the national campaign for large-scale social and political reforms gaining headway, with Theodore Roosevelt and his "square deal" in the forefront. Having succeeded President McKinley—assassinated in Buffalo in 1901—T. R. was elected President in 1904; then, having retired in favor of Mr. Taft in 1908, he fought for the nomination in 1912, and failing to secure it, he formed his Bull Moose party and staged an uproarious campaign. Behind the intrigue and clamor of politics the issues at stake were the regulation of railroads, breaking up trusts, workmen's compensation laws, social welfare legislation for women and children in industry, extension of civil service, pure food and drug laws, governmental responsibility for slums, factory conditions, shorter hours, better wages, regulation of insurance companies, banks and saving institutions, limitation on the use of injunction in labor disputes, income taxes, the postal savings bank and parcel post. The choice on such issues seemed clear to me. When Theodore Roosevelt in 1912 pictured an immigrant steel-worker bargaining with the United States Steel Corporation and asked what the American doctrine of equality meant in that situation, when he backed laws on housing, hours of labor, and workmen's compensation against the judicial decisions which had nullified them, I was all for him. I still recall the disapproval I faced in conservative Montclair when I spoke at a mass meeting supporting his candidacy.

Such social liberalism was to me essentially Christian, and Walter Rauschenbusch, whose *Christianity and the Social Crisis* appeared in 1907, furnished welcome force to this conviction. I was strongly influenced by him. He was an inspiriting person to meet—an impressive six-footer, charming in his friendliness, handling his deafness with such patience and skill that he seemed all the more engaging because of it, and obviously a man of dynamic energy. He is remembered now as the author of influential books and as a famous professor at the theological seminary in Rochester, but to understand his passion for the Christian social gospel one must go back to that decade, beginning in 1886, when he was pastor of a little church in "Hell's Kitchen" in New York City. There in the overcrowded, health-destroying, crime-breeding slums was lighted his burning conviction that a merely individualistic gospel, taking no responsibility for the social conditions that condemn multitudes to physical and moral ruin, was both practically futile and profoundly unchristian. His social outlook came, as he said, "through personal contact with poverty, and when I saw how men toiled all their life long, hard, toilsome lives, and at the end had almost nothing to show for it; how strong men begged for work and could not get it in hard times; how little children died."

Henry Van Dusen, president of Union Theological Seminary, said once that Walter Rauschenbusch had exerted "the greatest single personal influence on the life and thought of the American church in the last fifty years." He certainly made a momentous appeal to the social conscience of the Christian churches in the early nineteen hundreds. Undoubtedly my early preaching caught some of its flavor from his influence. None of us, however, then foresaw what lay ahead, nor guessed how much more resistant to the Kingdom of God human nature is than we supposed. For the dark shadows were closing over Europe and World War I was at our doors.

Along with Walter Rauschenbusch another personality deeply influenced me—Rufus Jones, the Quaker. His book, *Social Law in the Spiritual World*, was published the year I came to Montclair and reading it was a memorable event in my life. After that I devoured everything he wrote. I was far from being a Quaker then, so far as war was concerned, but in the message of the Society of Friends, especially as Rufus Jones interpreted it, I found such vitality —what William James called "a religion of veracity rooted in spiritual inwardness"—combined with such fearless and practical application of Christian principles to social problems, that I was gripped by it.

I little guessed then what warm friendship I was to enjoy in later years with Rufus Jones and his family. He was a radiant spirit concerning whom we in our household would say what a colleague at Haverford College said: "To meet him was to feel set up for the day." He did more than believe in the "inner light"; he possessed it. Moreover, along with this vital inwardness that made his life luminous was a social passion that made him the principal founder of the American Friends' Service Committee, whose extraordinary program of world-wide usefulness has won multitudes of contributing supporters, and has gained such recognition as the Nobel Peace Prize for the Quakers.

Rufus Jones wrote fifty-seven books. It was a labor of love when after his death I prepared an anthology of his writings, the title of which seems to me still to tell the truth: *Rufus Jones Speaks to Our Time.*

No picture of my eleven years in Montclair would be true to the facts if it left out the play and fun which eased the days and kept my spirits buoyant. Music and the theater helped a lot—I never can forget that evening when first I heard Fritz Kreisler or that enchanted night when I saw Sir Henry Irving play Shylock—and golf helped too. One Saturday I picked up a game with a stranger and we finished with a tie, so that he suggested another game the next morning to settle the matter. I said that I never could play on a Sunday because I had a job which compelled me to work that day. "What kind of job is that?" he asked. "What the hell do you do on Sunday mornings?" When I told him that that was a good question, that I had often asked it myself, and that he would have to come to the First Baptist Church some Sunday morning to discover the answer, we became fast friends.

The community was kind to me and my reminiscences of that far-off time are full of humor as well as of labor. One friendly family talked so favorably about me that their

Negro maid became interested too, and was urged by her mistress to come and hear me. In those days I had a head of bushy, curly hair, and the maid's report about that Sunday service centered on that. "Fo' the Lawd, ma'am," she said to her mistress, "his very hair do proclaim him to be a man of Gawd."

It was that " 'ayrick 'ead of 'air" which gave me the best chance I ever had to get back at a toastmaster. A bald-headed presiding officer introduced me at a banquet as "the man with the crocheted hair," to which I responded, "Mr. Toastmaster, I would far rather have hair that is crocheted than hair that is nit." That story must have spread for not long ago one of my old students, meeting me by chance, looked at my thinly covered head, and remarked sadly: "Neither crocheted nor nit!"

Happy and fortunate though my years in the Montclair pastorate had been, I was growing ready to leave. The reasons were inward, not outward. The church gave every indication of being loyally united behind my ministry, and everything a church could do to persuade a minister to stay was done. I felt sure, however, that I had done in Montclair all I was likely to do and I urgently desired the stimulus of a new situation.

In 1908 Union Theological Seminary had appointed me lecturer on Baptist Principles and Polity, and in 1911 had made me an instructor in homiletics. When in 1915 the seminary invited me to a full-time position there I accepted, and became Morris K. Jesup Professor of Practical Theology.

Chapter 6.

❦

A Professor at Large

DURING OUR first summers together my wife and I
had rested in New England or had taken trips—two to
Europe I particularly recall—but when Elinor and Dorothy,
our daughters, arrived we wanted to settle down, and on
the recommendation of a friend we rented a cottage, sight
unseen, at Boothbay Harbor, Maine. My wife had known
the Maine coast before; her mother's family had come from
Calais, and her great-grandfather had been a leading figure
in the state's politics. To me, however, the coast was new,
and that first summer it became, as it has been ever since,
my first love among all places on earth.

For more than a decade we lived in a rented cottage,
used a rented boat, and for the purposes of my writing
found some isolated room in an unoccupied house. The time
came, however—we had left Montclair then—when a home
of our own seemed justifiable. Some two thousand feet off
the coast, with a deep ship channel intervening, lies Mouse
Island. It is a lovely bit of typical Maine coastland some
sixteen acres in extent, beautifully wooded, its rocky, irregular shores inviting the trees down to the water's edge.
For many years there had been on the island a hotel, which

113

burned in 1913. The owner, an elderly man, did not care
to rebuild and World War I spoiled the market for the
island's sale. So in 1919 a friend of ours joined with us in
its purchase for a sum so small that it came within our
means. There later our partners and longstanding friends,
Mr. and Mrs. G. Ellsworth Huggins, and ourselves erected
our summer homes. The Fosdicks spent their first summer
there in 1924, and during all the succeeding years the peace
and beauty of that island have been a refuge and delight.
I am writing these recollections now in my study on the
end of Slim Point, with the sea on three sides and the
woods on the fourth.

Physical recreation has always been for me a prime necessity. Squash and tennis in my earlier ministry and golf in
later years literally saved my life. I recently came upon
some letters written to my father, two quotations from
which will sufficiently light up a very important aspect of
my life:

I have just come in from a glorious game of golf with two of
my fellow ministers and, having achieved the lowest score that
was made today, I am feeling very complacent about life in
general and hopeful about the future of the world.

I am just back from a glorious game of golf, and I am sure
that the air was never fresher nor the autumn colors more beautiful than they were today. I must say that I played a perfectly
abominable game, but I covered myself with glory on the last
hole by running down 610 yards in four, one under par and too
good to be true. Consequently, forgetting the other seventeen
holes, I am perfectly happy.

Along with games, however, and now outlasting them, has been my love of walking. I never have driven an automobile. I must confess that once I tried to. Deciding to buy a car, I took my daughter's auto out on a lonely Maine road to practice in preparation for the great event. There was not a person in sight. There in complete safety I could try out my skill. The immediate result was that I backed into a telephone pole and brought pole and wires crashing down upon the car. After that, with the relieved approval of the family, I decided that driving an automobile was not my special forte, and ever since I have stuck to walking. That, too, has been a lifesaver, and if now I am growing old vigorously I give the credit in no small measure to the long walks which for years have been my almost daily habit.

It was the Maine coast, however, where my love of the out-of-doors had its most complete fulfillment, and even amid the tensions of the city, dreams of Mouse Island have been salutary medicine.

In these recollections I cannot possibly name all my friends whose affectionate loyalty has been a lifelong benediction, but as I think of our neighbors on the Maine coast, some faces inevitably present themselves: Edward and Elizabeth Jenkins, for example—my memories of "Ed" go back to my student days at Colgate when he used to visit the college as a representative of the Y.M.C.A.; Charles and Geraldine Gilkey and their family—he was lately Dean of the Chapel at the University of Chicago, and my memories of "Charlie" go back to student days at Union. The Maine coast is not only one of nature's masterpieces but, at Boothbay Harbor, it gathers a stimulating and congenial company of friendly folk who have enriched our lives. The natives are endlessly interesting and attractive, incarnating as they do the old-fashioned American way of life, with its independence and love of liberty; and with some of them especially friendship has grown in warmth and admiration for over forty years now. Once a newcomer, a "city slicker," needing wood for his fireplace, drove in his automobile to a woodsman's home and announced: "I have come to give you an order." The answer was typically Maine. "I never take orders," said the woodsman, "but sometimes I accommodate my friends."

As for interesting visitors, the impression grows with the years that sooner or later almost everybody comes to Maine. Once Sarvepalli Radhakrishnan visited the Gilkeys. He was a professor at Oxford University then; now he is Vice-President of India. That day in a small sailboat, when Gilkey, Radhakrishnan and I had a few hours of intimate conversation about the meaning of religion, is one of my most unforgettable recollections. I felt much closer to him, Hindu though he was, than to many Christians who forget the wise words of William Penn: "It were better to be of no church than to be bitter for any."

As for the Maine coast itself, I long ago lost my heart to the sea. I tire of a lake. It may be beautiful, but it is always much the same. The sea, however—especially along a broken coastline like Maine's—is endlessly varied, never twice the same, sometimes delectably lovely, sometimes tremendous and awe-inspiring.

So our island has been to us an endless blessing. It is a

long sea mile from being great poetry, but when Rachel
Field, our Maine novelist, wrote the following lines she
spoke for all the Fosdicks too:

> If once you have slept on an island
> You'll never be quite the same;
> You may look as you looked the day before
> And go by the same old name.
> You may hustle about in street and shop,
> You may sit at home and sew,
> But you'll see blue water and wheeling gulls
> Wherever your feet may go.
>
> You may chat with the neighbors of this and that
> And close to the fire keep,
> But you'll hear ship whistle and lighthouse bell
> And tides beat through your sleep.
> And you won't know why and you can't say how
> Such change upon you came,
> But once you have slept on an island
> You'll never be quite the same.[1]

Certainly, when I tackled that professorship at Union
Seminary, I was going to need this summer resort for the
body and winter resort for the mind.

Under the terms of the professorship at Union my special
responsibility was to help the students to use the Bible
intelligently in their preaching. I gave expository courses
on Jeremiah and the Epistle to the Hebrews and criticized
student sermons in the chapel. My major course of lectures

[1] From *Taxis and Toadstools* by Rachel Field. Copyright, 1926, by
Doubleday & Company, Inc., and used by permission.

tackled an urgent problem which then was puzzling modern-minded preachers: the distinction between the ancient and often outgrown ways of thinking used in Scripture, and the abiding truths and experiences which those ways of thinking enshrined. I owe my friend and teacher, James Everett Frame, an endless debt of gratitude for suggesting that theme. One day, perplexed and baffled in trying to begin the preparation of my lecture course, I talked with Frame, and that conversation turned out to be one of those decisive few moments on which so often one's life and thinking hinge. The Bible, he reminded me, was written in ancient times when many of our modern concepts had not been dreamed of. The word "nature," for example, meaning a vast universal system of law-abiding order, does not occur in Scripture. The ancient writers had to express the truths they saw in the mental frameworks of their time. Couldn't I, in one area after another, make clear what those ancient categories were, trace the changes by which new mental frameworks had arisen, and make evident both how wrong the reactionaries are when they treat the old conceptual forms as binding on us and how wrong the radicals are when they suppose that because an old way of putting truth has been outmoded the truth itself has been out-grown? So a theme which had met my own personal need before I presented it to the students—abiding truths and experiences in changing mental categories—became the keynote of my major course at Union, and years later the result was my book, *The Modern Use of the Bible*.

Moreover, this theme was relevant not only to changes in mental concepts between Biblical and modern times but also to similar changes within the Bible itself. In the twelve centuries during which the Scriptures were being written profound alterations in outlook took place, from primitive ideas to the larger vision of the Hebrew prophets and the New Testament. The tracing of these developments within the Scriptures also was included in my lectures, and my book, A Guide to Understanding the Bible, reveals how impressed I was by what seemed to me the valuable help which this approach to the Scriptures gave the preacher.

I plunged into my work at the seminary with trepidation but with enthusiasm too. I hope that I helped the students, but I am unable to express how much they helped me. Their friendship has been an inspiration all the years since. Around the globe, whether in positions humble or conspicuous, they are rendering invaluable service to the Christian cause, and I am proud of them.

I was still deeply concerned about what theologians call "apologetics," the endeavor to present a reasonable, credible, defensible interpretation of the Christian gospel. The Meaning of Faith, published in 1917, two years after I entered on the professorship, reveals this continuing interest, and I wonder that with all the new courses I had to prepare I found time to write it. It came boiling up out of the stir of my own spirit. It was as easily readable a statement as I knew how to make concerning some of the questions about faith's meaning that bothered me and that I was sure must bother others.

Meanwhile, free week ends opened the door to itinerant preaching, generally in some college pulpit, and between the challenge of the seminary classroom and the stimulus of

speaking to university audiences, I was happy. All the
time, however, World War I was in the background, and in
the end it made me more a professor at large than I had
anticipated.

From the beginning of the war in Europe in 1914 I had
been increasingly anxious that we should get into it. At a
union service of the churches in Montclair before I left
I preached an atrocious sermon on "Things Worth Fighting
For." As affairs went from bad to worse, I became impatient
with President Wilson's notes of protest unaccompanied by
deeds of resistance. To be sure, I had long been a peace
advocate after the fashion of the mid-Victorian liberals,
taking it for granted that war, along with other evils, was
bound to be outgrown, until at last

> . . . the battle flags are furl'd
> In the Parliament of man, the Federation
> of the world.

When war actually came, however, I was all for it. When
the President used phrases like "too proud to fight," I was
indignant. When he ran for re-election against Charles
Evans Hughes on the appeal that he had "kept us out of
war," I wrote a letter of protest to Mr. Hughes because he
was not, in opposition, definitely promising to take us into it.
In the spring of 1917 I preached a series of sermons,
covering three Sundays, at Leland Stanford University.
David Starr Jordan, the lately retired chancellor, an ardent
pacifist, remarked to a friend of mine afterward that some
of my sermons were better than others. From his point of

view, at least, that certainly was true, for when I got going on the war, I was belligerent.

After the session at Leland Stanford, my wife and I spent two weeks tenting in the Yosemite Valley, and there I wrote *The Challenge of the Present Crisis.* It is the only book I ever wrote that I wish had not been written. To be sure, it is not so bad that it could not have been worse, and I applaud some passages in it for their endeavor to discourage hate, their fairness to opposing views and their attempt to remain as Christian as possible even while dedicating the Christian gospel to the support of war. But the book's main objective, the defense of war, I now repudiate. I was never more sincere in my life than when I wrote it, but I was wrong. What I was mainly driving at in that book was not the business of a Christian minister to be saying.

The book met with cordial welcome. Over two hundred thousand copies of it were distributed and it was brought out in a British edition. I took none of the proceeds for my private use but devoted them all to the public cause. So far as my small influence went, I did my best to back up and even idealize the war. What a temptation war is to a preacher! He could not be a preacher if he did not love the response of attentive audiences, the kindling answer of many minds rising to meet his message, and of many hearts moved in unison. War provides a medium of deeply stirred and well-nigh unanimous emotion in which the preacher's work can become thrilling. One of the most moving sermons I ever preached was in Harvard Chapel shortly after we entered the conflict. The patriotic sentiments of the congregation were waiting to be played upon that Sunday morning and I played upon them. I used a great text—"Jesus took the cup, and gave thanks"—and appealed to strong emotions and sacred faiths. I was exhilarated then but I am ashamed now.

When we had formally entered the combat but while the spirit of the people was still limp and apathetic, I stumped New York State with a team of speakers—an ex-governor of the state, a British officer back from the front, and others—whipping up the enthusiasm of great audiences to get into the fight. To be sure, I pleaded for world federation as the ultimate hope. I was for a league of nations before there was a League. Some of my fellow speakers did not like the idea of an international organization, and the audiences did not understand it or respond to it. I did not drop the plea, but before the trip was over I learned how to bring down the house with out-and-out militaristic appeals, and never more successfully than at the final meeting in my old home town, Buffalo, where in the Sixty-fifth Regiment Armory—I had drilled there as a boy—a great assemblage blew the lid off.

Feeling thus about the war, when ex-President Taft organized a group of speakers to go to England under the auspices of the British Ministry of Information to interpret to the British people the American attitude, I welcomed the chance to join the company. President Wilson put thumbs down on the project and the group never went, but when the Y.M.C.A. offered to send me over as an itinerant speaker to the troops in France, I coupled with it the opportunity to speak also under the British Ministry of Information. Obtaining from the seminary a semester's leave of absence, I sailed for England on a troopship early in 1918.

On the way over I taught a group of Y.M.C.A. secretaries in a course of studies on the historical backgrounds of the war. I must have kept some perspective in my thinking, for I recall how surprised and even shocked some of them were at the hard facts which I emphasized, proving joint responsibility and guilt for the conflict. At least, I did not think that the allies had come into court with clean hands. That we were rightly in it, however, and that when the Kaiser said "Gott mit Uns" we could go him one better, I had no doubt. Indeed, I must have been positively bellicose, because a letter has recently come to me, thirty-five years after the event, from a person who made that crossing on the *St. Louis*. "Everyone," says the letter, "was so inspired by what you said that all would have eagerly torn into the enemy barehanded, had they been able to come in contact with them."

We sailed up St. George's Channel in the light of the full moon. For some reason we missed our convoy and passed through the danger zone on our own. The submarines were busy that night and, as I recall it, got a Cunarder on the Irish side. We zigzagged through the moonlight, some of us sleeping peacefully, but some spending the night on deck, carrying life preservers and bothered with wild rumors. I remember one young lieutenant, lately out of Harvard, rather miserable at his first taste of fear, who in the morning told me that when he heard we were safely in, "I rolled over and said the Lord's Prayer. I was mighty glad that I knew it." We landed in Liverpool, went at once to London, and that night I saw for the first time, against the face of the full moon, the German airplanes flying in to bomb the city. One recollection stands clearly out from my memories of those first days in London—a stirring address by Lloyd George, then prime minister of England, toward the close of which the sirens began blaring out their warning that the Germans were flying in for another strike. How swiftly that audience scattered! That night the Germans hit the headquarters of one of the city's newspapers and ruined it.

The next four months I spent in Britain, France and Belgium. In England and Scotland I spoke in many of the camps. I had lived my life for the most part in academic environments, and an army is anything but that. No theological course, no suburban pastorate, no professorship could ever have taught me what I learned with the troops in wartime.

Among the British I talked to all sorts of audiences besides soldiers. In one of my letters home, written from Leeds, I told of addressing a gathering of working men one morning, a general audience of citizens in the evening, a luncheon of business and professional men the next noon, with the Lord Mayor presiding, after which I was going to York for an afternoon assembly of nonconformist ministers, followed by an assemblage of Anglican clergy presided over by the Bishop of Hull. My letter home ended: "My remains will be carried to London tomorrow morning."

One Sunday spent in Inverness, Scotland, is fairly typical. I preached at the morning service in one of the churches. Those were dark days; the Germans were making their last desperate bid for a break-through and victory, and were well-nigh achieving it. The Scottish troops especially had been hard hit and their losses terrific. That morning in Inverness most of the families knew that sons, husbands and brothers were in the thick of it. When the congregation which packed the church stood up and sang the Forty-sixth Psalm, I came as near as I ever did to losing control of myself:

> God is our refuge and our strength,
> In straits a present aid.
> Therefore, although the earth remove,
> We shall not be afraid.

In addition to that morning service I spoke four times more that day—at the dedication of a new Y.M.C.A. hut, at a mass meeting for soldiers in the afternoon, at vespers in one of the churches, and at a civilian mass meeting in the evening. The next day I sought a chance to sleep up at the home of a friend, John Kelman, on Deeside.

The spirit of the British people in that crisis was magnificent. If, as Sir Winston Churchill says, the test of a nation is what it can do when it is tired, they measured up. I visited the home of Sir George Adam Smith, the famous Biblical scholar. Lady Smith received me in her husband's absence. The pictures of her three older sons, already killed in action, stood on easels in the living room, and without a quaver she spoke of them and of her one remaining son, a boy of nineteen, just leaving for the front. "He will make a good soldier," she said.

My relationship with ex-President Taft's nonexistent mis-

sion brought me an invitation to dine with the American
ambassador, Walter Hines Page. I vividly recall that informal
dinner with his charming family, and, in particular, one
story that he told. He had recently dined with the king, who
had asked him—as though he did not know—"How long a
term is it that your American president serves?" "Four years,"
answered Mr. Page. "My God!" said the king. "If I could
get through in four years, I would never stand again!"

It was living with the troops themselves, however, that
meant the most. There were great camps of Australians, New
Zealanders, Canadians, and men from the British Isles in
the Southampton plain. What I said to them I do not recall—
doubtless I talked about interpretations of America's spirit
and attitude, analyses of the issues of the war and of hopes for
the postwar world, and always the basic faiths that would
undergird morale and see men through the toughest stints.

I crossed the English Channel three times, and can see
yet the protective destroyers on either side and the blimps
overhead as we made the crossings. I spent nearly a week at
British Great Headquarters near St. Omer, and there, for
the first time, touring the battlefields in a headquarters' car,
saw what war really results in. A day spent on the Somme
battlefield revealed unmitigated desolation, so complete that
no bird, it was said, had been seen there since the ruin fell.
Cities like Arras stand out in vivid recollection, not a building
left standing and the only remaining resident one lone
old woman who refused to leave her impoverished den
beneath the fallen walls. I visited Ypres, where nothing
stood erect except the battered shaft of the old clothiers'
hall, and I saw the hospital trains come rolling into the

channel ports, loaded with wounded soldiers bound for England.

When the time came to visit the American forces, the center of operations shifted to Paris. Those were the days when "Big Bertha" was sending her shells into the city from a location sixty-five miles away. On some days and nights a shell came about every twenty minutes. The damage done by each explosion was not great—the walls of the shells were too thick and the charge too small to blow anything to pieces—so that the effect was mostly psychological. Sitting in the American Club one day a group of us heard a shell burst nearby and, going out, found that it had hit a house on one side of a square and ricocheted around the entire square to explode in a tailorshop.

The nearest I ever came to the enemy was on a trip to the front-line trenches. There I saw the kind of service rendered by the Y.M.C.A. during World War I—a service which in certain uninformed quarters was grossly misunderstood and unappreciated. Early one afternoon we started —two Y.M.C.A. men, three soldiers and I—from our dugout in the second-line trenches, and for three hours sloshed and careened over the duckboards and between the plaited sticks and wire netting of the trenches until we came to our first line in a little hamlet which had been hammered to smithereens, and then went on to dubious ground, held by our men by day but from which they retired at night. In a letter to my wife I pictured the scene:

Here we found boys who had not been paid for weeks and weeks and were all "broke." We blew ourselves—gave away tobacco, chocolate, cookies, to the whole town. The news spread.

Out from the dugouts down between the ruins, along the paths and streets the fellows streamed in to get the coveted goodies. It was great sport; I haven't had so good a time in a long time.

From this first-line town, our second-line town was plainly visible, sitting on the ridge. The Germans put on a show for us, and shelled our town again as evening came. Once more we could hear the boom of the German guns, the song of the flying shells above our heads, and the burst when they struck their mark near the old tower in our village. It came at sunset time —a wonderful sunset after a perfect day—and for a little while the show was very interesting.

Then after dark, armed with the password, we walked quickly up the road to our own billets, traversing in a half-hour what had taken three hours by trench. Perhaps I wasn't tired!

One of the first talks I made in France was in an old barn just behind the front. A group of American boys were going out that night on a foray across No Man's Land to raid the German trenches, and if the average held, a large proportion of them were bound to be casualties before morning. They were a serious group and I did the best I knew how for them, feeling all the time like a hypocrite and a coward to be bucking them up for such a task when I could not go with them. What I recall most clearly is that when I had finished talking, one of the boys said: "Would you mind offering a prayer for us?"

It was back of the lines that one had the best chance to get at the men and see what war was doing to them. I saw one of the first contingents of gassed Americans brought into a hastily improvised first-aid station, and I understood what a British sergeant meant when under similar circumstances he said: "This sort of thing makes me want to suffer everything for everyone once and get it over." I talked to a large audience in one of the venereal isolation camps. It takes more than "apologetics" to prepare one for that. I grew accustomed to stepping into a prize ring when the bout was over and "preaching" from there, and sometimes a service with a great assembly of men was staged, with high officers presiding and all the pomp and circumstance available supporting them. I was sent out to isolated details on special assignments, such as the group that took over L'Aber Wrack, a little islet off the French coast used as an outpost to watch for submarines. The commanding officer was a Wall Street man but was evidently a jack-of-all-trades, too, for that small contingent of Americans had "civilized" the barren island, putting in even waterworks where no water had been. It was here that the censor, so he told me himself, came on a letter written by one of the men to his wife back home: "Stop those nagging letters! You are 3,000 miles away and it don't do no good. Do let me enjoy this war in peace!" How much good I did the men by what I said I cannot be sure, but I have always cherished one remark that the commanding officer of a flying squadron reported a sergeant as making after one of my talks: "I don't know what religion he belongs to, but he has a hell of a lot of sense."

One evening in Brest I took dinner with Admiral Wilson of the United States Navy, and he complained that the American people knew all about the Army but had no idea what the Navy was doing. "That is your own fault," I replied. "We who return to tell the story of what we have seen here know about the Army, but have never had a chance even to

see the Navy. Let me go out on one of your destroyers, and
I will go home and talk about the Navy." So I spent a few
days with a destroyer flotilla, going out some seven hundred
miles into the Atlantic to escort into Brest a convoy of
American troopships. The commander was Taussig, afterward
Admiral Taussig, and his officers were as fine a group of men
as I have ever bunked with. As we came into Brest Harbor on
our return, I was on the bridge with one of the officers. "We
have all been wondering," he said, "just who you are and
what your occupation is. Some of us think you are a lawyer
and some a businessman. What are you anyway?" "A minister," I said. "Well, I'll be damned!" he exclaimed, and then,
as a lame afterthought, he added, "My mother is a Baptist."
Strange as it may seem, in view of the reputation sailors have,
that exclamation was the nearest approach to profanity I
had heard from any officer on board, and we had lived on top
of one another for nearly a week.

Returning home by way of England I paused in London
and, wanting to see the City Temple where Joseph Parker
once had preached, I wandered into the empty sanctuary
and, climbing the pulpit platform, sat there thinking of the
influential history of that famous church. An American,
Joseph Fort Newton, was the minister then and the verger,
concerned about this unknown visitor, went to his study and
warned him about my presence in the pulpit. So I met Fort
Newton and, indeed, preached for him the following Thursday. Years afterward when he was in New York, I used to go
to hear him when I had a free Sunday, for he was to me
the most satisfying preacher in the city then. Alas! the City
Temple was destroyed by bombs in the next war. Now,

however, in its rebuilding Leslie Weatherhead is seeing his ministry fulfilled in a dream come true.

What these experiences in World War I did to my thinking is more easily imagined than expressed. An article published in the *Atlantic Monthly,* January, 1919, entitled "The Trenches and the Church at Home" summed up part of it. I have just reread it and am astonished to remember what an uproar that article caused. I was assailed from every side— not by fundamentalists alone but by liberals and personal friends. Of course I was warmly supported too, but in general the religious press cannonaded me. What I said in gist was simply that the Army and Navy were a cross section of America, that they were grand stuff, that they were up against the stark realities with which war confronts men, and that their attitudes toward, and feelings about, religion were a scathing commentary on the average run of American churches in which they had been reared. I went into detail about these criticisms—the egocentric, save-one's-own-soul type of religion, the irrelevance of our petty sectarian divisions, and the trivial negativeness of much of the church's moralism. I think now that what I said in that article is true. Certainly it indicates that my own long-drawn-out inner conflict with conventional religion was becoming for me much more than a personal affair. I was indignant at the caricature of Christianity presented in our average stereotyped church. I had seen in France, in the attitudes of the typical American rank and file, the results of this sorry misrepresentation of the gospel. I came home not inclined to pull my punches any more in dealing with it. I recall saying in more than one address that I wanted to go on speaking to the average run of Americans, as I had spoken to them in France, and that if I could not do that freely within the church, I would do it outside.

Still my most vivid recollection of coming home that late summer of 1918 is seeing my two children dancing up and down on our cottage steps in Maine, crying, "Daddy! Daddy!" while my wife beamed over their heads. I took up home life and my professorship again as though nothing had happened —but something had. My preaching before the war never had had the drive that it had afterward.

Three Presbyterian churches in midtown New York—the Old First, the University Place and the Madison Square— had decided to combine. They were in the same general neighborhood and many of their members had moved else-where as the business section of the city crept northward. The three ministers, Dr. George Alexander, Dr. Howard Duffield and Dr. Charles Henry Parkhurst, had all reached the age of retirement, and the time seemed opportune to make one church out of the three. Concerning all this I knew little, but when I was asked to take four Sundays in the pulpit of the Old First Church where the combined congregations were meeting, I accepted because of personal ties with members there. The new church was looking for a minister—a Presbyterian, of course—and it never occurred either to me or to them that we were stepping into trouble when I promised those four Sundays as an interim supply.

The upshot was a complete surprise. They asked me to become the minister of the newly formed church. I declined because I could not make the creedal subscription necessary to be a Presbyterian clergyman, and had no desire either to leave my professorship or to change affiliation from a comparatively free to a very stiff denominational system of ecclesiastical control. Then they called me to be simply the Guest Preacher. Dr. Alexander would be made minister, one or more associates would be called to carry the parish work; my responsibility would be preaching alone, and I could retain my professorship—such was the proposal. It was very attractive. I had had four years at large without a parish. The experience had been richly worth while, but the thought of having again my own congregation, with an opportunity for consecutive ministry and the chance to combine the two vocations I had always cared for most, teaching and preaching, was alluring. I told the church that I knew nothing about Presbyterian law, that they must take full responsibility on that score, but that if such an arrangement as they suggested were permissible, I would accept.

So began six years of ministry which, although they ended in violent controversy, were, while they lasted, among the happiest in my life.

Dr. George Alexander was one of the most admirable and lovable men I ever knew and my relationships with him were completely satisfying. Along with Guthrie Speers, our colleague, we made a harmonious team. The congregations packed the church. There was no sign of objection to the arrangement from Presbyterian sources outside, and within the congregation enthusiasm was high. One year we moved to the University Place building while the Old First's auditorium was made over into a singularly beautiful place of worship. Old families that had been slipping away from the midtown churches came back and new members were steadily added. Moreover, the new combined church took over four pieces of social service, including the Madison Square Boys' Club and the Bethlehem Chapel, inherited from the previous congregations, so that seven days a week, at the home church and its branches, our ministry went on. I was proud of the spirit and program of the church and threw myself into my share of it with a full heart.

Meanwhile the fundamentalist movement was rising. War is naturally followed by reactionary trends in religion, as in society at large. People long disturbed want to get back to what they think of as "normalcy," and in religion this commonly takes the form of retreat to orthodoxy. That trend has been evident since World War II in neo-orthodoxy's influential vogue, and after the earlier conflict it took the form of fundamentalism. All this, however, did not touch us at the Old First. The spirit of the church was liberal. Some of its most important leaders were on the Board of Directors of Union Seminary. I had a free pulpit and was conscious of no restraint.

The effect of my experiences during the war was evident in my preaching. It was much less theological and much more practical than it had been. Not so much apologetics as personal and social ethics became my chief concern. The war ended, the League of Nations was founded; the practical problems of the nation and the world loomed large. This shift of emphasis is evident in *The Meaning of Service*, published in 1920. In one form or another what I was driving at in that book—the ethical application of the Christian faith and spirit to personal and social problems—was presented in the pulpit at the Old First. I am glad, however, that I put it into book form. Across the years one of the most gratifying rewards of my ministry has been the stream of letters, often from out-of-the-way places all over the world, bearing messages of appreciation for help received from these earlier books of mine. One such letter came from a father whose son, a captain in the Medical Corps of the United States Army, had written him from Iceland: "The book that has influenced me more than anything I have ever read in my life I found entirely by accident in a little dusty corner of an old abandoned bookcase on a tiny island off the coast of Iceland. It is called *The Meaning of Service. . . .*"

While my responsibility at the Old First Church was restricted to preaching, I became increasingly interested in the outreach of the church's practical service in the community and, discontented with preaching to people without meeting them in intimate personal conferences when they desired help, I began hours of individual consultation.

Meanwhile I did not altogether stop being a professor at large. In the summer of 1921 my wife and I went to China and Japan. At Kuling, Mokansan and Pei ta Ho in China and at Karuizawa in Japan I faced assemblies of missionaries gathered for conference. It was one of the most informing and revealing experiences I ever had. For one thing, I saw fundamentalism for the first time in its full intensity. The missionary community was split wide open—on one side, some of the largest personalities and most intelligent views one could meet anywhere; on the other, such narrowness and obscurantism as seemed downright incredible. It was like walking a tightrope to address such audiences. The tension was terrific. I managed to hold the conferences together while I was there, rather than widening the cleavage, but it was a strain.

What the trip contributed most to me was, of course, a chance to see the Orient firsthand, however hastily. I cannot be grateful enough for that. In these days when China and Japan have become of primary, critical importance, I can at least see, in terms of actual experience, some things that else would be mere words to me, and when the estate of subject Asian peoples is debated I can visualize the pathos and humiliation of Korea crushed under the heavy overlordship of Japan. I came away from China feeling that despite the appalling problems of such destitute masses as I had never imagined before, no race on earth has more potential greatness in it.

How little I guessed, however, what was really going on behind the scenes in that vast land! Only a decade before, Sun Yat-sen had launched his revolution; the old Manchu dynasty had been deposed and a republic had been formed. Not the republic, however, but the local war lords were in the ascendancy when I was there; and when Sun Yat-sen died four years afterward, his republic was still an unrealized dream.

A part of the blame was Japan's. In 1915, while the Western powers were absorbed in World War I, Japan had made her outrageous demands which would have brought China under Japanese domination had not the Nine Power Conference in Washington, a year after our visit, restored at least some measure of her independence. Now, in retrospect, one can see how easily then China might have slipped into almost colonial subservience to Japan. Even the Chinese war lords were in many cases playing the game with her, each hoping thereby to strengthen his own local domination.

Meanwhile the angry spirit of revolt, especially against Western foreigners, was flaming ever higher, and it was justified. If now the so-called "free nations" have lost China, the basic reason goes far back to the arrogant humiliations— the Opium Wars, the Unequal Treaties, the extraterritorial rights, the insolent assumption of racial superiority, the signs like "No Chinese, no dogs allowed," and all the rest—to which Western foreigners had long subjected the Chinese. No wonder that even when I was there in 1921 the Bolshevik revolution in Russia was making a strong appeal in China! Something like *that* many of the Chinese leaders wanted for themselves. By 1920 the Russian communists had fairly well solidified their control over Russia, and even then they began to play their hand for China. First among the nations, they offered to renounce their extraterritorial rights and to treat China as an equal. For years Sun Yat-sen had appealed to one country after another for help in establishing his republic, but, met everywhere else by refusal, he finally in 1920 accepted the aid of Russia. China would not adopt the communist style of government, he said, but she would welcome communist aid and would permit a Chinese Communist party.

All this I write now in retrospect. I did not guess then what was afoot nor what was coming out of it. At that time young Mao Tse-tung was an assistant in a university library in Pekin, while in Paris a youth named Chou En-lai was a member of the first group of Chinese communist students there. During that year when I so innocently addressed the missionaries at Kuling, Sun Yat-sen sent one of his able young soldiers, Chiang Kai-shek, to Moscow to perfect his military training. A volcano was preparing to erupt; one could feel the ominous tremors; but no one then guessed what catastrophe lay ahead.

Indeed, we Americans were especially optimistic. Had we not used the indemnities paid us because of the Boxer War for scholarships, enabling Chinese students to come to American universities? We had not fought the Opium Wars, nor seized Chinese land, nor launched the Unequal Treaties; and while we had taken advantage of special privileges, such as extraterritorial rights which other nations had arranged, we thought of ourselves as good friends of China, occupying a preferred position there. At the time of my visit my friend, John Leighton Stuart, was founding Yenching University in Pekin, and my former student at Union, Timothy T. Lew, was beginning his outstanding career as a public leader and teacher there. What a happy day my wife and I spent in the Lews' home, and how unshadowed by prophetic foreboding our hopes for China were! There, too, was the Pekin Union Medical College with its gorgeous new buildings in process of construction and with The Rockefeller Foundation assuring its future as the foremost training center of physicians in all Asia. When now I think of China's defection to the communists, I feel not alone the tragic problem with which it confronts the world, but more intimately I am heavyhearted at the frustration and defeat of the unselfish plans which in 1921 made the missionary enterprise in China a

thrilling adventure in helping to put a great people on their
feet. The Edwin Lobenstines, the Thomas Carters, and all
the other large-minded missionary leaders who were our
friends—what a devastating debacle their hopes have suffered! And who then could have pictured John Leighton
Stuart, our last American ambassador, facing the tragic
situation which a few years later confronted him?

As for Japan, I was charmed with the land and the people,
and even during the horror of Pearl Harbor and its aftermath,
I was glad to remember the great-spirited Japanese whom
I had met, such as Yukio Osaki. He was a liberal and an
internationalist, and had been minister of education in the
Emperor's cabinet. He stumped Japan for the League of
Nations and was one of the most enlightened and thoroughly
admirable men I ever met. In a long evening's conversation
in Karuizawa he shared his hopes with me, and years afterward he called on me in New York when our vicious Oriental
Exclusion Act had worked its deadly mischief. Still he kept
his unconquered international mind even though he expected
to be assassinated for it when he reached home. As a matter
of fact, assassins tried it when he landed.

I have no special competence in international affairs and
have no reason to pride myself on any gift of prophecy in
that realm. On my return from the Orient, however—on
October 9, 1921—I preached a sermon in the Old First
Church on "Do We Want War in the Far East?" Reading it
now, I am surprised to see how apparent even then were
the factors that issued in World War II. To be sure, Lieutenant-General Sato was saying: "In order to place our
Empire on a firm, permanent foundation of peace, an Empire

which has never once submitted to the insult of a foreign
nation for three thousand years of her history, we should
not permit the Japanese-American relations of today to
remain merely as a verbal quarrel across a river. We should
by all means appeal to arms and be done with it at once."
On the other side, Dr. Ebina, the venerable leader of Christian Japan, was saying: "Like a chick within the shell,
struggling to be born, young liberal Japan is growing up
inside the strong, encrusted traditions of her militaristic
state and she wants help from without as well as power from
within to burst through." Sato's mad policy won the day in no
small measure because "help from without" was lacking.

In 1924 I went to Britain as one of the exchange preachers
who were being sent back and forth between Britain and the
United States. My wife and the children accompanied me,
and especially because it was the children's first foreign
trip we had an interesting time.

My first address in England was delivered in the City
Temple before a missionary convention. Two hundred years
before, that same missionary organization had sent to New
York the funds with which to launch the First Presbyterian
Church, and my thankful recognition of that fact gave me a
toe hold to start with. That first meeting was an inspiriting
start for my weeks in Britain.

I thoroughly enjoyed speaking to British audiences of
many sorts, from a luncheon of the Liberal Club in London
to the congregation of "Free St. George's" in Edinburgh.
The schedule was heavy and the kind of addresses needed
diverse—today Queen's College, Oxford, tomorrow a Wes-

leyan chapel in the poorer section of Manchester, the next day a congregation of the Church of England at St. Martin's-in-the-Fields, London, the next a garden party at Lord Leverhulme's, the next a ministers' conference in Nottingham. I count my friendships in Britain among the most satisfying of my life's experiences, and this trip widened the circle of them. Two days spent in the home of Sir Angus Watson—he was not knighted then—I especially recall, both because of the gracious hospitality which greeted us and because, with a prophetic insight that still amazes me, he foretold the difficult changes in England's economic status and in the structure of the British Empire which were bound to come as a consequence of the war.

The University of Glasgow gave me a D.D. It was one of the most deeply appreciated honors that ever came to me. I felt very humble about it, knowing that it was not so much a tribute to me as to Union Seminary where increasing numbers of Scottish students were studying. As I marched down the aisle of the great hall with James Ramsay Mac-Donald, Prime Minister of England, as my companion in the academic procession, I was in a serious and subdued mood, but that frame of mind was soon dissipated. I had not realized what a pandemonium of roughhousing the commencement exercises at Glasgow University were. The students took possession of the galleries and from beginning to end shouted wisecracks at the speakers, drowned out with catcalls the most impressive passages in the addresses, hooted at the recipients of degrees, and even threw things at the audience —my wife was hit with a roll of toilet paper! Prohibition being then in the fore in Britain's thought of America, the galleries burst out singing when I rose to receive my degree:

How dry I am, how dry I am,
Nobody knows how dry I am.

At the luncheon afterward I remarked in my brief speech
of thanks that the exercises had sounded like a man with a
wooden leg having a fit on a tin roof, and I have wondered
ever since whether this bit of impudent American humor was
taken by that Scottish audience as Americans would take
it. Certainly, the occasion left me endlessly grateful, and
on special academic occasions I still wear with satisfaction
that red robe from Glasgow.

In September, 1925, in St. Peter's Cathedral in Geneva
I delivered the sermon at the opening of the League of
Nations session. Loyalty to the League was a family matter
with us. My brother, Raymond, during the war had been
associated with the Secretary of War as director of all extra-
military camp activities in the United States and abroad,
and he served as civilian aide to General Pershing in 1919.
He was given the Distinguished Service Medal and was made
a Commander of the Legion of Honor in France. What with
the Young Men's Christian Association, the Knights of Columbus, the Jewish Committee, and the Salvation Army operating
in the camps, he had his hands full and he did a great job.
When the League was founded and President Wilson was
still taking it for granted that we would join, he appointed
Raymond Under Secretary General of the League to represent the United States, and Raymond helped set up the first
organization in Geneva. Even in the middle-twenties, when
I preached there, hope was not dead that someday the
disgrace of our refusal to co-operate would be redeemed. It
was later that the Senate, in one of the most deplorable

legislative actions in the world's history, having turned down the League in 1920, turned down the World Court also in 1929.

These years of combined teaching, preaching and itinerant speaking passed swiftly, and despite the fact that fundamentalism in the country at large was growing increasingly self-conscious, well organized and cantankerous, it did not occur to me during the early years at Old First that the arrangement we had entered into would not continue indefinitely. Thunder clouds, however, were gradually filling the sky. One Sunday in May, 1922, I preached a sermon on "Shall the Fundamentalists Win?" Then the storm broke.

Chapter 7.

🍃

The Fundamentalist Controversy

THE CONFLICT between liberal and reactionary
Christianity had long been moving toward a climax. There
were faults on both sides. The modernists were tempted to
make a supine surrender to prevalent cultural ideas, accepting
them wholesale, and using them as the authoritarian standard
by which to judge the truth or falsity of classical Christian
affirmations. The reactionaries, sensing the peril in this shift
of authority, were tempted to retreat into hidebound obscurantism, denying the discoveries of science, and insisting on
the literal acceptance of every Biblical idea, which even
Christians of the ancient church had avoided by means of
allegorical interpretation. As Reinhold Niebuhr neatly sums
it up: "That part of the church which maintained an effective
contact with modern culture stood in danger of capitulating
to all the characteristic prejudices of a 'scientific' and 'progressive' age; and that part of the church which was concerned
with the evangelical heritage chose to protect it in the armor
of a rigorous biblicism."

When the storm did break, chance placed me near the
center, and I tell the story of the controversy, as I experienced it, not because my share in it was more important

144

than many others', but because I did have an interesting opportunity to see it from the inside.

My sermon, "Shall the Fundamentalists Win?" was a plea for tolerance, for a church inclusive enough to take in both liberals and conservatives without either trying to drive the other out. I stated the honest differences of conviction dividing these two groups on such matters as the virgin birth of Jesus, the inerrancy of the Scriptures and the second coming of Christ, and then made my plea that the desirable solution was not a split that would tear the evangelical churches asunder, but a spirit of conciliation that would work out the problem within an inclusive fellowship.

Since the liberals had no idea of driving the fundamentalists out of the church, while the fundamentalists were certainly trying to drive the liberals out, the impact of this appeal fell on the reactionary group. "Just now," I said, "the fundamentalists are giving us one of the worst exhibitions of bitter intolerance that the churches of this country have ever seen. As one watches them and listens to them, one remembers the remark of General Armstrong of Hampton Institute: 'Cantankerousness is worse than heterodoxy.' There are many opinions in the field of modern controversy concerning which I am not sure whether they are right or wrong, but there is one thing I am sure of: courtesy and kindliness and tolerance and humility and fairness are right. Opinions may be mistaken; love never is."

If ever a sermon failed to achieve its object, mine did. It was a plea for good will, but what came of it was an explosion of ill will, for over two years making headline news of a controversy that went the limit of truculence. The trouble

was, of course, that in stating the liberal and fundamentalist
positions, I had stood in a Presbyterian pulpit and said
frankly what the modernist position on some points was
—the virgin birth no longer accepted as historic fact, the
literal inerrancy of the Scriptures incredible, the second
coming of Christ from the skies an outmoded phrasing of
hope.

There might have been no unusual result had it not been
for Ivy Lee. Head of one of the nation's foremost publicity
organizations, he was a liberal Presbyterian, and the sermon,
printed in pamphlet form by the church, caught his attention.
He asked the privilege of distributing it to his nation-wide
clientele, and I consented. Mr. Lee cut out a few innocuous
sentences of the homiletical introduction and conclusion,
provided a fresh title, "The New Knowledge and the Christian Faith," broke up the sermon into sections with attractive
subcaptions, and distributed it with a commendatory message
calling attention to its importance. None of us foresaw the
stormy consequence. Mr. Lee and I subsequently became
warm friends, and I know that he always took pride in the
way he put that sermon over.

The attack that followed was launched by Clarence Edward Macartney, then minister of a Presbyterian church in
Philadelphia. He was very decent and dignified in his attitude. While his theological position was in my judgment
incredible, he was personally fair-minded and courteous.
Indeed, when the storm was just breaking, he wrote me
directly, in order to be sure that he was not misquoting me.
After that we had some frank and not unfriendly correspon-
dence, in which he presented his own unbending orthodoxy,

shocked at my doctrinal looseness; and I, still hoping that tolerance might win, tried in a conciliatory way to make him see that while I differed from him in my intellectual formulations, I was endeavoring to maintain, just as much as he was, the timeless values and truths of the gospel. It was, however, a vain attempt.

I returned to my preaching after a summer's vacation in 1922 to face a tense situation. The congregation at the church was solidly behind me, but around the horizon storm clouds were gathering. Fundamentalism, especially among Presbyterians and Baptists, was fighting mad, and I was an easily accessible object of attack. One immediate result was that the congregations at the church, which always had filled the auditorium, now overflowed all available auxiliary spaces and took up every foot of standing room. This went on until even the chancel steps were crowded, and when I went into the pulpit someone sat down in the seat I vacated until the sermon was finished.

Among fundamentalist Presbyterians the attack naturally took the form of a determined endeavor to get me out of that pulpit. It was bad enough, they thought, to have heresy preached in a Presbyterian church, but to have a Baptist do it was intolerable. The General Assembly of the Presbyterian Church which met in 1923 had before it overtures from ten presbyteries wanting something done to stop my heretical preaching. William Jennings Bryan, then at the top of his form as a defender of the faith against evolution, was one of the leading figures of the Assembly, and his oratory helped to achieve a fundamentalist victory. Anyone who ever heard Bryan speak can understand that. I had the privilege twice, once at Westfield in 1896 when a crowd of us, carrying goldenrod, heard him plead for free silver, and once at Harvard where, before an audience which jammed Sanders Theater, Bryan attacked evolution. It was an extraordinary performance. What he said was nonsense, but the way he said it—his voice, his inflection, his sincerity—was fascinating. At any rate, he dominated the General Assembly in 1923.

The Committee on Bills and Overtures brought in a majority report, referring my case to the judgment of the New York Presbytery; but, by a vote of 439 to 359, a minority report was adopted, expressing "profound sorrow that doctrines contrary to the standards of the Presbyterian Church" were being proclaimed in the Old First pulpit, and directing the Presbytery of New York to take such action "as will require the preaching and teaching in the First Presbyterian Church of New York City to conform to the system of doctrines taught in the Confession of Faith." Moreover, the minority report specified five doctrines, in particular, which they had in mind: the inerrant Bible; the virgin birth; the substitutionary atonement, Jesus' death "a sacrifice to satisfy divine justice"; the physical resurrection of Christ "with the same body in which he suffered"; and Christ's supernatural miracles.

Both as a gentleman and as a Christian I found myself in a difficult position. I was a guest in a denomination to which I did not belong and was causing trouble in the household of my host; and I was a lover of peace and harmony, wanting a church more united, not more divided, who instead was occasioning vehement discord. Upon hearing of the General Assembly's decision, therefore, I presented my resignation to the session of the church. The fact remained, however, that I was being attacked as a representative of liberal Christianity—"modernism's Moses" one humorous fundamentalist dubbed me—and I had an obligation not to leave my fellow liberals in the lurch with a defeat on their hands when patience and persistence might yet win a victory. When, therefore, the session unanimously declined to present my resignation to the congregation, I let them have their way, to see if the conflict, whose first battle we had lost, might turn out to be a war whose ultimate victory might be ours.

That next church season, 1923-24, was one of the most strenuous I ever spent. The part of it which I recall with greatest distaste was the political maneuvering, the drafting and redrafting of statements, and all the questionable compromises involved in trying so to present the matter to the next Presbyterion Assembly that our arrangement at Old First could somehow continue. I found myself caught in a long process of ecclesiastical intrigue which I thoroughly disliked.

I had seriously and, I think, rightly committed myself to a tolerant policy, believing that the belated doctrinal issues then crowding into the center of attention were really marginal and would so turn out to be, and that, therefore, the church ought not to split because of them but hold together and ride out the storm. My mind and conscience were thus on the side of conciliation, but in the end it involved more than I had bargained for.

The committee of the New York Presbytery, under the chairmanship of Edgar Whitaker Work, at once started to prepare for the General Assembly in 1924 a report that would mollify the opposition. Appeasement was their policy, and I presume inevitably so. They were my stanch friends; they wanted my ministry at Old First to go on; they saw that it could not go on unless they won over a majority of the next Assembly; and so they began painting my portrait in as orthodox outlines as possible and portraying the background situation at Old First to make it seem innocuous.

Dr. Work's committee wanted a statement from me to include in its report. I sent a tentative draft. They were very complimentary about it, calling it "a straightforward, manly and magnificent statement," but that exaggerated praise was only setting for their discontent. They were troubled by the "absence of any even remote hint or suggestion of admission or concession" in it. They wanted me, so they wrote, to "express some doubt as to your own judgment in preaching the sermon, 'Shall the Fundamentalists Win?'" They very much wanted me to rephrase my affirmation of faith, using words with a more orthodox aroma than the ones I had employed, and in general they wanted me to assume that the aggrieved party in the dispute was not myself but the General Assembly, and so to approach the Assembly with concession and even apology. Of course I could not do it. I recall yet my struggle over that letter for Dr. Work, torn as I was between the desire to help my friends and my entire unwillingness to say what they wanted me to say.

The covering letter which I sent along with my formal

statement reflects my difficulty. I regretted the necessity of disappointing Dr. Work's expectations. I protested that while he pictured my statement being read by conservative Presbyterians, I pictured it being read by young men and women who had looked to me in some measure for spiritual leadership and who would be wondering whether I had "stood by my colors" or had "trimmed, hedged, and compromised." I was glad to calm down a few phrases "needlessly aggressive and perhaps strident," but "putting a positively apologetic and concessive note" into the letter, I could not do. So far as the troublesome sermon was concerned, I said that "far from having searching of conscience because I preached the sermon, I should have had desperate and intolerable searching of conscience if I had not preached it or something like it"; and I added: "I have thought and rethought the problem in the hope of finding some way of making a statement for your purposes, but every time I tried, I framed a statement even less concessive than the one I thought of at first." The best I could do was to omit all reference to the sermon. I was willing to substitute "deity" for "divinity" in affirming my faith about Christ, "because they mean the same thing," but I could not make the other verbal changes he asked for. And I ended by saying:

Even if I could write the letter which you have suggested, I am positively certain that it would do no good whatever, and for the simple reason that I must not take in this letter a tone which I don't take anywhere else. No one who knows me personally, hears me preach, lecture, or reads my books, can for a moment suppose that I take an apologetic and deprecatory attitude toward the gospel which I preach. Upon the contrary, I am proud of it; I believe in it; I stand by it. With all the inevitable limitations and mistakes, I am sure that it has in it the seeds of hope for the future generation. I do not apologize for it; I proclaim it; and everybody knows it. It would therefore convince nobody (even if it were honest) for me to take in this letter to you under these special circumstances a tone of voice which I never take anywhere else. The letter which I am now sending you seems to me to be a natural and straightforward expression of the thing that I say in my private conversation, in my sermons, lectures, and books. Whether you can use it or not I do not know. If you find it impossible to use it I shall of course understand thoroughly.

And all this fuss was about a statement in which if I erred at all, I erred on the side of conservatism.

Meanwhile, as the months passed the controversial uproar grew ever louder and more obstreperous across the country. The headlines screamed and even the Episcopalians entered the fray, so that in 1924 Bishop William T. Manning of the New York Diocese begged his clergy to observe a truce during the Christmas season. My own situation became correspondingly warm, with three groups throwing fagots on the flame.

First, the fundamentalists themselves grew increasingly vehement. In pulpits, magazines, pamphlets and mass meetings they assailed the liberals and called on them to leave the evangelical churches. Their slogan was concisely stated in a mass meeting of Presbyterian fundamentalists in New York: "We have a right to demand that those who serve as pastors of our churches shall 'hew to the line' in matters of faith." When my ministry came within their range of fire another factor added ammunition. "Dr. Fosdick," cried an outraged Presbyterian at another New York mass meeting, "is a foreigner within our gates, without standing or credentials that have been considered; one who is considered a usurper and whom the Supreme Court of our Church has told very plainly he was not welcome."

If the Presbyterian fundamentalists disliked me, their Baptist brethren went them, if anything, one better. They held a series of mass meetings of their own, at the opening session of which John Roach Straton, pastor of the Calvary Baptist Church in New York, tore loose. "We are driven," he said, "to the conclusion that Dr. Fosdick is not only a Baptist bootlegger, but that he is also a Presbyterian outlaw; without the slightest personal ill will and with no desire to injure him personally, I nevertheless declare, in the light of Bible teaching, and in the name of eternal truth, that Dr. Harry Emerson Fosdick is a religious outlaw—he is the Jesse James of the theological world."

One incident I had almost forgotten until recently I ran upon an account of it in an article by my friend, Arthur Baldwin. The reader must remember that he is my friend— he succeeded me in the Montclair pulpit, then went to a long pastorate in Philadelphia, and for years has been our neighbor in the summer community in Maine—so that one must take his estimate of my preaching prowess with more than one grain of salt. His article reminded me of the ferocity with which the attacks of the Baptist fundamentalists began. Said Arthur Baldwin:

When I came back from France after World War I, I found
our Baptist folk in turmoil. Dr. Fosdick was to preach the annual
sermon before the Convention in Denver and the fundamentalist
faction was up in arms. Judge Freeman, a Denver jurist and a
pronounced conservative, was leading the opposition. In the
spirit of "Curfew shall not ring tonight" they were pulling every
wire and denouncing the denominational leaders who had foisted
this evil on them. Nevertheless Dr. Fosdick preached as planned.
Before a sharply divided audience he took as his theme, "The
Unshaken Christ." Considering the time and place, the intensity
of feeling, that sermon stands out in my memory as the greatest
sermon I ever heard. . . . One of the conservatives told me afterwards that he sat there simply shaking with emotion. Judge
Freeman did the handsome thing afterwards. He did his best to
persuade Dr. Fosdick to leave the Presbyterian Church he was
serving in New York and take the pastorate of The First Baptist
Church of Denver.

Alas! That chastened mood among the Denver Baptists
proved to be transient. When later I was called to the Park
Avenue Baptist Church in New York, they resolved "that
we use all honorable means to prevent the seating of delegates from the Park Avenue Church at the coming Northern
Baptist Convention."

Much of the attack on me, especially in Presbyterian
circles, was maintained upon a dignified level. It represented the honest concern of dogmatic minds to keep the
church static in doctrine, and it stated its case without
descending to personal abuse. Indeed, the idea that the
membership of the evangelical churches was sharply divided
into two groups, convinced liberals and militant reactionaries, grossly misrepresents the situation. There were all

sorts of liberals and all sorts of fundamentalists; and many more who were neither one nor the other regarded the whole controversy with mystification and distaste. Most liberals were not nearly so modernistic as their foes pictured them, and most fundamentalists were not nearly so pugnaciously reactionary as the liberal portrait of them commonly made them out to be. I recall with respect and gratitude the stanch conservatives who did not agree with my opinions but who were gracious, fair-minded and courteous. What Carlyle said after his talk with Sterling I would say of my friendly relationship with them: "except in opinion not disagreeing."

As the controversy went on, however, and angry passions became overheated, the vocabulary of invective sometimes became unrestrained. This excerpt from the *Western Recorder*, a Baptist publication, is fairly typical of many fundamentalist broadsides:

It will be remembered that the said Fosdick professes to be a Baptist preacher, and is the pastor of the First Presbyterian Church of New York City. It goes without saying that Presbyterian cash looks good to him, and withall covers a multitude of Baptist doctrines. Yet, after all, so far as this world is concerned, what is doctrine compared to dollars?

As is well known, Mr. Fosdick denies the virgin birth of Christ, the inspiration of much of the Bible, and believes he has brute blood in his veins. Baptists have nothing to do with his antecedents, though confessedly they are bad enough, but certainly he is pretty "foxy." A preacher who can draw a fat salary for being, and not being a Baptist, at one and the same time, is certainly "walking about Zion," and telling things, other than towers.

In addition to his other chameleon accomplishments, the floriferous Fosdick is a professor in, probably, the most heretical and heterogeneous theological seminary in all the round world. There is little doubt that he fills the position without grace but with distinction, to the extinction of the truth of the Scripures. And while he lacks faith in the fundamental truths of Christianity, it's "dollars to doughnuts" that he has faith enough in the monthly pay check to deposit it at the bank.

We are told that Esau sold his birthright for a "mess of pottage," but this was a mere bagatelle compared to what some men receive for renouncing the once delivered faith. Of course Mr. Fosdick is anxious to please a certain clientele, and surely he has his reward. It is a safe guess that the spiritually unfumigated Fosdick will not vacate his profitable pulpit until his congregation "tenders him his resignation." In the meantime we may expect to hear him raise a howl (the language of his professed ancestors) about the "narrowness," "bigotry" and "unbrotherly spirit" of the Northern Presbyterian Church. It will also be surprising, if some uniontarian, latitudinarian, broad-as-all-outdoors Baptist does not bob up to express his sincere sympathy with this "lovely spirit." Selah!

Such fundamentalist fulminations repeatedly recalled Dryden's remark about Jeremy Collier: "I will not say 'The zeal of God's house has eaten him up'; but I am sure it has devoured some part of his good manners and civility."

Preaching Sunday after Sunday amid such angry denunciations was not easy. I did my best not to let the controversy dominate my ministry or make me forget what preaching was really meant to accomplish. Charles Clayton Morrison, then editor of the *The Christian Century*, wrote an article about me at that time, two sentences of which I have always especially appreciated: "What I like most about Fosdick the heretic is that he does not seem to care about capitalizing his heresy. He keeps on capitalizing his catholicity, just as if he were an unnoted and humble pastor directly responsible for the souls of the modest flock which the Father had given him to tend."

That, at any rate, was what I tried to do, although of course I was blasted for *that* by radicals who wanted me to shout shocking heresies every Sunday.

Meanwhile, my foes were raising the winds of controversy to ever-increasing fury.

The second party in the conflict was made up of my friends. They did not all agree with me doctrinally, but they were in general on the liberal side, and in particular were deeply concerned about maintaining personal freedom in the church. The outcome that would follow a fundamentalist victory was clear. As one typical Presbyterian reactionary put it: "How can men who are honest stay in the Presbyterian Church when they no longer believe in her doctrines? There is only one honest way for these brethren to act. Let them get out!" This meant, however, that the church's doctrines were finally to be frozen in terms which the fundamentalists chose and that both all liberty of interpretation and all possibility of progress were to be denied. This raised an issue much larger than any individual; I was only by chance thrust into a representative position, standing for a kind of Christian liberty that all liberals had to stand for if they were not to be driven from the evangelical churches.

My friends, therefore, were contending not so much for
me—although personal loyalty often warmed their efforts—
as for the essential liberties of the Christian ministry. To
have the General Assembly try to enforce five such defini-
tions of indispensable belief as it was requiring the New York
Presbytery to impose on me was more than they could
stand. They rose in revolt and fought for their freedom.

On the first Sunday after the 1923 Assembly John Kelman,
a Scottish Presbyterian, then minister of the Fifth Avenue
Presbyterian Church, New York, made a typical statement:

When I came here in 1919 I had never heard of that declaration
of the Assembly. In the questions which were addressed to me
no reference was made to any such declaration. If there had
been any such reference and if it had been necessary for me
to profess my agreement with it, I could not have accepted a call
to any church in America.

The impression that ministers of this church are bound to consider these forms of statement as essential is one which would
have the most serious consequences upon the minds of thinking
men and women around us, and especially upon the mind of the
rising generation. For their sake, as well as for my own, I therefore feel it my duty to associate myself with those who entered
their protest against the action of the General Assembly.[1]

Many of the most impressive voices in the Presbyterian
church, such as Henry Sloane Coffin and William P. Merrill, spoke in similar fashion. Henry van Dyke, then a professor at Princeton, came back for a Sunday in his former
pulpit at the Brick Presbyterian Church, New York, to say
roundly: "These famous 'Five Points' of the Assembly . . .

[1] *New York Times,* May 28, 1923.

are not valid as a definition of the fundamentals of Christian faith. They have no binding force. You do not need to trouble about them." And Presbyterian editors such as Nolan R. Best and James E. Clarke risked serious damage to their publications and the loss of their own positions to take their stand for freedom in the church.

Altogether it was a hot situation for me, caught as I was between the attacks of my foes and the defenses of my friends, and compelled Sunday after Sunday to face over-flowing congregations expectantly awaiting some message worthy of the occasion. I had been reared in a church which has no authoritative written creeds and which gives to each congregation autonomous control over its own affairs. As I watched the operation of the Presbyterian system, making individual congregations subservient to the Presbytery and the Presbytery subservient to the General Assembly, with a written Confession of Faith that modern minds can subscribe to only with mental reservations, I was ill at ease.

Nevertheless, fundamentalism was no peculiarly Presbyterian problem; it was an urgent peril in all the evangelical churches; and by the selection of the reactionaries I had been made for the time being a symbol of liberalism. It would have been easy to insist on my resignation from Old First, but had I done so my liberal friends would have called me a quitter. It clearly looked as though I could best serve the cause by staying on and fighting it out.

Meanwhile, I never knew before that I had so many friends. A letter signed by several hundred professors and students of Cornell University strongly backed me up, writing, they said, "in solemn protest against these misinformed and unchristian attacks and in pledging our unqualified loyalty to you as the leading American interpreter of the Christian religion for men and women of scientific training." Letters of similar import came from institutions as far apart as Mount Holyoke College in Massachusetts and the Southern Methodist University in Texas, and one that I especially valued was sent by five hundred and sixty professors and students at Columbia.

President John Grier Hibben of Princeton, himself a Presbyterian minister, came to my defense in a baccalaureate sermon, saying that "a part of the Christian church has recently been stampeded through fear of a great teacher and prophet of righteousness in New York City, because the group which would call him to account does not speak his language or understand his thought." President W. H. P. Faunce of Brown gave me his spirited support: "Nearly all Christian ministers with whom I am personally acquainted and all the college teachers that I know believe substantially what Dr. Fosdick has been preaching with such lucidity and power as to win the approval of two continents. If any particular denomination does not wish to hear his message, that denomination is the loser and not Dr. Fosdick."

As for the secular press, I never can be sufficiently grateful for the loyal backing of men like John Finley, of the *New York Times*. The outrageous escapade of the Scopes trial in Tennessee, backed by William Jennings Bryan, was to come in 1925, but its foreshadowings were apparent and many citizens who would ordinarily have given a religious controversy only amused or disgusted attention were awakened to the public menace involved in rampant fundamentalism, so that the secular press commonly reflected sympathy with the liberal cause.

I marvel yet at editorials such as one that John Finley wrote for the *New York Times* when it became apparent that my days at Old First were numbered:

It is plain that the whole loss will fall not upon Dr. Fosdick, but upon the Presbyterian Church. It will have convicted itself in the eyes of the lay public not only of a certain denominational narrowness, but of the folly of giving up the services of a preacher whose good report has filled the whole city, become known throughout the entire country and reached the knowledge of the churches in England. Such a voice as that of Dr. Fosdick's is in no danger of being silenced by any technical ecclesiastical veto. He has but to speak, anywhere, and people will flock to hear him. Without artifice in the pulpit, or the slightest trick of ministerial sensationalism, he has moved thousands by the quality of his thought and the depth and sincerity of his religious emotions. When a church, no matter of what denomination, has at its disposal such a preacher of spiritual power in a time of dominant materialism, it is so stupid as to be almost wicked to let him go. It seems very close to a violation of the Scriptual injunction to quench not the spirit. But Dr. Fosdick need not think of abandoning his great following or his high mission. If not in one pulpit, then eventually in another, his exceptional vocation for the ministry will, no doubt, be exemplified so long as strength and life do not fail him.[2]

With a good deal of hesitancy I include these tributes, not only because they are part of the record, but because

[2] *New York Times*, Oct. 7, 1924.

I wish to remove any possibility of supposing that in this
bitter controversy I was in any sense a martyr. Some of
my too enthusiastic friends were tempted to add that halo
to me, but there was no occasion for it. I thoroughly disliked the whole contentious and embittered episode; at
times I seriously wondered what the ultimate effect upon
my opportunities as a Christian minister would be; but I
was all the time supported by powerful backing from those
by whom one would most choose to be backed, so that
there was never any occasion for developing a martyr com-
plex.

Especially at the Old First Church I was unanimously
sustained by a friendliness for which I can never be sufficiently thankful. My colleagues in the ministry there, Dr.
Alexander and Mr. Speers, bore a heavy load on my behalf,
and their loyalty never failed. Dr. Alexander was a great
personality, more conservative than I in his theological
opinions, but devoted to large-spirited, inclusive Christianity. Under his leadership the whole congregation rallied
around my ministry, and amid the tumult on the outside, the
parish within was not only harmonious but vigorously
active in its work, as though the best answer to attack was
not recrimination but a practical illustration of what a
church like ours could mean in a modern metropolis.

It was not alone the fundamentalists and liberals, however, who heated the fires of controversy; a third group,
smaller in number but vociferous in expression, added to
its vehemence. This group was made up of left-wing religious radicals. Many of them had been ministers or members

of evangelical churches, and finding the constraints intolerable had left them. They took the same position the fundamentalists did on one point: that the liberals should leave the evangelical denominations. Common honesty, they thought, demanded that the liberals get out. No criticism of my attitude from the fundamentalists was more harsh than some that came from this left-wing group. They insisted that my only decent course was to do as they had done— shake the dust of the evangelical denominations from my feet.

The difference in point of view between the evangelical liberals and this left-wing group was important. The radicals, motivated by disgust with the evangelical churches, wanted them left to their own hidebound, obscurantist devices. We, on the other hand, were determined not to surrender to the fundamentalists the control of the great historic denominations. We saw in them priceless values; we treasured the Christian heritage of which, with all their faults, they were the most influential conservers; we felt ourselves one with them in the abiding, substantial truths they stood for, despite our disagreement with their outgrown theological formulas. For all the liberals to desert them, leaving their long-accumulated prestige, their powerful influence and their multitudes of devoted Christian people in the hands of fundamentalist leadership, seemed to us an unthinkable surrender and an intolerable tragedy to the Christian cause.

Moreover, the left-wing group, so we thought, lost their perspective in exaggerating the importance of the controversy. They commonly saw it as the crack of doom for

the old denominations, the beginning of a final split that
would line up the evangelical churches under reactionary
control, on one side, and all honest, outspoken modernists
on the other. I recall a conversation with one of these radicals. He could with difficulty repress his contempt for my
attitude. He thought the controversy was one of the most
momentous events in the church's history, a kind of new
Reformation that would force the withdrawal of all intelligent, sincere modern minds from the old-line institutions. He thought this, in part, because he wanted it, and the
popular tumult of the controversy encouraged him to see
his hopes in process of fulfillment. As for evangelical liberals
in general and for me in particular, we seemed to him
to be trimming. Why did we not see that the great split
had now come, that the time for toleration and conciliation
had passed, and that the only honest thing for all of us to
do was to quit the old denominations?

We, on the other hand, thought that the controversy,
despite the noise it made, was an ephemeral affair, with
the matters in dispute, such as the five points the General
Assembly raised, insufficient in importance to disrupt the
historic churches. I often confided to my friends my sense
of shame that I was unwittingly made the front and center
of a controversy over such belated issues. The questions
in dispute were not the great matters that confronted
modern Christianity; they were trivial in comparison with the
real issues of the day; and the whole uproar was not the
noise of the main battle but the flare-up of a rear-guard
action. The idea of splitting the great churches over such
obscurantism as William Jennings Bryan stood for seemed
to us absurd; the slow but inevitable processes of education

were bound in time to put an end to such outdated thinking;
and meanwhile our place was inside the evangelical
churches, patiently standing our ground, claiming our
liberty, and biding our time. The outcome, I am sure, has
validated our stand.

The left-wing group, however, who thought me a trim-
mer because I did not accept their policy, had sharp tongues
and pens. I sympathetically understand the difficulty which
they felt in my position. I had been troubled too deeply
by the hemming and hawing, the backing and filling, of
evangelical liberals caught in creedal churches where the
fact of theological progress had not been recognized and
the right of doctrinal reinterpretation had not been granted,
not to have felt the desire to flee the whole tangled situation.
Nevertheless, I was sure then, and am sure still, that these
radicals were mistaken about the main issue: for the liberals
to have deserted the old-line denominations and to have
surrendered them to reactionary leadership would have
been a recreant and craven policy, with tragic conquences.

A typical champion of the radicals was Albert C. Dieffenbach, editor of *The Christian Register*, an influential Unitarian magazine. He had been a minister in an orthodox
church until, revolting against the theology imposed on him,
he had become a Unitarian. He had the zeal of a convert:
"We must have the reformation which was never completed
in Luther or any of the churches since his time except the
Unitarian Church."[3] To him the major glory of the Unitarian
movement was not its fight for liberty but its stand for a
specific set of doctrines: "As a church we owe whatever
vitality and usefulness we have in the world to our distinctive

[3] *The Christian Register*, March 9, 1922.

theological stand."[4] To be a liberal, as he understood the term, was to hold these specific doctrines and fight for them, so that to him an evangelical liberal was an impossibility: "An evangelical Christian is not a liberal, in the accepted use of both words. They are mutually exclusive terms."[5] He, therefore, as much as the fundamentalists, made uniformity of doctrine the basis of a church, and he wanted a theological fight that would split the old-line churches on a doctrinal basis and drive the liberals out.

It is not surprising, therefore, that he took his gloves off and went for me with a vengeance. "If our sympathy goes over completely to Dr. Fosdick for his spirit," he wrote, "our intelligence goes over quite as completely to Dr. Macartney for his impregnable defense of the orthodox Presbyterian faith;"[6] "I have the profoundest respect for a man who is consistently a Roman Catholic, or for a man who is consistently a fundamentalist, but I have no respect for the attitude of Dr. Fosdick."[7] I found myself, therefore, raked by fire from two directions—the fundamentalists and the radicals—and which was fiercer I do not know. Dr. Dieffenbach painted in flattering terms qualities in me that would have made me, so he thought, an ideal messiah to bring in the kingdom of modernism, if only I would belligerently take up the role; and he deplored as cowardly surrender what he called my choice instead "to be a popular preacher."[8] He accused me of insincerity. "When he goes

[4] *Ibid.*, Oct. 30, 1924.
[5] *Idem.*
[6] *Ibid.*, Dec. 14, 1922.
[7] *The New York Times*, Nov. 29, 1924.
[8] *The Christian Register*, Nov. 29, 1923.

to Cambridge," Dr. Dieffenbach said, "he speaks in terms of liberalism and when he comes to New York he says, 'I am an evangelical Christian,' "[9] whereas the fact was that I never preached a sermon at Harvard which I had not first preached in my own pulpit. He asserted that the sermon which Ivy Lee sent out was not the sermon I had actually preached, but was "an amended version, which omits a great deal of the challenging, indignant and militant tone of the other."[10] This was completely untrue; nothing was omitted in Ivy Lee's "version" except a few sentences of homiletical introduction and conclusion.

I suppose that I should have felt complimented by all this, for what Dr. Dieffenbach wanted was that I should join him in becoming a Unitarian. His methods, however, were certainly not persuasive. He even wrote: "Dr. Fosdick has never, to the best of our knowledge, told us a word that would imply that the Bible from beginning to end is other than perfect, absolutely inerrant in its ethical and spiritual content. Think of that!"[11]—which was a howler to all who followed my teaching at the seminary or my preaching in the church, and certainly was strange news to my fundamentalist foes.

I recall now these attacks of Dr. Dieffenbach with genial good will; he was fighting with holy zeal what he thought was the battle of the Lord; but, fortunately for me, some of the strongest voices in the Unitarian fellowship were lifted in my defense. Professor Francis Peabody, of Harvard, wrote a letter to *The Christian Register* warmly supporting

[9] *New York Times*, Nov. 9, 1924.
[10] *The Christian Register*, Jan. 24, 1924.
[11] *The Christian Register*, June 7, 1923.

my stand, and his covering personal message to me when he sent me a copy of it reads:

I do not wish to inflict on you any more literature, but am tempted to send you the enclosed letter, which is, indeed, much more restrained and temperate than in its first draft, when my indignation got loose. The Unitarian communion has always suffered from adherents who bring with them the traditions and habit of mind of rigid Protestantism, and feel bound to perpetuate the same contentions to which they are accustomed. This militant editor is, in short, a Lutheran by instinct, and conceives all Liberalism as agreement with him, just as the fundamentalists define Christianity as agreement with them. Free churches must tolerate these reversions, which are really signs of an inbred orthodoxy. They are entirely alien to the traditions of Unitarians, and I should commend to this editor not only some devout reading of the writings of Fosdick, but also a closer acquaintance with the writings of Channing and Martineau, both of whom have with constant reiteration reported their vision of a Holy Catholic Church, with diversity of administration but the same spirit and Lord.

I have no right to press any advice on you; but I earnestly hope you will not be betrayed into further controversy, but will simply deliver your message with the courage you have always shown.

So the debate grew increasingly warmer, and meanwhile, not only in the parish but outside it, I went on trying to saw wood. In the spring of 1924 I delivered the Lyman Beecher Lectures on Preaching at Yale University on *The Modern Use of the Bible*. The lectures came out of the background of my major course at the seminary, but when

they were delivered in Battell Chapel at Yale, everyone
was thinking of them in terms of the current controversy. As
one of my friends who read the printer's proof of them
said—thinking of the General Assembly's demand that I
assent to the Presbyterian creedal requirements—"Anyone
who read your Yale Lectures and then heard you assent to
the first constitutional question would call you an unmitigated liar, and would be perfectly justified in doing
so." He was right about that. I could gladly have affirmed
my faith that "the Scriptures of the Old and New Testa-
ments" *contain* the word of God but not that they *are* the
word of God, and certainly I could not have applied the
word "infallible" to the whole Bible.

Between the meetings of the General Assembly in 1923
and 1924, these three groups I have tried to describe—
fundamentalists, evangelical liberals, and left-wing radicals
—kept the pot boiling, with all of us wondering just what
was being cooked. When the news of the Assembly's action in
1924 broke, I was in Britain. It was in Manchester, I recall,
as I was about to go on the platform to address a mass meeting, that a cablegram came, telling me that the Assembly
had invited me to become a Presbyterian and begging me
to postpone response until I heard the case presented by
my friends. I knew the answer then, but I waited patiently.

What had happened at the General Assembly was briefly
this: a defense of my ministry, made as conciliatory as
possible, was presented by the Presbytery of New York
along with a minority report attacking my ministry, signed
by twenty-two of the Presbytery's ministers and elders;
these two reports were submitted to the Judicial Commis-

sion whose recommendation the Assembly adopted, that if I were to continue in the pulpit of the First Presbyterian Church, I should regularize my position by becoming a Presbyterian minister "subject to the jurisdiction and authority of the Church." "If he can accept the doctrinal standards of our Church," said the Judicial Commission, "as contained in the Confession of Faith, there should be no difficulty in receiving him. If he cannot, he ought not to continue to occupy a Presbyterian pulpit." The Commission, therefore, recommended that the New York Presbytery, through the proper channels, "take up with Dr. Fosdick this question to the end that he may determine whether it is his pleasure to enter the Presbyterian Church and thus be in a regular relationship with the First Presbyterian Church of New York as one of its pastors."

The *New York Times* headline "FOSDICK DECISION PLEASES BOTH SIDES" fairly well represented the immediate reaction among Presbyterians. Mr. Bryan exclaimed exultantly: "We have won every point"; and, on the other side, Dr. William Merrill said: "The decision reached seems to me to be one with which all should be reasonably satisfied, and it is particularly pleasing to friends of Dr. Fosdick that the invitation to enter the Presbyterian ministry is so cordial and courteous." Certainly that invitation was pressed upon me with persuasive vigor by my Presbyterian friends. Never before or since have I been under such pressure. It was not easy to have loyal Presbyterian supporters say: "We have backed you through thick and thin, now you must back us up." They saw in my acceptance of the invitation the end of the controversy; I knew that it would be only the beginning. The reason for Mr. Bryan's satisfaction in the Assembly's decision was only too evident. Once within the regular ranks of the Presbyterian ministry I could be tried for heresy the first time I uttered a liberal conviction, and obviously many irritated and watchful men were itching for the chance. Indeed, Dr. Mark Matthews of Seattle, a leading fundamentalist, said so explicitly. Cornelius Woelfkin, then minister of the Park Avenue Baptist Church, New York, wrote to a friend about three months after the Assembly's meeting:

I see the Presbyterian fundamentalists are putting on the war paint again for Dr. Fosdick. A Dr. Matthews of Seattle, who has the largest church in the country, has gotten out his tomahawk. William J. Bryan said to a friend of mine six weeks ago, "We will not have any preacher in our church who is not within reach of our stick."

Dr. Parkhurst, who is here, said to me, "It is too bad, but I cannot see how Dr. Fosdick can join the Presbyterians. It will keep the church stirred up all the time."

To the urgent letter of the Presbytery of New York, therefore, pressing upon me the acceptance of the Assembly's invitation, I sent a declination, and the salient paragraphs in it so clearly reflect my thinking at the time that I include them here:

My decision not to become a Presbyterian minister is not at all due to denominational reasons. Were the transfer of my membership from one denomination to another the only question involved, I have no sectarian loyalties that would make the change difficult. But that is not the only question involved. The proposal of the General Assembly calls for a definite creedal subscription, a solemn assumption of theological vows in terms of the Westminster Confession.

In answer to this proposal I must in all honesty set my long-standing and assured conviction that creedal subscription to ancient confessions of faith is a practice dangerous to the welfare of the church and to the integrity of the individual conscience.

There have been two historic attitudes toward creedal subscription among evangelical Christians. Some have welcomed it, have founded their churches upon acceptance of definite formulations of faith, and then with the passage of time and the coming of new ways of thinking they sought liberty from the literal meanings of their confessions by emendation and interpretation.

Others, equally evangelical, have felt that this practice is perilous to honesty and hampering to the free leadership of the Spirit. They have distrusted the ethics and feared the effect of subscription to ancient forms of statement, involving successive reinterpretations of the meaning attached to the words. They have refused to require this in their churches and, as individuals, they have not submitted to it. To this second way of thinking I unreservedly belong.

There are many creedal statements, such as the Augsburg Confession, the Westminster Confession, the Thirty-nine Articles, which express in the mental formulas of the generations when they were written abiding Christian experiences and convictions. I honor all of them; they represent memorable achievements in the development of Christian thought. But for me to make a creedal subscription in terms of any one of them would be a violation of conscience.

Let me add also that this general and long-standing attitude toward creedal subscription is necessarily heightened by the particular situation in which I now find myself.

In theology I hold the opinions which hundreds of Presbyterian ministers hold. I am an evangelical Christian. So many men of my position have been cordially welcomed into the Presbyterian ministry, as holding the substance of doctrine for which the church stands, that I have no reason to suppose that the Presbytery of New York would fail to receive me. But after two years of vehement personal attack from a powerful section of the Presbyterian Church, I face now an official proposal which calls on me either to make a theological subscription or else leave an influential pulpit. Any subscription made under such circumstances would be generally and, I think, truly interpreted as moral surrender. I am entirely willing that my theology should be questioned; I am entirely unwilling to give any occasion for the questioning of my ethics.

One further reason for my declination remains. I undertook my present relationship at the First Church with entire good faith. Knowing nothing about Presbyterian regulations with regard to the employment of ministers from other denominations, I refused to take responsibility for any decision in the matter. When, however, the Session of the Church, the Presbytery and the Synod had passed upon the proposed arrangement without a dissenting voice, I supposed that my relationship with the church was without taint of irregularity.

It was the interdenominational character of the arrangement which chiefly attracted me. Here was an object lesson in the new freedom with which Christians could disregard denominational lines and work together. The arrangement at the First Church has been so regarded in popular thought, and I have rejoiced in that aspect of the relationship.

The proposal of the General Assembly, however, would reverse all that. I recognize that the Assembly's decision concerns the particular relationship at the First Church and cannot fairly be interpreted as a general rule excluding the ministry of non-Presbyterians from Presbyterian pulpits. Nevertheless, the principle involved in the decision, if logically applied, would certainly tend to discourage the employment of any except Presbyterian clergymen as ministers in Presbyterian pulpits.

It may not enact a rule, but it suggests a precedent. It encourages a return to the principle of a denominationally "closed shop." It represents, so it seems to me, a retrograde sectarian movement. As a convinced interdenominationalist, therefore, who does not believe in an exclusive but in an inclusive church, I must not consent to the decision. To concur with it would be to agree with an attitude with which I radically disagree, to fall in with a denominational spirit which I regret and deplore.

As you see, my reasons for declining the courteous invitation which you have extended to me spring from my conscience. I must not do what for me would be a disingenuous and fictitious thing, under the guise of taking solemn vows. I am sure you would not have me do it.

I supposed that the Old First Church's acceptance of my resignation, which was the necessary consequence of this letter, would end the matter, but it did not. I could no longer hold any official place in the ministry of that church, but no one had ever doubted the right of a Presbyterian congregation to invite such preachers as it pleased to occupy its pulpit. To that right the congregation of Old First appealed as the last chance of continuing something like our former relationship. "Therefore," they wrote, "after your resignation as Associate Minister takes effect, we invite you to make it your custom when not otherwise engaged to preach in our pulpit on Sunday mornings." The letter that carried this invitation was as warmhearted and persuasive as any I ever received but, of course, an affirmative answer was impossible. With the concurrence of the New York Presbytery, in order to give the church time to prepare for the inevitable break and in the hope of guiding the church's spirit into a constructive attitude that would override the immediate rebelliousness that many felt and save the parish's membership from threatened withdrawals, I agreed to preach for them until the first of the following March, 1925.

Those last months in the Old First pulpit were strenuous. I note a headline in the *New York Times* of October 27— "JAM FIFTH AVENUE TO HEAR DR. FOSDICK—CROWDS TIE UP TRAFFIC AT HIS FIRST APPEARANCE SINCE RESIGNATION WAS ACCEPTED." That kind of thing in greater or less degree went on, despite the fact that I steadfastly declined to descend to any sensationalism or to capitalize the controversy in order to draw a crowd. I was bent on one major aim: to leave the parish harmonious, vigorous and united in its determination to continue without a break its important ministry to the city.

My last Sunday in the pulpit I will let the *New York Times* describe:

A great wave of religious emotion swept over the crowded congregation of the First Presbyterian Church, Fifth Avenue and Eleventh Street, yesterday morning, when the Rev. Dr. Harry Emerson Fosdick preached his "Farewell" sermon. Most of the women in the church were in tears, and many of the men struggled to hide their feelings, when the minister who had preached to them for five and one half years reached the end of his final sermon. . . .

No one left the church after the benediction, which closed the service. Everyone remained standing in the pews or in the aisles. Dr. Fosdick started to descend from the pulpit to mingle with the congregation as has been his custom. Before he could leave the pulpit the emotion of the men and women in the front rows overcame them. They hurried forward and ascended into the pulpit, all that could get in. For fifteen minutes they stayed there, surrounding Dr. Fosdick and assuring him of their unending support.

Then the preacher got down from the pulpit and a double row of people filed past him to shake his hand. He remained an hour to exchange good-byes and listen to the heartfelt words of men and women, some with tears in their eyes, who echoed the hope that it was not farewell but only au revoir.

Dr. Fosdick in his sermon had all but crushed the hopes of his followers. He told them frankly that he did not share the expectation that the General Assembly of the Presbyterian Church could be persuaded to let him return as special preacher.

"When I leave this pulpit today," Dr. Fosdick solemnly declared, "I do not expect to return."

In his sermon Dr. Fosdick defied the men who had accomplished his defeat. He implied that those who had beaten him had won only a pyrrhic victory. All they had done, he went on, was to build a sounding board that carries his message further than it had ever gone before.

"They call me a heretic," he said. "Well, I am a heretic if conventional orthodoxy is the standard. I should be ashamed to live in this generation and not be a heretic."

The retiring preacher thanked the First Church for the liberty of speech given him, extolled the experiment of church unity made there as a success, despite the interference of outsiders, and begged the congregation to "stand by" the church and not to "mind" him.

Chapter 8.

༄

The Riverside Church

As MY MINISTRY at Old First drew toward its close, other opportunities began opening, none more improbable at first than the proposal from the Park Avenue Baptist Church in New York. John D. Rockefeller, Jr. invited me to lunch and broached the matter: Would I consider succeeding Cornelius Woelfkin whose retirement was imminent? I thanked him and said that I did not see how I could do it. When Mr. Rockefeller asked why, I replied that while the Park Avenue Church had an associate membership for unimmersed Christians, baptism by immersion was required for full membership and I was unwilling to conduct a pastorate under such a restriction. He asked whether, in case that restriction were removed, I would consider an invitation, and I answered that such an action on the church's part seemed to me highly improbable, but that even if it were taken, I would still say No. Once more he asked why, and I replied that the Park Avenue edifice, seating about eight hundred people, was situated in one of the swankiest residential areas of the city, and that if I accepted the pastorate there, I would be justifiably accused of surrendering a real opportunity for public influence to become private chaplain to a small group of financially privileged people. Mr. Rockefeller patiently inquired whether, in case they moved to another site and built a church amply equipped to serve the metropolitan community, I would take the pastorate then. My answer seemed obvious. They had just built the Park Avenue edifice—the first service there was held in 1922—and it was incredible that the church would do what he suggested; but, I added, even if they did, I could not become their minister. Once more Mr. Rockefeller asked why, and I answered: "Because you are too wealthy, and I do not want to be known as the pastor of the richest man in the country." Dead silence followed, and then he said: "I like your frankness, but do you think that more people will criticize you on account of my wealth, than will criticize me on account of your theology?" The laughter following this sally helped at least a little to grease the ways for the launching of the Riverside Church.

To my immense surprise the Park Avenue congregation met the conditions—eliminating all sectarian restrictions on membership, thus opening the church to all Christians on equal terms, and undertaking to build a new and ample edifice equipped for community service. To these decisions there was surprisingly little opposition within the church, the action so nearly unanimous that it opened a door I could not refuse to enter.

Because Mr. Rockefeller was the best-known member of the church, and because my relationship with him has occasioned curiosity, I may comment on it here. I had known him personally for a decade. Frederick T. Gates, that extraordinary personality who for years had been the guiding spirit in distributing the benefactions of John D. Rockefeller, Sr., had been my friend in Montclair, and in 1916, three years after its organization, he had seen to it that I was made a member of the Board of The Rockefeller Foundation. I had retained that position until in 1921 my brother, Raymond, was elected to the Board, when I retired because one Fosdick was enough. So I had known Mr. Rockefeller, Jr., and had watched him at close range. When, therefore, he invited me to the pastorate of the Park Avenue congregation, I told him that if I shrank from the kind of misinformed talk my becoming his minister was likely to cause, it was not at all because I feared him. One of the most considerate, friendly, self-effacing, co-operative persons I have ever known, he was so far from desiring to dominate either the church's policies or the minister's utterances that he has always leaned over backward to avoid either. I have known him as a trustee of the Riverside Church to argue strongly against a proposed policy which the official boards were considering, and then when outvoted, I have seen him take the chairmanship of the committee appointed to put the policy into operation, and at the cost of hard work carry the matter he had voted against to a successful conclusion.

In personal relationships he liked best those who stood up to him; he thrived on honest opposition, respecting the opinions of those who differed from him, just as he wanted his own opinions respected. No minister could have had a better partner than he has been, and I look back now on many years of association with him with grateful appreciation. He has been a devoted believer in the interdenominational policy of the church, and his breadth of view and inclusiveness of spirit have been a constant inspiration and support. Certainly he has never lifted a finger to limit my liberty, and I trust him completely, as I have every reason to. As for using his money as a means of influence over the church, it is characteristic of him that he early put his annual contribution to the budget at Riverside Church into a capital fund and gave it outright to the church, thus surrendering personal control over it. Whatever influence he has had in the church is due to his own character and wisdom, and to the gratitude of his associates for the loyal support he has given to the whole enterprise.

A minor but typical incident reveals his habitual attitude and manner. One Sunday morning a member of the congregation, waiting to be shown to her seat, found Mr. Rockefeller, who had arrived later than usual, standing beside her. She overheard him say to the usher, as he looked at the already crowded nave: "I'll not disturb the congregation by going up to my usual pew; I'll find a seat in the balcony." Whereupon an aggressive, pompous stranger, not recognizing Mr. Rockefeller, said to the usher: "Show me a seat downstairs. I am not the balcony type." That story went the rounds, not only because of its humor, but because everybody who knew him recognized in it Mr. Rockefeller's characteristic spirit.

Another personal friend in the Park Avenue Church, James C. Colgate, made the new relationship agreeable. As a student in college I had met the Colgate family, and had shared the affectionate devotion which many generations of students had felt for "Jim." When as a senior at Union Seminary I was assistant at the Madison Avenue Baptist Church, I found

Mr. and Mrs. Colgate and their family there. I was a poor, struggling theologue then and there was no reason why they should have paid me special attention, but they did. For a year I had dinner at their home almost every Sunday; they were endlessly kind to me; I loved their children and have counted them my good friends ever since. One never forgets a thing like that. Since I came to maturity and public notice I have made many friends, but here was a family that took me in when I was an obscure youth. Mr. Colgate was one of the best backers I ever had—in later years he was chairman of the committee that supervised and guaranteed the support of my radio program—and when he died it was, in a real sense, the end of an era for me.

The terms on which I agreed to become minister of the Park Avenue Church were worked out one evening at a conference between Mr. Rockefeller, Mr. Colgate and myself. They found me rather difficult. I had been caught once in a position where I could not be honest without raising an ecclesiastical storm, and I recalled Bill Nye's saying that a man who is bitten twice by the same dog is better adapted to that occupation than to any other. It was fortunate that we were friends to start with. We came to an agreement, and due in no small measure to Mr. Colgate's persuasive presentation, the church confirmed our proposal.

It is useless to begin naming others whose leadership in those first days made our venture possible—men like Edward L. Ballard, president of the Board of Trustees at the start, and Albert L. Scott, his successor. Never was a minister surrounded by an abler and more loyal group of men and women.

At the Park Avenue Baptist Church it was understood that Dr. Woelfkin was to carry on until I returned from a sabbatical year abroad; that then, in addition to my service at the church, I was to continue my professorship at Union Seminary; that colleagues were to be called to the church's ministry who would carry major responsibilities in the new program; and that I declined to accept more than five thousand dollars a year as salary. Fantastic rumors long were circulated and believed concerning my financial relationships with the Riverside Church. Dr. Dieffenbach during the fundamentalist controversy wrote in *The Christian Register*: "It is reported that Dr. Fosdick receives for his service at First Church $1000 a month,"[1] whereas the fact was that my salary there was five thousand dollars a year, and in passing from Old First to the new relationship I refused to accept more recompense than I had been receiving. I had my professor's salary anyway and to have paid me in addition what ministers of prominent churches in New York commonly received would have been too much. In later years, as under the pressure of responsibilities at the church I surrendered gradually my teaching and salary at the seminary, the church correspondingly increased my recompense, but no similar church in New York, I think, has paid its minister a more moderate salary than the Riverside Church at my insistence has paid me.

Before starting for Europe I preached one Sunday morning in the Park Avenue Church, on May 31, 1925. I note the *New York Herald Tribune* front-page headline the next morning: "FOSDICK OPENS HIS 'THRILLING ADVENTURE' IN 'FREE' PULPIT." It was certainly a memorable day for me, the more

[1] Mar. 20, 1924.

so because Dr. Woelfkin was in the pulpit to introduce me
to the pastorate of the congregation he had served long and
well. Dr. Woelfkin was a strong, vibrant, radiant personality.
Before I ever dreamed of coming to the Park Avenue pulpit
we used to play golf together. I recall with amusement now
that during the fundamentalist controversy, when on the
links we wanted an especially long shot, we would say to the
golf ball, "Your name is John So-and-So," and then we
would swat it. Without his preceding ministry and his strong
desire that I should be his successor, all that has followed
since would have been impossible. It was not I who made
the Park Avenue Church what it turned out to be, a liberal
fellowship ready for an adventure into unrestricted interdenominationalism. From the days of Thomas B. Armitage,
1846 to 1888, the church had had a series of broad-gauge,
free-minded, outspoken ministers—W. H. P. Faunce, afterward president of Brown University, notable among them—
and Dr. Woelfkin stood worthily in their succession. That
first Sunday in the Park Avenue Church was crowned by his
presence, and at Riverside I have been proud to preach in
a pulpit bearing this inscription: "This pulpit is given in
memory of Cornelius Woelfkin, Pastor of the Park Avenue
Baptist Church 1912-1926, whose wise and progressive leadership made this church possible."

The next year, spent abroad, was a notable experience.
We put our daughters in a Swiss school and then launched
out. Our trip up the Nile to the First Cataract was made the
more significant because James Henry Breasted, the Egyp-
tologist, was there and opened to us the archaeological treas-
ures of the land as only he could do. From Egypt we went

to Greece, where Mr. and Mrs. Henry Morgenthau, Sr.—he
had formerly been American ambassador in Athens—were
our hosts. They outdid themselves in generous hospitality,
and we saw all that then was seeable in Greece. Returning
to Geneva, I left the family there and sailed for a brief visit
to New York to review the plans for the church's new edifice
which were then maturing. Everything was going well. I
discovered what all the years afterward confirmed, that I
was associated with a group of laymen whose wisdom and
ability were equal to any task imposed on them. I returned
to my family in Geneva reassured and enthusiastic about
the prospects of the new venture.

The high point of our trip was our visit to Mount Sinai and
the Holy Land. From the Red Sea port of Tor we went into
the Sinaitic Peninsula on camels, and after a thrilling experience, living in the Monastery of St. Catherine on the traditional mountain, we rode our camels to Suez, an eight-day
trek through the desert, seeing in reverse the probable route
of the fleeing Hebrews under Moses' leadership. We had
good companions, Maynard Owen Williams, of *The National
Geographic Magazine*, Henry Soulen, an artist for the *Ladies'
Home Journal*, and "Brother Jacob" Vester, of the American
Colony in Jerusalem. Altogether the trip was everything we
could have dreamed, and now, over thirty years afterward,
I can vividly recall our happy, jolting company on camelback,
singing at the top of our voices:

> Oh, we're waddling through a wadi, with our
>   camels in a string,
> Full of tea and lemon toddy and 'most every
>   liquid thing,

We are headed in for Suez, for a hotel
    and a tub,
And we've seen a lot of thrilling sights
    from Sinai to a dubb.[2]
Oh, we're waddling through a wadi,
    fellahin and fellahs too,
We are slowly learning everything that
    camels ever do,
And when at last we reach our homes,
    and ride by gas and steam,
We'll waddle through a wadi still in many
    a wistful dream.

After our return from Sinai my wife and I for two months made our headquarters at the American Colony in Jerusalem, and from there went out to the most rememberable places in the Holy Land. What those two months have meant to me during all the years since I dare not try to estimate. The Bible gained fresh vividness and animation. From the fall of Jericho to the crucifixion of our Lord the events narrated in Scripture fit the landscape and are carved and sculptured in its hills and valleys. We sailed the Dead Sea and built our campfires on its shores, watching the sun go down in glory behind towering Olivet, and there from thirteen hundred feet below sea level we saw, as the invading hosts under Joshua saw, the snow-crowned crest of Mount Hermon, nine thousand feet above. The Hebrew prophets came to life again as we visited their ancient homes, and step by step we followed the Master's ministry from Nazareth to Golgotha.

An American visitor in Jerusalem once remarked that if she had known Palestine was talked about in the Bible, she

[2] A hideous desert lizard.

would have brought a copy with her! Well, not only is Palestine talked about in the Bible, it illumines and explains the Bible, until one visualizes its personalities and its events as though one were seeing them afresh. To spend a moonlit night on Mount Tabor, to walk with memories of the Master over the hills of Nazareth or beside the Sea of Galilee, to stand on Neby Samwil and see Bethlehem and Calvary only five miles apart, to see the amazing acres of wild flowers, which Jesus saw, fairer than Solomon in all his glory, to rest beside the very well where Jesus talked with the woman of Samaria, to sit under the olive trees on the hill where he made his decision in Gethsemane—such experiences left an indelible impression on my thought and life. I wrote a book about our visit—*A Pilgrimage to Palestine*—which still is being used by those who travel there, but even a whole book cannot adequately express what those two months meant to me.

As for Zionism, it was vigorously getting under way. Rabbi Judah Magnes, president of the Hebrew University in Jerusalem, took us on a tour of the new Jewish settlements, and I was deeply moved by the courage, ardor and devotion with which those pioneers were tackling the renovation of the land. Rabbi Magnes had high, idealistic hopes of the service which his people would render, not to Jews alone, but to the Arabs also. "So far as I am concerned," he said, "I am not ready to try to achieve justice to the Jew through injustice to the Arab. I would regard it as an injustice to the Arab to put them under Jewish rule without their consent." He believed in a cultural Zionism that would put at the disposal of the Middle East modern agricultural and industrial techniques and methods of social service with which the Jews would usher in a new day for all the people. Ominous portents of trouble, however, were obvious even thirty years ago. On both sides the leadership was slipping from men like Judah Magnes, and aggressive, chauvinistic, even violent Zionists were being met by fearful, angry, resistant Arabs. On the Jewish side the radicals, called "Revisionists" then, were formulating policies which issued years afterward in such horrors as the assassination of Count Bernadotte and the massacre at Deir Yassin. On the Arab side the Grand Mufti in Jerusalem, Husseini, said to me once at dinner: "I am a man of religion and therefore a man of peace, but if the percentage of Jewish population in Palestine rises above a certain level, there will be war."

"While tragedy is obviously possible," I wrote, "I personally hope that Zionism may succeed." When I wrote that, however, I was distressed, as I still am, by foreboding doubts. "If the partisans of political Zionism, as now seems probable, are allowed to force the issue," I said, "I am willing to risk my reputation on prophecy: Zionism will end in tragedy." I can only hope that the deplorable tension and hatred, assassination and massacre, which have made Jewish-Arab relationships one of the most explosive perils in the world may somehow find a constructive solution.

We made our homeward journey from Palestine by way of Syria and Turkey. Then we picked up the children in Geneva and sailed to face the challenging opportunity to which the rest of my active ministry was to be given.

The plans for the new building were drawn in 1926, but five busy years passed before the Riverside Church was dedicated. I am often asked how we came to select the site on

Morningside Heights. The major reason, I suspect, was the fact that already so many educational and religious institutions had begun moving to the Heights that it was clearly going to be one of the foremost cultural centers in the nation, and no adequate Protestant parish church was there to minister to the countless thousands who were being drawn to the neighborhood by its unique opportunities. Columbia University already was there, with its affiliated institutions, Teachers College and Barnard College. The Union Theological Seminary was across the street from our chosen site, and the Jewish Theological Seminary was erecting its new buildings a block away. The Juilliard School of Music was our immediate neighbor and International House was across a small park from our proposed building—an interracial, international institution where five to six hundred students lived, coming from at least sixty-four countries and studying in some forty-seven colleges and professional schools in the city. St. Luke's Hospital had already moved to the Heights, and the Cathedral of St. John the Divine, having laid its cornerstone in 1892, was slowly beginning its progress toward becoming one of the two or three largest cathedrals in the world.

Our family, after three years in Englewood, New Jersey, had lived in a professor's apartment in the Union Theological Seminary since the end of World War I, and I had seen this amazing aggregation of cultural institutions develop, with more in the offing sure to come. Perhaps I had something to do with choosing the church's site, but when once the proposed location was suggested, I recall only a favorable consensus of opinion in the congregation. At first we selected a block overlooking Morningside Park, a half-mile away from our present site, but Columbia University begged us to let them have it for their much-needed expansion and, fortunately for us as well as for them, we shifted our attention to the then unpromising bluff above the Hudson River. Two private dwellings and an unsightly apartment house occupied the site. I remember inspecting it one day and hearing a man—a resident, I suspect, in the apartment house—loudly telling a friend his low opinion of the folly and stupidity of building a church there. "What good will it do?" he shouted.

It was indeed a venture to move from a settled residential area like Park Avenue to this new location, but I used to take comfort from the experience which a previous minister of the church, Dr. Thomas Armitage, had when in the eighteen-sixties the congregation began planning to move from Norfolk Street up to the wild fringes of civilization on Forty-eighth Street just off Fifth Avenue. Said Dr. Armitage:

> I was by common consent written down as absolutely insane for leading the church outside the bounds of civilization. There was one kind-hearted brother in the church who seriously doubted whether, after all, I was in my right mind. One day he gently hinted at the matter, saying: "Pastor, I have great faith in phrenology; will you go down to Fowler and Wells to have your head examined?" "Oh, yes!" I said, "William, anything to oblige you." I went. Fowler went over the hard bumps and gave me a written report, dated June 24, 1864. The brother was delighted with it and believed in my up-town project afterwards right heartily.

At any rate, venturesome though our proposal was, we faced no such doubt and reluctance. Indeed, during those years of waiting before the new edifice was ready for occupancy our membership nearly doubled.

One incident which graced those intervening years I recall with relish. Having sold our Park Avenue property to the Central Presbyterian Church, we had to move out, and the trustees of Temple Emanu-El offered us freely the use of their former synagogue, Temple Beth-El, at Fifth Avenue and Seventy-sixth Street, which they had just vacated to go to their new edifice. We worshiped in Temple Beth-El until our new building was completed, and the courtesy and generosity of our Jewish hosts knew no bounds. One of our trustees was so moved by this exhibition of fraternal good will that, meeting a friend of his, a member of Temple Emanu-El, he exclaimed, "That was a very generous thing you did in offering us the use of your synagogue"; and then, forgetting himself, he added, "That was a Christian thing to do." "Christian!" said his friend, "What do you mean—'Christian?' That was a Jewish thing to do!"

Another incident during those intervening years I recall with anything but relish. Dining one evening with friends in the neighborhood, I was called to the telephone by my daughter and told that the new church was on fire. It certainly was —a spectacular blaze that called out tens of thousands both in the city and across the Hudson in New Jersey to view the sight. The wooden scaffolding, which then filled the nave, had been set afire by a carelessly strung electric wire, and the result cost us nearly a year of extra waiting before the damage was rectified and the church completed. One good result of our misfortune was a new law, making wooden scaffolding illegal and requiring steel.

Meanwhile, the most painstaking thought was being given to making the new building not only a fully equipped center for practical service to the community, but as beautiful a sanctuary for worship as we could construct. Early in the planning of the new church Mr. Rockefeller, who was chairman of the building committee, said to me—a bit apprehensively, as I recall—that he supposed I wanted a spacious auditorium primarily fitted for preaching to large congregations. Upon the contrary, I answered, I wanted a sanctuary primarily fitted for worship. We had the unique opportunity to build all at once not only a center of social service but a cathedral, where one could preach to be sure, but where not the pulpit but the high altar would be central and where beauty of proportion and perspective, of symbolism and color would speak to the soul even when the voice of man was silent. To that end Mr. Rockefeller, ably backed by Eugene C. Carder, one of the church's ministers, devoted himself with unstinted care and labor.

The major inspiration for the new sanctuary came from Chartres Cathedral—the clerestory windows were actually made in Chartres—but one who studies in detail the church's iconography will see that it reflects the interests and judgments of the modern world as well as the cherished values of the ancient Christian heritage. Among the statues in the chancel screen Sir Joseph Lister and Louis Pasteur stand with Hippocrates and others around Christ the healer; Henry Drummond and Pestalozzi are in a group around Christ the teacher; Abraham Lincoln, Florence Nightingale and General William Booth, along with fifteen others, surround Christ the humanitarian. I suppose that I am responsible for the

fact that the carvings which crown the pillars in the nave
narrate the major events in the life of Jeremiah—to me the
greatest of the Hebrew prophets—and Eugene Carder, I am
sure, chose the six preachers whose figures stand in niches
on the nave's south wall: Chrysostom, Augustine, Savona-
rola, Latimer, John Wesley and Phillips Brooks.

The sculptures over the west portal attracted the most
public comment, for there, with Christ triumphant above the
doorway, was an arch covered with carved figures—a series
representing scientists, including Charles Darwin and Albert
Einstein; another representing philosophers from Pythag-
oras to Ralph Waldo Emerson; another representing religious leaders from Moses, Confucius, Buddha and Moham-
med to John Milton, William Carey and David Livingstone.
When Dr. and Mrs. Einstein landed in New York City on
December 12, 1930, they visited the Riverside Church that
very afternoon. The news that he was sculptured over the
doorway of a Christian church had reached him in Germany,
and he had been reported in the press as wanting "to see
that oddity." He was a charming guest and I recall the feeling in his voice when, looking at that arch of the world's
foremost scientists with himself the only one there still living,
he exclaimed: "That could not have happened anywhere
except in America." He was impressed also by the "scholars'
window" in the nave, and when he saw in the stained glass
Immanuel Kant walking in his garden, attended by his faith-
ful servant carrying an umbrella, he said with a laugh: "I
will have to be very careful for the rest of my life as to what
I do and what I say."

In 1929 we began using the lower levels of our new edifice

for the Church School, and at last on October 5, 1930, we occupied the completed structure, dedicating it formally on February 8, 1931. That was a crowning day after a long wait. Looking forward to it, I had written a hymn which was sung at the dedicatory service:

> God of grace and God of glory,
> On Thy people pour Thy power;
> Crown Thine ancient church's story,
> Bring her bud to glorious flower.
> Grant us wisdom, grant us courage,
> For the facing of this hour.

That was more than a hymn to me when we sang it that day—it was a very urgent personal prayer. For with all my hopeful enthusiasm about the new venture there was inevitably much humble and sometimes fearful apprehension. One day Dr. Carder and I sat together on the foundation walls of the new edifice, which had just reached the street level, and said to ourselves with anxious foreboding: "What a tragedy if all this should turn out to be a flop!" Moreover, even if it were not a "flop" the possibilities were dreadfully present that it might not be the kind of success the Master could approve. While we were still in the Park Avenue edifice, I preached a sermon in which I said:

You know it could be wicked for us to have that new church— wicked! Whether it is going to be wicked or not depends on what we do with it. We must justify the possession of that magnificent equipment by the service that comes out of it. If we do not, it will be wicked. . . .

Very frequently in these days people come to me and say,

The new church will be wonderful. My friends, it is not settled
yet whether or not the new church will be wonderful. That
depends on what we do with it. If we should gather a selfish company there, though the walls bulged every Sunday with the
congregations, that would not be wonderful. If we formed there
a religious club, greatly enjoying themselves, though we trebled
our membership the first year; that would not be wonderful. . . .

If all over the world, at home and abroad, wherever the Kingdom of God is hard bestead, the support of this church should
be felt and, like an incoming tide, many an estuary of human need
should feel its contribution flowing in, that would be wonderful.
If young men and women coming to that church should have
Isaiah's experience, seeing the Lord high and lifted up, his train
filling the temple, and if they too should discover there their
divine vocation—"Whom shall I send and who will go for us?"
—and should answer, "Here am I; send me," that would be
wonderful. If, wherever soldiers of the common good are fighting for a more decent international life and a juster industry, they
should feel behind them the support of this church which, though
associated in the public thought with prosperity and power, has
kept its conviction clear that a major part of Christianity is the
application of the principles of Jesus to the social life, and that
no industrial or international question is ever settled until it is
settled Christianly, that would be wonderful. And if in this
city, this glorious, wretched city, where so many live in houses
that human beings ought not to live in, where children play
upon streets that ought not to be the children's playground, where
unemployment haunts families like the fear of hell, and two weeks
in the country in the summertime is a paradise for a little child,
if we could lift some burdens and lighten some dark spots and
help to solve the problems of some communities, that would be
wonderful. If in that new temple we simply sit together in

heavenly places, that will not be wonderful, but if we also work together in unheavenly places, that will be.

Such, at any rate, was our ideal when we dedicated the Riverside Church.

When we at last settled down to work in the new edifice the membership grew rapidly, the congregation overflowed the nave, the community on Morningside Heights gave us a warm welcome and organized under our roof some of the most worth-while enterprises of the neighborhood. I can speak without immodesty of this gratifying development because I had so little directly to do with it. No minister, I am sure, ever had a better staff. I often have said to my friends that I am a genius as an organizer, and that my genius consists in disliking organization, recognizing that I know little about it, and so picking out able colleagues, turning the task of organization over to them and forgetting it. Dr. Carder had been associated with Dr. Woelfkin for nine years before I came to the church, and it was a supreme piece of good fortune that he was there for me to depend upon. C. Ivar Hellstrom came to the staff shortly afterward with special responsibility for the church's department of religious education, of which he made an outstanding success, winning the affection and admiration of thousands of children, and of their parents. When Dr. Carder resigned, Norris L. Tibbetts brought to our common tasks an extraordinary personality and competence without which the fruitfulness of the church's work would be unthinkable. George Heidt was called from a responsible position at Brown University to be our business manager and he has carried that burden with conspicuous ability. This group, a harmonious co-operative team, gathered around them church workers for whose able, loyal support I am endlessly grateful. The temptation is strong to go on mentioning names, but I must resist it, for I shall not know where to stop.

Doubtless someday someone will write a history of the Riverside Church. In these intimate recollections I can only note a few of the problems that we faced and tried to deal with.

We set out to create a nonsectarian, inclusive church. All Christians, from whatever denominational background, were welcomed to our membership on equal terms. This meant that the control of the church by any denominational group could not be guaranteed or even expected. After we had been going a few years, investigation revealed that less than a third of our members had Baptist backgrounds. Representatives of all the major and many of the minor Protestant denominations were soon in our company, along with others from Roman Catholic and Jewish antecedents. When gathering information to explain to my successor the situation he was coming into, I found what no one had apparently noticed, that the president of the Board of Trustees and the chairman of the Board of Deacons at that time were both Methodists.

The cause of Christian unity works toward its goal by two methods. First come large-scale overhead endeavors to achieve organizational union, along with co-operative enterprises such as the National Council of Churches and the World Council of Churches. There is, however, a second field of endeavor immediately at hand, not needing to wait for the overhead union of great denominations: individual congregations, namely, where Christian union can be put into effect at once and given persuasive illustration. The achievement of large-scale interdenominational union will depend in no small measure on such foundation work in individual churches. So far as it goes, it makes of Christian union a realized fact. The multiplication of such congregations provides an increasing number of Christians who on the basis of actual experience believe in union and demand its extension, and it furnishes a growing number of churches which illustrate its value and possibility.

One danger confronting an individual congregation which adopts this policy is that it may become an isolated unit, lacking effective relationship with the Christian church as a whole. The leaders at Riverside decided, therefore, that until a better method appeared delegates would be annually sent to the Northern Baptist Convention, and since Baptist polity protects the freedom of the local congregation, this method of keeping in working touch with the Church Universal has been maintained; but there was nothing to prevent similar association with other denominational bodies, and since my retirement the church has joined the Congregational denomination also.

With the increasingly interdenominational character of our membership, it became obviously unfair to channel our gifts through any one denominational budget. The policy therefore was adopted of giving to specifically chosen causes in the community, the nation and the world, each cause individually investigated and selected. The philanthropic and

missionary contributions from Riverside Church go without
sectarian bias to various denominational and interdenominational causes around the world. Here is a typical annual list
of causes supported by our gifts: a rural project under the
Kyodan (United Church of Christ) in Japan; the education
of forty girls from an Arab refugee camp near Tyre; Korean
refugees; Bacone, the Indian college in Oklahoma; the International Christian University in Japan; the Vellore Christian
Medical College in south India; a school of social work in
Delhi; Y.M.C.A.s in Portuguese East Africa and at Dakar;
a settlement house in Tokyo; the migrant workers' program
of the Home Missions Council; the work of an agricultural
missionary in China; Union Theological Seminary in Tokyo;
the radio and rural work of the Philippine National Christian Council; the Agricultural Missions Foundation; the
Interdenominational Board of Christian Work in Santo
Domingo; and many philanthropic projects in New York
City such as the Manhattanville Community Centers and the
East Harlem Parish.

Another result of our nonsectarian policy was that we
could not admit into full membership families from all denominational backgrounds and then deny them the forms
and customs of baptism that were sacred in their heritage.
Our forms of observance, therefore, are as varied as the
demands of our people. Some little children are dedicated
to the Christian life without baptism; some are baptized.
Some adults joining the church are immersed; others are
sprinkled; still others, such as the Quakers, join on verbal
profession of faith without baptism. Never, so far as I know,
has this interdenominational character of our membership

and ministry had the slightest controversial result within the congregation. I have never heard a member of Riverside Church express regret at our stand or desire for a changed policy.

I wish we could have been as successful in including all economic and occupational classes in our congregation. To be sure, the widespread idea that we are a group of wealthy folk, or ever have been, is nonsense. The Park Avenue Church was located in the city's best-known residential area, but its people, for the most part, did not live there. When the present site of Riverside Church was chosen, we discovered to our surprise that it was almost exactly in the geographical center of the widespread dwelling places of our members. The number of people in the church who could be called wealthy has never been large, and in proportion to the whole that group has grown smaller year by year. Our people are, for the most part, physicians, lawyers, social workers, students, teachers, civil servants, white-collar workers, various kinds of engineers, housewives, men and women in executive positions and in small businesses. It is a notable group whose varied abilities we have never been able to put to proper use within the church, but only a few are rich. To my great regret, however, there are few representatives of labor unions among us, nor is it my regret alone. I recall Albert Scott, then president of the Board of Trustees, deploring this situation, wishing we could somehow raze the barrier that commonly makes of our Protestant organizations in this sense "class" churches, much as they may desire otherwise.

The Riverside Church is an interracial fellowship. Mem-

bers are admitted one by one, on the basis of their Christian
faith and of their motives in coming to us, and no child of
God is shut out from our membership because of race, color
or nationality. Chinese, Japanese, Negroes, Slavs, Jews, South
Americans of various nationalities, and others are in our
fellowship. Racial and national background is no proper test
of membership in a Christian church and we have never
made it such.

Moreover, so far as our experience goes, it is a mistake to
think of such an interracial policy as constituting a problem.
It is a privilege and an opportunity, and our fellowship has
been enriched by the racial and national variety of its
members. To have maintained a segregated church across
the square from International House, where representatives
of many races and nations live together, would have been
incredible. A racially segregated church is in my judgment
wickedly unchristian anyway. To profess devotion to the
task of winning all races and nations to Christ and then to
shut out those thus Christianized from our fellowship is
downright apostasy. We deserve no special credit, therefore,
for our interracial policy, but should rather be grateful that
we are situated where we can practice it freely with a minimum of difficulty and a maximum of advantage to all concerned.

The type of program we should carry on in the new
building gave us deep concern. A generation ago there were,
in general, two kinds of churches in the city, and while
many congregations combined features from both, the two
types are readily distinguishable. One conducted a program

centered in worship and preaching, with little else going
on. Sunday services and a midweek prayer meeting, along
with a few occasional gatherings, constituted the activities
of the congregation. This type of church has been described
as one where Christianity is talked about one day a week
and where for the other six days the church is the background for an undertaker's sign. While this is caricature,
there is some truth in it. This kind of church was the natural
result of carrying over into metropolitan life the setup of a
small country congregation of the simpler sort. What made
a church was a building, a preacher and an audience that
listened to him once or twice a week, and as a by-product
maintained fellowship in social gatherings, conducted a
Sunday School and a few organized societies—especially
of young people and of women—and financially supported
philanthropies and missions. This type of church often
wielded a powerful and worth-while influence, especially
from the pulpit, but it tended to be a self-contained club,
membership in which was highly beneficial to those who
joined it, but whose service did not reach out to all sorts
and conditions of people.

In revolt against this self-contained type of congregation
the institutional church arose. It often went to the opposite
extreme, minimizing worship and preaching, and glorying
in practical expressions of Christian service to the underprivileged and unchurched. I recall one such prominent
church whose policy was represented in its building—the
sanctuary for worship small, ill-favored and architecturally
pushed to one side, while the clubrooms, the gymnasium,
and all the typical equipment of a settlement house were

prominent. The invaluable service it rendered to the constituency it reached made it famous, and yet, while it took justifiable satisfaction in practicing Christianity seven days a week instead of talking about it one day, it has become clear with the passing years that the future does not belong to that setup.

In planning the building and the program of Riverside Church we endeavored to combine the best features of both types. Certainly no one entering our edifice can suppose that we minimize worship and preaching. Not simply on Sunday at eleven o'clock, but in many other services, as of the Church School and the Men's Class in the Chapel, the beauty of our sanctuaries has encouraged the spirit and practice of worship.

Indeed, we have deliberately sought to make our services of worship inclusive of varied religious temperaments, so that under Riverside's roof are housed week by week types of worship commonly housed under separate sectarian roofs. Each week we conduct one major congregational preaching service of the kind familiar in most nonliturgical Protestant churches; we conduct one liturgical service without sermon, composed mainly of music and litany; on every Sunday of the year we sponsor a Quaker service, run by the Friends themselves, some of whom are members with us; we conduct worship services where religious drama is central, and others where free discussion of religious problems is carried on. All these types meet real human needs and represent valid varieties of temperament, and we have put them under one roof.

Far from minimizing worship, therefore, we have stressed

it, but at the same time, like the institutional churches, we
have not wished to be a self-contained religious club. We
have wanted to express our Christianity in service to the
community at large as well as to our own membership. We
desired this, first, because in a city like New York no other
kind of program meets the issue. On every side of every
metropolitan church is need—physical, financial, psychological, spiritual. There is loneliness needing fellowship,
mental sickness needing wise counsel, sometimes unemployment needing organized help; there are little children wanting nursery care, boys and girls wanting recreation, young
men and women wanting opportunity to play as well as
worship together, adults to whom creative work in arts and
crafts would be a godsend, and others still with abilities in
music, drama, social service, wanting groups of kindred
minds to work with for their own sake and for the sake of
others. The Riverside Church set out with a seven-day-a-
week program to meet these needs.

While this kind of program sprang from our belief in it
as a matter of principle, it was urged on us with special
insistence because we were being trusted with so costly an
edifice. Our building represented a large expenditure and we
were criticized for the lavish outlay. Only if we could make
it a center of public service, all the week long gathering
under its hospitable roof people who needed what we could
give and reaching out into the city and the world with varied
usefulness, could we justify the building with which we
had been trusted.

In implementing this idea we did not so much impose a
prearranged program on the community as ask the com-

munity what it wanted from us—with results that surprised us. One area of our program after another came into being not because with foresight we planned it, but because the community, organizing itself under our roof, created it. Many elements in our program we did, of course, foresee, and we provided such equipment as bowling alleys, a gymnasium, a playground, theatrical stages, to meet them. For many years now the Riverside Church has been throughout the week a scene of varied activity and our problem has been not so much to solicit attendance and create working organizations, as to choose wisely between alternatives and to give priority to the most vital and important needs.

Of course we planned a Church School but it soon outgrew all our expectations concerning it and all the predictions from the community as to the number of children who would attend. Dr. Hellstrom and his staff soon had our facilities bursting at the seams with hundreds of boys and girls who came to the church for three hours on Sunday morning and all Friday evening; and, with various attendant enterprises such as family counseling and classes for parents, the Church School has had a flourishing history. Even so we were not meeting the needs of the neighborhood's children. A weekday nursery school was demanded. There were missionaries on furlough, married students, and families where both parents worked—a five-day-a-week nursery school would be a benediction to them. So we organized one and today some two hundred children are enrolled.

A department of social service was a must from the beginning, for the economic depression of the nineteen-thirties was at its depth when we occupied our new building. "I have nothing left except courage," said a letter from one of our unemployed members, "and sometimes, like a weak heart, that beats so low one cannot count its pulse." Something had to be done about *that,* and under the leadership of Mary Downs something was done so efficiently, in co-operation with the Charity Organization Society (now the Community Service Society), that during five years over seven thousand places were found for unemployed persons who appealed to us for help. Since then the department—now under the guidance of Mrs. Edwina Hazzard—has been handling about every kind of problem that individuals and families in New York City face.

At the start we never dreamed of the Riverside Symphony Orchestra, but the commuuity soon was asking for it. Similarly one organization after another—the Epicures, for example, a group of young married couples that has added liveliness and warmth to our fellowship—was self-created rather than officially planned. Nor did we foresee what an important spiritual ministry the creation of beautiful things in an Arts and Crafts department would bring to many lives in a city like ours. We planned a small program especially for children, but under the inspiration of Mrs. Alma Guillet and her successors the work has expanded until some four hundred persons are taking courses under our roof.

Early in our occupancy of the new building Myra Vance of our staff told me that a few women of the congregation were thinking that a business and professional women's club would be useful. I had no idea what was going to happen when we gave the green light to that suggestion, for now over five hundred "B's and P's" are rendering such varied and efficient services within the church and beyond it, that one who knows what they are doing can only with difficulty imagine the Riverside Church without them.

Similarly the Riverside Guild—a body of more than three hundred young people—has outgrown all the best hopes we cherished concerning it at the beginning. New York can be one of the loneliest places on earth, especially to a young man or woman who lands there without friends. I have before me a letter written by a mother in a distant city:

Dear Dr. Fosdick:

Some months ago I wrote you about my son. I told you he was a lonely boy in the "big city" with no place to go and asked you to send him literature of your young people's activities. You not only did that but you wrote to him and saw him personally and got a member of your staff on his trail.

I have been waiting for an opportunity to send you real evidence of his transformation, and I can think of no better way of doing so than by enclosing parts of his last letter to me.

I feel that words are inadequate to tell you how much I thank you. . . .

What the young man had written to his mother was in part this: "Boy! I've been having a grand time doing this, that and everything else. Life has more meaning in it and I have a host of friends, thanks to the Guild. I don't know what I should have done without it. The Spring is in my bones again." That kind of incident has been repeated uncounted times in the Guild's history. Nor has the Guild's ministry been social only, for its services of worship on Sunday evenings have been among the most moving I ever attended, and the discussion groups on Thursday nights have helped numberless youths to find faith and vocation.

The Men's Class under Dr. Tibbetts' leadership is carrying on a great tradition. Among the class's former teachers were Charles Evans Hughes and John D. Rockefeller, Jr., and what they started is going forward now in a program of worship and practical service in which some three hundred men are finding personal enrichment and challenging opportunity for usefulness.

The Women's Society is a dynamic organization which has branched out into many types of serviceable work. In Riverside Church women are now members of the Board of Deacons, and alike in leadership and in detailed projects of neighborhood and missionary service they are a very influential part of the picture.

Sir Wilfred Grenfell once appealed for a religion of "action, not diction." We certainly have not despised "diction," but we have encouraged "action," and sometimes visitors, strangers to New York, are mystified and amused by our methods. There are ten kitchens in the church. I have seen many a visitor take for granted such churchly things as Hofmann's lovely pictures and "the largest carillon in the world," but ten kitchens! Nevertheless, they are significant, for quite apart from all the gatherings at luncheons and teas, how could we expect to make the church a real headquarters for varied groups, engaged in study, worship, recreation, service, until ten to fifteen thousand people come weekly to our activities, if when their daily work was done they had to go home to Long Island, New Jersey or Westchester and then return to the city again? No! Those kitchens have served a useful purpose in helping to make possible a seven-day-a-week program.

Even this inadequate sketch should indicate why it is that

now, ten years after my retirement, the Riverside Church
is larger and stronger than it ever was when I was active in
its ministry. Gloomy predictions were sometimes made about
what would happen to the church when its first impetus
was spent. Such forebodings were mistaken. Those who
harbored them did not know what was really going on at
Riverside. Granted our errors and failures! Yet many hundreds of people were deeply involved in the church's program; we were a fellowship of active, devoted laymen and
laywomen; throughout the year worth-while enterprises
were afoot that challenged the loyalty and won the enthusiastic participation of increasing numbers of people; and
many were finding the solution of their personal problems
in a vital faith. It takes more than a change of steersmen
to sink a ship like that—especially when the new steersman
is a master pilot.

The public has always been curious about the financial
support of our church, and there has never been any reason
why that curiosity should not be satisfied. A common impression has been that its bills were paid by a group of
wealthy persons. That never has been true, and with the
passing years the support of our program has been carried
by an increasing number of contributors. The church belongs
to all its people and I think they feel that, from the children
up. One toddler from our nursery group, seeing me pass on
the street, said to his mother: "That man goes to my church."
At any rate, that is the kind of church we have aspired to be.
   One unintentional tribute to this human quality at Riverside I specially relish. *The New Yorker* magazine thought

that Riverside Church offered a good target for one of its whimsical articles. Another church in New York, where a friend of mine was minister, had suffered painfully from one of these clever, scarifying write-ups, and I was disturbed when I heard that we had been selected for another. Dr. Carder welcomed the appointed writer with open arms and gave him the run of the church. Day after day he saw from the inside what we were doing, talked with anyone he wanted to talk with, visited any group he chose from the Day Nursery up, and the more he saw, the less the article got under way. For several Sundays he attended our services, and one Sunday morning after the service he came to the chancel steps, and standing close to Dr. Carder and myself, listened to the people who came in a long line to shake hands with us. Last of all, he heard one of the women of the church say to Carder: "Gene, can you help me? Marshall and I have been invited out to dinner and he has forgotten his handkerchief. Have you got a clean one you can lend him?" Dr. Carder produced the needed article and handed it over—at which our journalist visitor threw up his hands. "That's the last straw," he said. "I'll be hanged if I write that article about this church. It is altogether too human."

The trouble is that Riverside Church looks expensive, and we have often been criticized for that. I tried to answer that charge once in a sermon, saying in part:

This is one of the least expensive churches in the United States. For how would you estimate the expensiveness of a church if not by the per capita cost for all the individuals who during the year come to the church's doors to be served by it?

Here, for example, is a little country church, with a modest meeting house and a small congregation, spending a few thousand dollars a year. One jumps to the conclusion that this is a simple, homely inexpensive church. But suppose now, that, figuring up the cost per capita for all who during the year come to that church's door, you find that it is two dollars. That is a very expensive church.

A competent survey by H. Paul Douglass has recently been made covering just such factors in our American churches. Here is one congregation where the per capita cost of those who are served by the church in the course of a year is over two dollars. That is a very expensive church. Here is another, one of the most efficient city churches in the United States, where the cost per capita is 48¢. Even that is expensive. Indeed, the least expensive church which Dr. Douglass found in the United States had a cost for each entrance of 35¢. Where, then, does our cost stand in view of our proposed budget? At 37¢. Believe it or not, we are within two cents of the least expensive per capita cost reported in the United States. And when we abstract from consideration our income from endowment and think simply of what we have to raise, which would fairly represent the situation in most churches, it would be about 25¢. We are one of the least expensive churches in the United States.

One kind of public usefulness which our building made possible we had not clearly foreseen. Requests came streaming in from the community and from the city at large, asking for the use of our auditorium, our gymnasium, our dining rooms. We found ourselves hosts to all sorts of worth-while enterprises, and the business office was soon put to it to reconcile our own program with the needs of our visitors.

Some of these visitors were exciting—Toyohiko Kagawa from Japan, for example. He came to this country in the early

nineteen-thirties, when communism was busily infiltrating
the Japanese community in the United States. He had been
dangerously attacked by a group of communists in San Fran-
cisco, so that the police across the country were on the alert
whenever he appeared. The Japanese Christian leaders in
New York had asked for the use of our nave for a meeting
at which Kagawa would address his fellow countrymen, and
both they and we were amazed when some twenty police-
men turned up to see that the speaker was unharmed. Their
presence was justified, for hardly had Kagawa begun to
speak before one agitator after another rose to interrupt
him and shout him down. Kagawa, however, proved master
of the situation. As the police moved in, ranging up and
down the aisles and forcing the remonstrants back into their
seats, Kagawa—unperturbed, smiling, gracious, assured—
requested that they retire and leave the matter to him. The
incredulous police retreated to the vestibule and then in a
remarkable exhibition of moral force Kagawa, by patience
and fairness, wore out his tormentors, made them look
ridiculous, and finally silenced them, ending, so his Japanese
auditors testified, by delivering a powerful and moving
evangelistic appeal. When he finished, his audience thronged
around him with warm and friendly greeting, and even some
of the men who had been trying to shout him down cheered
him with cries of "You win! You win!"

One of the most dangerous problems that faced the Riverside Church sprang from the fact that crowds came to its
services. Crowds can be the most deceptive and ephemeral
measure of a church's usefulness. A really Christian church

must be "personality-centered," its criterion of value the saving experiences which come to individuals. "The genius of Christianity lies in reverence for personality"—I found that easy to write, but in Riverside Church, with its rapidly growing membership and its attendant crowds, we set ourselves with anxiety and hard work to put that into practice. In one staff meeting after another we reiterated the admonition: keep your eyes on individuals; nothing in the long run matters in this church except what happens to them.

This cardinal principle affects everything a church does. I must not here portray the varied ways in which we tried to live up to it. I hope that we have deserved a little what one stranger wrote about us in a magazine article. It certainly represented what we were aiming at. "Incredible as it seems," said the article, "this is the miracle that Riverside Church has accomplished—a simple, small-town church in the largest city in the world; a friendly gracious cordiality in an architectural setting suitable for a coronation."

So far as I was concerned, the most intense application of this personality-centered policy came in individual counseling. While we were still in the Park Avenue edifice I made an after-dinner speech before a group of New York ministers, which raised an unexpected storm. I pointed out the insufficiency of pastoral calling, as Protestant ministers commonly practice it, to meet the real needs of the people, especially in a large city, and I stressed the urgent necessity of a better method of personal helpfulness. In particular, I called attention to the Roman Catholic confessional, where people individually come to the priest, in contrast with our Protestant pastoral calling, which helps indeed to hold together the church's fellowship but seldom offers opportunity for dealing with intimate, personal problems. I pleaded that just as folk in legal difficulty seek the lawyer, and folk in illness seek the physician, and Roman Catholics, disturbed in conscience, seek the priest, the Protestant church needed some recognized, easily accessible time and place for personal consultation, where the people could find the minister. I wanted a Protestant version of the Catholic confessional. What a howl that caused in certain areas of the religious press! Having lately been accused of being a destructive radical, I now was accused of going over to popery.

In my student days in the theological seminary I can recall no mention of personal counseling, and certainly it was not treated as a central function of the Christian minister, requiring serious preparation. The new dynamic psychology had not then arrived. My college course in psychology, as I remember it, consisted mainly of a tripartite splitting of the psyche into intellect, emotion and will, with analytic comment on the operation of each section and an assumption that the three were yet somehow one. Indeed, one theological professor of mine tried to illustrate the divine Trinity on the basis of that analogy. The mental hygiene movement in the United States may be dated from 1892, with Adolf Meyer as the principal founder, but it was years before the influence of men like Freud and Jung—both of whom first lectured here in 1909—was felt in the United States, and many of the chief figures in developing American psychotherapy are still alive today. As for the relations between the new psychology and religion, I vividly recall the thrill of the pioneering books, such as James' *The Varieties of Religious Experience,* Starbuck's *Psychology of Religion,* Coe's *Psychology of Religion,* Pratt's *Psychology of Religious Belief,* and Ames' *Psychology of Religious Experience.*

With the advent of psychiatry's vital, dynamic understanding of personality, the ministry's need of methods by which the resources of religion, illumined by the new insights, could be mediated to individuals through direct personal consultation, became acute. Today, while much remains to be done, the best theological seminaries seriously train their students for personal consultation; the applications of psychology to pastoral service every year become more important; clinical training in hospitals and asylums is provided for theologues who specially desire it; the minister and the psychiatrist increasingly recognize their partnership in a common task; and the churches, according to the special needs of their communities, more and more provide means to make such co-operation available and effective. I certainly acknowledge an unpayable debt to the psychiatrists to whom I have referred cases that were beyond my depth.

I envy young ministers who today are trained in the disciplines that make personal counseling effective. My generation of theologues started with none of that—only a serious love of people, a deep discontent with preaching as the sole means of reaching them, an increasingly clear perception of critical needs in individuals with which the church should be dealing and of the urgent want of a Protestant "confessional." I am commonly thought of as a preacher, but I should not put preaching central in my ministry. Personal counseling has been central. My preaching at its best has itself been personal counseling on a group scale. Of all the rewards of my work I prize nothing so much as the remembrance of miracles I have witnessed as the result of Christian truth brought to bear privately on individuals.

One night a young man—a complete stranger to me— came to my home. He had just tried to commit suicide by hanging and the strap had broken. Hesitant about attempting it again, he came, a very crumpled, desperate fellow, to see a minister of whom he had merely heard. It took a few minutes for me to establish confidential relationships with him—by not being shocked at his suicidal desires, by taking them for granted as a familiar experience, by being quietly sure that there was both a reason for them and a cure. Then he began to talk, revealing a psychological history full to the brim of self-contempt and self-hatred. That inward slant which made every experience of his, however trivial, bounce off in the direction of humiliated self-deprecation must have begun in childhood. If he knew what had happened in his early boyhood to start this chain reaction of shame and self-scorn, I told him, then we could find the cure ourselves; if not, we would have to seek the help of a psychiatrist to discover it.

"My God!" he said. "I know only too well what it was." A brutal father, who used to beat him mercilessly until his back was covered with welts, was the beginning of his trouble. Some boys respond to such treatment by rebellion; he responded by humiliation. So I reconstructed for him his psychological history, tracing the consequences of that early emotional ordeal until he exclaimed: "Do you mean that *that* is all that is the matter with me?" Then we went down to his deeper levels. He had admirable qualities. He had known experiences which made possible his intelligent response to the meaning of vital religion. Before we were through, a few hours later, he had gained a perspective on his character and spiritual resources which made a picture of himself very different from that which had led to his attempted self-destruction. When he left me that night, he exclaimed: "I'm a new man in a new world!" The next time I saw him was by chance in a hotel lobby, where he embraced me, saying: "I am on top of the world." And later he sent me a copy of a trade journal containing an article praising him for some especially effective work which he had done.

That kind of experience with individuals I regard as central in my ministry.

Indeed, I distrust a preacher to whom sermons seem the crux of his functioning. The temptations of a popular preacher—if he is only that—are devastating. He is applauded by fans, credited with a Christian selflessness he cannot claim, and enticed by many listeners to think of himself much more highly than he ought to think; what may be mainly ingenious rhetoric and well-trained eloquence, motivated by subtle exhibitionism, is taken for divine afflatus. To preach a "successful" sermon, to feel the rouse of a responsive audience, to hold in one's hands the concentrated attention of spellbound congregations, is a thrilling experience. Let any preacher who has such an experience go humbly home and pray to be delivered from its seductions! Only the grace of God can deliver him—that and a genuine care for persons, so that to him, as to Jesus, all that matters in a crowd is the opportunity to get vitally in touch with some individual.

This desire to handle personality at firsthand, to deal directly with individual needs, is at the very heart of the minister's vocation. In some callings one deals first with things and only secondarily with persons. An engineer building a bridge primarily handles materials, and then uses persons as means to his end. In other callings, however— the teacher, the physician, the nurse, the psychiatrist, the minister—one deals directly with the needs of persons. After long years of interviewing, often being asked for advice about the choosing of a vocation, I have learned to divide men and women into two camps. Some will be contented in professions and businesses whose tasks are primarily focused on things, statistics, abstract ideas, or large affairs of government; others will be utterly miserable unless they directly handle human life, dealing immediately with personality's urgent needs.

This personality-centered quality is indispensable to a good teacher or physician or minister. Henry Schindall describes a scene where a group of boys bade farewell to a great teacher. " 'Sometimes,' said the teacher, 'I think teaching is a heartbreaking way of making a living.' Then as he glanced down the line and saw the boys looking at him reverently, he added with a wistful smile, 'But I wouldn't give it up for all the world.' " Unless a minister feels thus about his calling he had better quit. That teacher lived in his boys, as a good physician lives in his patients, or a good minister in his people, and how a minister can be content without dealing privately and intimately with the deep-seated problems of those whose servant he is supposed to be, passes my understanding.

At any rate, this firsthand dealing with individuals has been the creative center of my ministry and a fruitful source of my preaching. Pastoral calling has its essential place in a metropolitan church, but only when it is informed and made vital by continuously maintained personal relations between the church and its members. It is painfully easy in New York for lonely members to slip away into a vague, formal connection with the fellowship, empty of real meaning and of effective consequences. So Riverside's widespread membership is divided into seventy-five "zones," with one hundred and thirty zone leaders, and by means of careful follow-ups, zone gatherings, the use of the neighborly "grapevine," and constant personal inquiry, the church tries to see to it that none of its members strays away and is forgotten. Nevertheless, the most vital business of pastoral service comes to its climax when needy souls, within or without the church, seek help in individual conferences.

This fact had become startlingly real to me when at the First Presbyterian Church, where my responsibility was simply preaching, I became concerned about individuals who might wish to talk with me concerning their intimate problems. One Sunday, therefore, I announced hours when I would be in the church office for consultation. The first day I found fourteen people waiting in the anteroom, and had to deal first of all with a case of homosexuality. From that time on I had done my best to catch up on the new knowledge and the new methods of psychotherapy. What I owe to Dr. Thomas Salmon, for example, one of this country's pioneers in psychosomatic medicine, cannot be adequately told. My self-training was a poor second best to what is available now, but it opened doors to a kind of intimate service to needy souls that became of central importance in my ministry.

Ministers are sometimes supposed to be isolated and aloof from life's raw, hard facts, to be ignorant of its smut and dirt, its sordid sins and passionate debaucheries. To the casual observer they may seem to live in a world apart. No minister, however, who practices personal counseling can long remain in an ivory tower. I have shared vicariously in the "confessional" the struggles of human souls with every kind of guilt—murder, adultery, alcoholism, all manner of sexual perversion—until I can imagine no revelation of moral chaos and evil-doing that would surprise me. As for neurotic and psychotic disorders, only a psychiatrist sees more of them than does a minister to whom troubled personalities habitually come for help. To be sure, such intimate dealing with the dark side of human nature is far from being the whole story of the personal counselor's experience. He sees the best in human nature too. The emphasis today, especially in theological circles, rests on man's wickedness. That is all too obvious, but there is another aspect of human nature—extraordinary character in ordinary people, exhibiting amazing fortitude and courage in hazardous and tragic situations. I recall that girl, stricken by polio, to whom a sympathetic friend exclaimed: "Affliction does so color the life!" "Yes," said the girl, "and I propose to choose the color." I recall that invalided woman, so radiant that when tired and discouraged I used to call on her to be set back on my feet

again. "I am in the rough," she said, "but watch me get out.
Faith is my niblick." I recall the man who, desperately poor
and making a scanty livelihood as a sandwich man on lower
Broadway, found one day a wallet containing twelve hundred dollars and who brought it to me to be returned, if
possible, to its owner. Personal counseling made man's sin
vividly real to me, but it made man's nobility real also.

I distilled the essence of my experience in this field into
my book, *On Being a Real Person*. There, with all possibility
of individual identification concealed, I have told some of
the stories of human need that came to my "confessional."
One never could guess what would turn up next. A Boston
minister once said that he came to New York to see me,
bearing an invitation to deliver an important address with
a large fee attached, and that when he telephoned me for
an appointment I refused to see him because I was too busy
and declined his invitation. He was irritated at being, as he
thought, "high-hatted." I had brushed him off, he felt, and
he was indignant, so that, finding himself on the return train
seated next to a Negro, who turned out to be a minister
too, he let loose his disgruntled opinion of me. Whereupon
the Negro minister said that he had spent two hours with
me that day. I recall those two hours vividly. The Negro's
deranged wife had committed suicide upstairs, while he
was downstairs, and loving her devotedly as he did, he was
heartbroken. What happened during those two hours is
about as important as anything that can happen in a church,
for when the man left, he said quietly to my secretary: "He
has put the stars back into my sky."

No matter how much a counselor may help his "patients,"

the chances are that they do as much for him as he does for
them. If his sermons and books have point and relevance, if
they strike home to vital problems and hit real nails on the
head, the explanation lies in his clairvoyance, strenuously
gained by sharing the struggles of human souls, one by one.
At any rate, without this creative experience of personal
counseling I never could have preached for twenty years
in Riverside Church.

Such intimate dealing with individuals stands in apparent
contrast with so far-flung a ministry as radio preaching. We
take radio and television for granted now, but thirty years
ago radio was new, and its use for religious purposes was
in an experimental stage. As I recall it, S. Parkes Cadman,
minister of an influential church in Brooklyn, was about the
first to command what in those days was a fairly extensive
hookup, but soon afterward I started following the trail that
he was blazing. I was still at the First Presbyterian Church
when I began radio preaching and I had no idea of the possibilities involved. Frankly skeptical of its effect, I undertook
it rather listlessly. I used to go down to the studio on Sunday
afternoons and sitting at a table, talk into that strange con-
trivance, the microphone, with no vivid sense of contact with
the unseen audience. Later the microphone became to me
almost as stirring as a great congregation, no longer a thing
but an almost living symbol of multitudes of individual
people, and sometimes to the amusement of the technicians
I became as excited and physically active in addressing it as
though the unseen audience were visibly present.

At the Park Avenue Church a single station carried our

morning service, and as personal responses came in, the possibilities in radio of vital, spiritual usefulness became increasingly clear and challenging. In 1927 "National Vespers," a Sunday afternoon program over a continent-wide network, began, and for many years gave me an opportunity at once inspiring and humbling. "National Vespers" was a public service with no financial considerations involved. The National Broadcasting Company estimates that it contributed freely to this program between two and three million dollars' worth of radio facilities and, of course, I have never received a penny of compensation. The necessary expenses for music and secretarial help were at first covered by a committee of my friends, but later small gifts from appreciative listeners, ranging from twenty-five cents up, proved adequate to meet all bills, so that the budget was democratically carried by the voluntary contributions of those listeners who wanted to help.

The most obvious source of amazement to one who saw the beginning of radio preaching was, of course, the vast distances covered. Until World War II made it impossible, "National Vespers" went out over several short-wave stations. I never became used to the miracle involved in that. The records show that the sermons were heard in seventeen different countries. A girl whom I baptized in her youth, later a missionary, listened in at her post in Central Africa. A minister in New Zealand wrote that he tuned in regularly —with him it was nine o'clock Monday morning. Letters came from listeners in Persia and China; many came from Great Britain; and once when I told a story about what happened in Metlakatla, Alaska, an appreciative letter came from an auditor in Metlakatla, confirming what I had said. The present generation takes all this and more for granted. To me, who was in on the start of it, it will always remain half incredible.

Another deep impression that years of radio preaching made on me was the intense, intimate and influential meaning it has for multitudes of individuals. Of course there is plenty of casual, superficial listening. An old fisherman, living on an island off the Maine coast, once greeted me enthusiastically, saying: "I listen to you every Sunday." I felt quite set up, but then he added: "I turn the radio on early Sunday morning and keep it on all day." That kind of thing I had supposed might be general, but later the steady stream of letters—grateful, intimate, presenting vital personal and domestic problems—made the unseen audiences very real and human to me. Every speaker over the air gets routine responses, crazy letters, begging letters, abuse from critics and flattery from fans, but as increasing numbers of preachers using radio and television now know, another kind of response is much more impressive and revealing.

Even in those early days when radio was new, letters streamed in from all sorts of places and from all imaginable human situations, from prisons and hospitals, from universities and legislatures, from cities and from lonely homes on the frontiers. A leading historian in one of our universities wrote: "My wife listens to your sermons every Sunday afternoon, and yesterday I listened in with her, as I do occasionally, and was very much impressed with what you had to say. . . . I wish sometime that I might have the opportunity to have a few moments' chat with you." The same mail, however, might bring a letter from another kind of background altogether: "Being beauticians and coming in contact with as many people as we do in the course of the day, and of course discussing topics of the day, we were without realizing it expressing so many ideas from your sermons in different words of course. Then our clients ask where did you get your reasoning from and we in turn would either mention your broadcasts or bring in to them some of your sermons, or both. We have done the same with our friends, therefore we have been able to get in touch with the young and old. . . . It is utterly impossible to express the changes in these people and ourselves, therefore, I will not attempt to, but enough is said when one can say they have Hope today."

In the same mail might come a letter such as this from a minister: "Life had us down for a few minutes. We were helped by your sermon to smile, throw back our shoulders and thrust out our chins"; or a letter like this: "I have been here in a tuberculosis sanatorium for some time, and all during my stay I have listened to your broadcasts. From every one I have learned something that has thrown light on some phase of this complicated and often distressing business of living and maintaining a secure hold on the values of life"; or a letter like this from San Quentin prison in California: "Did you know that the quietest thirty minutes in this large 'Bay View' hotel is on Sunday evening when your sermon is rebroadcast? It is a pleasure to hear you, you make it so plain, so easy to understand. I am sure that all the fellows appreciate you as much as I do."

Such messages make clear why radio preaching ceased being for me a performance before a microphone and became a means of vital dealing with the problems of real people. "Perhaps you would be glad to know," said one letter, "of the real benediction your service this past Sunday was to a group of loved ones gathered around a sick bed. . . . The sufferer is fighting a losing battle with a dread malignant disease. . . . I do not see how your sermon could have been more appropriate if you had known to whom you were speaking." Another letter read: "May our family express their most sincere thanks for your help last Sunday evening. . . . When Mr. ——— came home from his office on Tuesday night he said, 'Dr. Fosdick's sermon kept me from doing one thing today and made me do another.' Last night as he sat here reading he suddenly laid down his book and said, 'That sermon was worth the whole cost of the radio.'" Evidently one could engage in individual counseling over the air. As a result, endless requests for advice streamed in by mail and often faced me with a perplexing task when I tried to send wise answers.

One opportunity which came with radio preaching I especially welcomed: it gave me the chance to speak directly to my fundamentalist brethren in their homes. I did not by any means persuade all of them—there are plenty left— but the radio ministry helped, as in the case of one listener who wrote: "I had always thought you were a devil with horns and a tail, but I have been listening to you over the air recently, and what you say seems to be Christian." "When I was a young woman," wrote another, "my father, who was an 'old-time' Baptist, was afraid 'that young Fosdick was a little too broad, a dangerous tendency.' Little could he know that that same 'dangerous' personage would

one day help to save 'the old faith' of his youngest child."
Even the criticisms of the orthodox have increasingly been
mollified by good will, as in the case of a professor of
homiletics in a leading Presbyterian seminary who told his
students to study my sermons for their style, but not to be
misled by their theology—although, he added, his wife had
lately read my sermon on "The Forgiveness of Sins" and had
exclaimed: "That would have been a good sermon, if Dr.
Fosdick had not written it!"

Whatever the effect of radio preaching may be on the
listener, the effect on the preacher is salutary. He is speaking
to all kinds of persons from all the social, racial and religious
backgrounds there are. Nothing narrow, sectarian, exclusive
and merely partisan will do. He must strike a universal
note and deal with elemental human problems. In response
to what he says letters will come from Roman Catholics,
Christian Scientists, Jews, agnostics and all sorts of Protestants. He must state his convictions—they would all despise
him if he did not—but he must be fair, inclusive in his understanding and sympathy, always a human being first and not
a partisan. I am profoundly grateful for the opportunity the
radio has given me to help others; I am just as grateful for
what the radio ministry has done for me.

Meanwhile, preaching at Riverside presented plenty of
problems. There were many plain people in the congregation
facing every sort of human difficulty, but there were eminent
"brains" too, with strong convictions about all the current
economic and social issues. Many a time as I went into the
pulpit I recalled Hugh Latimer's experience that Sunday
morning when, heading toward the royal chapel, he heard a

voice within him say: "Latimer, Latimer, be careful what you preach today because you are going to preach before the king of England"; then another voice said: "Latimer, Latimer, be careful what you preach today since you are going to preach before the King of kings."

A rather spirited debate is on today concerning the present condition of our American churches as compared with their estate at the turn of the century. On the pessimistic side many argue that while church membership has grown to a proportion of the population far larger than was ever achieved before, numbers have not brought commensurate strength and influence. So inclusive has the church's policy become, they say, that almost anyone can be a member; discipline has vanished, a "decorous worldliness" afflicts the typical congregation, and a Baptist, as one critic remarked, is simply "a person who, when he stays away from church, stays away from a Baptist church." A friend of mine at Columbia University asserts that never before have the churches "been materially more powerful and spiritually less effective," and a recent book glorifies the vitality of the nineteenth-century churches, in comparison with which we are now a poor second.

These critics are warning our present-day churches of a real peril. Too lax inclusiveness is a menace, and numbers are not a test of spiritual strength. I notice, however, that most of these critics are comparatively young; they never lived in those nineteenth-century churches, as some of us did; if they had, they would drastically qualify their enthusiastic praise. Thank heaven for the liberation which multitudes of our present churches enjoy from the petty bigotry, the obscurantism, the miserable legalism and the individualistic blindness to social problems which too often afflicted those old churches and drove into ecclesiastical exile souls whom Christ would have welcomed!

Our churches face new problems and fresh perils in a disheveled, threatening world, and no one should underrate our failures. But, in the light of my own retrospect, I am much more hopeful of the Christian church's future now than I could possibly be if we were anything like a reproduction of the nineteenth-century model. Faults and failures there are, and dangers manifold, but on the whole the church has been making headway toward a better day.

Looking back on my twenty years as a minister at the Riverside Church I often wonder how I got through them. The opportunities were always greater than I could compass, the demands heavier than I could carry. Whether my nerves would much longer stand the strain seemed at times questionable, and once a major surgical operation threatened to settle the matter. Being a minister can seem "a heartbreaking way of making a living," but always I knew that I "would not give it up for all the world." When aged sixty-seven I retired from the active ministry of the church and saw in the pulpit there my successor, Robert James McCracken, a great preacher and a most admirable and lovable personality under whose inspiring leadership the church has gone from strength to strength, an old gospel hymn familiar in my youth came alive again:

> Here I raise my Ebenezer,
> Hither by Thy help I've come.

Chapter 9.

❧

Winds of Doctrine

WHAT A GENERATION of doctrinal controversies I have lived through! They have rocked the churches all my lifetime. Charles H. Briggs, the famous pioneer of Old Testament critical scholarship in the United States, was still teaching in Union Seminary when I studied there; he had been condemned as a heretic by the Presbyterians and had taken refuge in the Episcopal Church. Arthur Cushman McGiffert, in church history, was one of my most revered teachers; he too had suffered from the Presbyterians' repeated attacks and trials, and had escaped to the Congregational Church. I have seen the churches and their seminaries live through many contentious decades, and my own struggle for liberation from the theological dogmatism in which I was reared has been only a pale reflection of a whole generation's revolt.

I am no technical theologian, but I cannot write an honest autobiography without recalling these gusty winds of doctrine which often made it difficult to steer a steady course in proclaiming the Christian gospel.

My adversaries, and even my friends, have sometimes had difficulty in defining just what my theological position is, and I think I know why. I have never been able to be either a theological reactionary or a theological radical. I could not be a theological reactionary because, so it seemed to me, the fact that astronomies change while stars abide is a true analogy of every realm of human life and thought, religion not least of all. No existent theology can be a final formulation of spiritual truth. Concerning every human experience theories of explanation and interpretation are essential, but however confidently they may be held, their probable insufficiency must be assumed and their displacement by more adequate ways of thinking positively hoped for. Cosmic theories and theologies are meant to change. Static orthodoxies, therefore, are a menace to the Christian cause. If the day ever comes when men care so little for the basic Christian experiences and revelations of truth that they cease trying to rethink them in more adequate terms, see them in the light of freshly acquired knowledge, and interpret them anew for new days, then Christianity will be finished.

Unable to be a theological reactionary, I could not be a theological radical either. The radicals always seemed to me to have decided that the stars had vanished because an old astronomy had gone. My own reaction has been the opposite: the old astronomy was wrong about something real and permanent, and to get at that reality afresh, to see it again more clearly and more truly was the only solution that in the end counted for anything. I have been commonly accused of taking theology too lightly because I have been eager for new ways of seeing and stating Christian truth. Upon the contrary, I take theology so seriously that whenever in the Christian tradition I see doctrine persistently struggling over some central issue, displaced by new doctrine but still tussling with the same old problem, I am sure that truth is really there, and that the combined transiency and persistence of doctrine in dealing with it is a testimony to its importance. So ideas of God change and ought to, but that fact does not mean that anything has happened to God; and theories of the atonement have followed one another in a long succession, but far from undermining the significance of vicarious sacrifice, that fact bears witness to its inescapable momentousness.

This attitude has given to my ministry a middle-of-the-road quality which can easily be misunderstood as compromise, but which springs from deeper sources. Toward the close of the eighteenth century President Ezra Stiles of Yale wrote: "I never was particular and exclusive enough for a cordial and close union with any sect, not even my own." Something like that has been my experience even with the liberalism with which my name has been associated. Looking back, I regard with satisfaction the difficulty my critics have had in classifying me. What I have done I would do again and try to do better: believe both in abiding stars and changing astronomies.

Basic in my thinking has been the conviction that theologies are psychologically and sociologically conditioned and that dogmatism in theology, whether "liberal" or "orthodox," is ridiculous. Dealing as they do with eternal verities, theologians are easily tempted to assume that their formulations also are eternal, whereas, if anything on earth is tentative, subject to the push and pull of changing science and philosophy and to shifting popular moods of optimism and despair, it is systems of theology. When I was graduated from the seminary my thesis concerned the historic doctrines that had been formulated to explain the death of Jesus, and I recall the strong impression made upon me by the fact that no doctrine of atonement in the church's history can be understood apart from the prevalent ideas and especially the legal and penological concepts of the society in which it arose. These theologies about the Cross of Christ, set forth with such elaborate argument, were not the everlasting truth they were often taken to be, but were temporary formulations of a great matter, made by men conditioned by their social culture and their psychological reactions to it.

This fact has had much to do with the quality of my liberalism. When in college I returned from agnosticism to theism, I was a Neo-Hegelian of sorts, but William James later called in question my too great confidence in that kind of absolutism. It was the study of theology itself, however, which finished the process. The theology of any generation cannot be understood apart from the conditioning social matrix in which it is formulated and this is as true for liberalism as it is for orthodoxy. When, therefore, liberalism was in full swing at Union Seminary, I always required from students in my preaching classes at least one sermon a term on the faults and failures of the liberal position; and when neo-orthodoxy became influential I welcomed especially sermons in criticism of that. These theological trends, and all others that will follow them, are partial, contemporary attempts to formulate great matters. To take the best insights of them all, to see the incompleteness and falsity in them all, to trust none of them as a whole, to see always that the Reality to be explained is infinitely greater than our tentative, conditioned explanations—that seems to me wisdom.

This attitude has, of course, made my ministry useful to some and not to others. Roman Catholics and Protestant fundamentalists commonly assume—often, it seems to me, with unconscious cynicism—that most people want a finished, static creed to be signed unquestioningly on the dotted line, so that dogmatic certainty is the only way to meet their need. That there are plenty of folk to support this thesis is clear. My experience has thrown me for the most part with another sort of person, often religiously ruined by such dogmatism. Taught to identify the Christian gospel with some form of orthodoxy, they have rebelled, and have either thrown over the whole business or else have struggled along, their faith at war with their intelligence and their Christian experience tortured by an unhappy sense of intellectual dishonesty. It is to such folk that my ministry has, I suspect, been most useful.

Here is a letter typical of hundreds that have come to me:

I was given the heritage of a deeply religious home, but after my Mother and Father were no longer there to guide me, my outlook on religion became warped, because I thought my Aunt's fanatical—yet deeply sincere—fundamentalism necessarily un-questionable and representative of all Christianty. So as my mind grew in scope I felt myself against my will being torn inch by inch away from the church I loved. And when in the Army I had forced upon me a great deal of time to read and think, it did not make me happy to realize that the breach was growing wider. Then one evening I happened upon a copy of *The Modern Use of the Bible,* and from then on I no longer had to apologize for Christianity to some of my more scientifically-minded friends, and passed from the defensive to the offensive as the chains that had held back my thinking began to break. I will not bore you by going over my manifold and deeply held religious convictions, nor recount all the details of my spiritual growth since then—but it could only be described as "colossal." However, I would like to say—with the utmost sincerity—that through your writings you laid a solid foundation for my religious beliefs and enabled me to restore my faith. For this I shall be eternally grateful.

Another factor in my struggle for a convinced faith has been emphasis on direct, immediate personal experience as the solid ground for assurance. Two major emphases are always found in organized religions: on one side, stress on the objective authority of church, Scripture and creed; on the other side, stress on "the divine-human encounter" within the soul, on personal experience of God's transforming and sustaining grace. Both are present in the New Testament, but there seems to me no doubt that the latter is primary. In Islam there are dogmatic creedalists and mystical Sufis, and always in Christianity, disguised under many different names, there have been dogmatists with their primary emphasis on logical doctrine and mystics with their primary emphasis on transforming personal experience, Romanists stressing the authority of church and creed and Quakers stressing the authority of the "inner light." All these emphases belong within the scope of an adequate Christianity, but it has been deplorably difficult to keep them in balance. Certain types of liberalism have so stressed inner experience that they have brushed aside the objective nature of eternal truth; and today certain types of dogmatism so stress the objective revelation of God in Scripture and creed that they belittle the "inner light" as mere subjectivism.

As for me, I stand with Canon B. H. Streeter, of Oxford: "I have had experiences which materialism cannot explain."

That expresses the fact which in my generation kept many within the Christian fold, even when current theologies insulted their intelligence. Out of a critical and to them momentous struggle on which the whole meaning of life depended, they bear witness that, granting the necessity and profound importance of Christian theology, Christian experience is the abiding continuum underlying vital faith. So Jeremy Taylor put it long ago: "Men cast out every line, and turned every stone and tried every argument: and sometimes proved it well and when they did not, yet they believed strongly; and they were sure of the thing when they were not sure of the argument."

We humans, despite our ignorance and sin, are experientially confronted with spiritual reality. Life is not, as one skeptic has called it, "only a physiological process with only a physiological meaning." We do face the moral imperative of conscience and high hours of revelation when "the spirit's true endowments stand out plainly from the false ones"; we do confront supreme personalities, Christ over all, whom we cannot dodge, deny or forget; and we all feel in our best moments the futility of man's endeavors to be content with a cosmos that comes from nowhere, means nothing and is going nowhither. Here Christian thinking, like all thinking, starts with experience which outlives all changes in doctrine about it, and constitutes the ever-recurrent test and criterion of truth, and the ultimate basis of religious certainty.

These facts of experience are objectively real. We do have hours of revelation, as Sidney Lanier says, when

> . . . belief overmasters doubt, and I know that I know,
> And my spirit is grown to a lordly great compass within.

We do face our intractable consciences—"something inside
a man that he cannot do what he wants to with." We do experience sin, guilty remorse and forgiveness; and moral victory, snatched from the jaws of defeat by the influx of a
Power greater than our own, is as real an event as sunrise.
We do confront man's tragic history where scientific brilliance
brings him no peace if, gaining the world, he loses his soul.
We do confront Jesus Christ—disturbed, provoked, challenged, fascinated by him and, if we will, ushered by him
into a new life.

Such experiential facts are no more unreal and illusory than
other objects of our thinking, and our thinking on spiritual
problems must start from them and return to them. They are
the revelation of God. We did not make them up; God took
the initiative; they were thrust upon us. They pursue us like
"The Hound of Heaven" in Francis Thompson's poem. Our
discovery of them is really our surrender to them. A wise
theology clarifies them, reassures our faith in them, deepens
our understanding of them, but, as for me, it is the experience
itself in which I find my certainty, while my theological interpretations I must, in all humility, hold with tentative confidence. As Karl Barth himself says: "Our concepts are not
adequate to grasp this treasure."

Such is the "liberalism" in which I have found a sustaining
and defensible Christian faith.

Looking at our contentious theological situation, it is important to recognize that as there are diverse types of orthodoxy, so there are varied types of liberalism. Calling a man a
"liberal" is no definitive description of his opinions; such

labels, as someone has said, are a "device to save talkative people from the necessity of thinking." The neglect of this fact has caused endless misrepresentation of liberalism. At any rate, I venture to protest on behalf of the very considerable number of liberals of my stripe against familiar misinterpretations of our position.

We do not believe in automatic, inevitable social progress, supposing that by some inherent necessity the world is growing better and better. That we took the optimistic color of our generation is undoubtedly true. Such optimism—not the creation of religious liberals—was the secular spirit of the age, the conditioning mood of scientists, philosophers and poets, which colored Christian thinking, as prevalent moods always color the religion of the time. It was no Christian liberal, but Herbert Spencer, an agnostic, who wrote: "Progress is not an accident, not a thing within human control, but a beneficent necessity. . . . This advancement is due to the working of a universal law; . . . in virtue of that law it must continue until the state we call perfection is reached. . . . so surely must the things we call evil and immorality disappear; so surely must men become perfect."

It is easy now to assemble fatuous expressions of naïve hope in which Christian liberals reflected this dominant temper of their generation. Newell Dwight Hillis, in Plymouth Church, Brooklyn, charmed his congregation by saying:

Laws are becoming more just, rulers more humane; music is becoming sweeter and books wiser; homes are happier, and the individual heart is becoming at once more just and more gentle. . . . For today, art, industry, invention, literature, learning and government—all these are captives marching in Christ's triumphant procession up the hill of fame.

Such optimism was familiar before the two world wars; its effect on Christian thinking is one of the major illustrations in history of the inevitable conditioning of religious thought by its social matrix; but to suppose that Christian liberals as a whole so far surrendered to it that they believed then or believe now in automatic, inevitable progress is fantastic.

In my seminary days there were classrooms, to be sure, where optimism reigned, where, for example, Thomas C. Hall talked beguilingly of the "Kingdom dream," but even then that was not the whole story. One of the critical turning points in my thinking came from a remark dropped by Professor George William Knox in a seminar: "Beware how you baptize evolution in terms of progress!" That clicked. I never escaped its peremptory challenge to the naïve social hopefulness with which my optimistic generation had infected me.

That remark, bearing fruit, profoundly influenced my lectures at Vanderbilt University in 1922 on *Christianity and Progress*. Those lectures antedated the influence of neo-orthodoxy in America and represented a major type of liberalism. In them I called the current "unmitigated enthusiasm about the earth's future" "a fool's paradise"; said that "the mid-Victorian confidence in an automatic evolution which willy-nilly lifts humanity to higher levels" was "a quite unjustified flourish of sentimentality"; argued that "upon the basis of a scientific doctrine of evolution, no idolatrous superstition could be much more lacking in intellectual support than

Spencer's confidence in a universal, mechanical, irresistible movement towards perfection"; denounced the "superficial, ill-considered optimism which has largely lost sight of the terrific obstacles in human nature against which any real moral advance on earth must win its way"; and added:

A recent writer considers it possible that "over the crest of the hill the Promised Land stretches away to the far horizon smiling in eternal sunshine." That picture is nonsense. All the progress this world will know waits upon the conquest of sin. Strange as it may sound to the ears of this modern age, long tickled by the amiable idiocies of evolution popularly misinterpreted, this generation's deepest need is not these dithyrambic songs about inevitable progress, but a fresh sense of social and personal sin. . . .

As liberals of my sort thus attacked Spencerian ideas of automatic progress, so we never believed that the Kingdom of God could fully come in human history on this planet. This denial that the Kingdom can be realized in history is now one of neo-orthodoxy's emphases, but Christian liberals were making that denial before neo-orthodoxy's influence had become potent in America. To be sure, Reinhold Niebuhr's haunting analysis of sin—even our best good corroded by egocentricity and pride—was not in our minds then, and our thinking would have been better balanced if it had been there. Nevertheless, we liberals too had long confronted what I called in 1922 "the same inescapable experience out of which the old doctrine of original sin first came . . . that humanity's sinful nature is not something which you and I alone make up by individual deeds of wrong, but that it is an inherited mortgage and handicap on the whole human

family." As I recall the matter, however, our first denials that
God's Kingdom could ever be consummated within human
history on this earth sprang not so much from our estimate of
sin's persistent and ingenious power to ruin our best endeavors as from the temporary nature of the earth itself.
Once uninhabitable, it would be uninhabitable again. The
sun would become hotter and burn it up or colder and freeze
it out. Whatever temporary progress might be achieved on
this planet, it would face unfulfilled an inevitable *terminus
ad quem.*

On a train between New York and Boston—I vividly recall
that day in my early ministry—I read in the newspaper a
report of an astronomer's address concerning the seven ways
in one of which the earth would end. That too was a turning
point in my thinking. Some time since at the Planetarium in
New York I saw pictured five possible ways in one of which
our planet will become uninhabitable. Extend man's probable
existence on earth as many billions of years as one may, the
problem is not essentially changed. Someday, unless there
is a fulfillment of man's life beyond history, the human
venture will be futilely finished and everything will be as
though nothing here had ever been at all.

This challenging fact had two effects on my thinking.
First, it became a major reason for my faith in immortality.
In my private feeling I have never eagerly desired my own
endless continuance. Indeed, in my boyhood some of my
most hideous hours came—quite apart from any thought of
"future punishment"—from contemplating the idea that one
could never die, that forever and forever he must live with
himself with no escape from his self-consciousness, no way

of ending it however he might crave an end, a billion billion years from now the inexorable necessity of continued life still confronting him, with unending billions of years ahead. Call this morbid if one will, but a very great religion, Buddhism, has been pretty much founded on it. Had I been born in the Orient, I might have been a good Buddhist, wanting above all else to escape the unending "wheel of rebirth" to Nirvana, the "peace of a candle that has been blown out."

If, however, death is the end of me it is of others too. Then all our ancestors are finally dead, and we and all our children will be finally dead, and with the planet's perishing, the last Robinson Crusoe on this wandering island in the sky will be finally dead, and nothing will be left, no value conserved, no purpose fulfilled from all that was endeavored and done on earth. That inevitability involves a senseless creation which in the end consummates nothing, wastes everything, preserves no values, fulfills no promises, has no meaning. My faith in immortality has been mainly a corollary from my faith that creation cannot be so utterly senseless and irrational. As for the meaning of immortality itself and the nature of the life to come, it must have dimensions far beyond our imagination's power to grasp; I have dropped my boyhood's anxieties about that; that is in the hands of God.

The second effect of our planet's transiency upon my thinking was to make impossible the prevalent vague optimism about endless social progress here. This earth can be a "vale of soul-making," as Keats called it; there has been progress and there can be progress still—far better, it may be, than our presently chastened hopes conceive—in reshaping human institutions for man's good and winning victories over his inherent evil; but no final consummation of divine purpose, no ultimate resolution of man's dilemmas can be expected on a temporary planet. God must have some further word to say; whatever approximations of his will on earth may be achieved, his Kingdom in its fullness lies beyond history, not within it.

Another favorite charge against liberalism has been that it reduces Christianity to mere ethicism as though nothing were left of the gospel except the morals of Jesus without his world view and his faith in God, but I never knew a liberal in the evangelical churches who would have consented to any such position.

When neo-orthodoxy had barely been heard of in this country I wrote as a liberal, in my book, *As I See Religion:*

Much current talk about morals without religion . . . proceeds upon the incredible assumption that there can be serious discussion of what man ought to be without serious discussion of what man is. *Oughtness,* however, is essentially related to *isness* . . . and on that simple fact the endeavor of morals to secede from religion will in the end wreck itself. For while morals deal with what men ought to do and be, religion is basically a message about what men are. They are not the scum of the earth, says a high religion, the accidental by-product of a merely physical cosmos; they are personalities, spiritual beings whose powers of intellection, purposefulness, good will, spring from the nature of the Real World and are necessary to interpret the full truth about it. They are, in a word, sons of God, and it does not yet appear what they shall be. To suppose that morals, dealing with what man ought to be, can blithely wave farewell to this basic problem regarding what men are, that the Ideal for man is un-related to the Fact about man, is to disregard obvious human experience.

The liberalism which I have known, therefore, has been profoundly concerned about man's world view. It has affirmed, with as much conviction as the orthodox ever could display, that Christian faith takes in the whole cosmos and is a gospel about its divine origin, purpose, destiny and mean-ing. On this point scores of my sermons bear witness to my conviction that without faith in God the whole climate of man's life would become so arctic that the best in man's ethical life would become impossible.

While liberals as a whole, however, have not been so naïve and gullible in their optimism as their opponents like to picture them, while they have never thought that God's Kingdom could be fulfilled by human progress within history, and have never considered the ethics of Jesus the whole gospel, there has been plenty in liberalism to criticize. In the Lyman Beecher Lectures at Yale in 1924 I stated, as candidly as I knew how, the modernist position in dealing with the Scriptures, but those who accepted the new views "with intellectual eagerness, coupled with spiritual super-ficiality" gave me concern. Orthodox "Bible Christians" were commonly dead in earnest, but some liberals took an attitude toward the Bible consisting mainly in rejecting the old views of it. This negativeness went on to a general denial of old theological formulations without creating well-thought-out, positive statements of liberal convictions in the realm of Christian faith, so that one New York newspaper hit off the situation by saying that the fundamentalists lacked charity and the liberals lacked clarity. "At this point," I said, "the defenders of ancient theology have an incalculable advantage over the modernists. . . . these defenders of old theologies know exactly what they think."

Indeed, the dangers facing the liberal movement went deeper yet. Quite apart from left-wing radicals who swung over toward, and even into, nontheistic humanism, the whole movement was conditioned by its major purpose: to adjust Christian thinking to modern knowledge. The liberal theology of my generation was not just unconsciously molded by contemporary philosophic, scientific and social pressures; it was consciously, deliberately, sometimes desperately trying to adapt Christian thought to, and harmonize it with, the intellectual culture of our time. That was the only way in which we could save our faith, and its achievement was a matter of life and death. Here was science's new world view, utterly diverse from the cosmic setting of traditional theology. Split clean in two by the conflict between science and contemporary religious thought, we became schizophrenic when we tried to be both Christian traditionalists and modern intellectuals. Fundamentalists saw that issue and made their choice, denying modern knowledge, from evolution up and down, for the sake of preserving their Christianity. We, too, saw the issue, but found no peace in such obscurantism. We were out to reformulate Christian thinking so that it could take modern knowledge in.

We won our battle. It was one of the most necessary theological battles ever fought. The neo-orthodox today may condemn liberalism as they will; they are nonetheless its pensioners and would not be here at all had not liberalism waged and won for them its indispensable campaign. We could be Christian without being deaf, dumb and blind in the face of modern knowledge. All truth, we said, is God's truth, and Christian theology can take it in, rejoice in it, and incorporate it into the understanding of the gospel.

A peril, however, was inherent in our endeavor, which liberalism as a whole was neither wise enough to foresee nor Christian enough to forestall. We were adjusting Christian thought to a secular culture. Unaware of the consequence, we made the secular culture paramount and standard. Was this or that factor in Christian thinking in harmony with the new science?—that was the test. The center of gravity was not in the gospel but in the prevalent intellectual concepts of our time. We surrendered our independent standing ground and became a movement of adaptation and accommodation.

Some of us saw the debacle coming and were deeply concerned. We were liberals through and through, but all the more with ominous forebodings we saw the inadequacy of our party and the certainty of revolt against it, unless we could plunge deeper and go farther than mere adjustment to current modern thinking. We began to drop our concern about fundamentalism and to take for granted the harmonization of scientific and Christian thought; some of our best scientists were Christians and some of our best Christians were scientists; and we began to shout warnings—as one of my sermons in the middle-thirties was entitled—that "The Church Must Go Beyond Modernism." We had then been through one world war and only God knew whether we could avoid another. Our current culture was no adequate standard, no supreme criterion, to which Christian truth must be adjusted; our whole civilization was in desperate need of being itself adjusted to Christian truth. So the entire scene shifted, and liberalism began saying—to quote the sermon just referred to—

We have adapted and adjusted and accommodated and conceded long enough. We have at times gotten so low down that we talked as though the highest compliment that could be paid Almighty God was that a few scientists believed in him. Yet all the time, by right, we had an independent standing ground and a message of our own in which alone is there hope for humanity. . . . We have already won the battle we started out to win; we have adjusted the Christian faith to the best intelligence of our day and have won the strongest minds and the best abilities of the church to our side. Fundamentalism is still with us but mostly in the backwaters. The future of the churches, if we will have it so, is in the hands of modernism. Therefore, let all modernists lift a new battle cry: "We must go beyond modernism," and in that new enterprise the watchword will be not, "Accommodate yourself to the prevailing culture," but "Stand out from it and challenge it." For this inescapable fact, which again and again in history has called modernism to its senses, we face: We cannot harmonize Christ with modern culture. What Christ does to modern culture is to challenge it.

I recall preaching a sermon in those days on "The Major Fault of Liberalism." A well-known liberal minister came to me afterward, very much grieved; I was deserting the liberal cause, he said. As a matter of fact, I was trying earnestly and ineffectually to help it. To many of its adherents, liberalism became a static orthodoxy; it dug in its heels where it was and merely stood its ground; it failed to see that the admonition "new occasions teach new duties" applies not to reactionaries alone but to modernists also. In order to move out into the terrific postwar generation with a gospel suited to man's staggering needs, it did not have to surrender a single one of its invaluable gains, but it did have to wake up, recognizing that reactionary liberalism can be as much a failure as reactionary traditionalism. So the inevitable happened and a theological revolt swept in.

Some of the consequences I witnessed during my final years as a seminary professor, listening to student sermons at Union. I learned to distinguish at once, without asking personal questions, between students who had come into their neo-orthodoxy through liberalism—as Reinhold Niebuhr did—and those who had taken their first plunge into theology under neo-orthodox auspices. The men with liberal backgrounds often presented valuable emphases and insights, gained from neo-orthodoxy, with such force and effectiveness as made me grateful. They were not accommodating the Christian gospel to anything; they were taking their stand on the Christian gospel and challenging the world. But the men who had never known theology until they learned it first in neo-orthodoxy! In a few cases especially I never had heard at Union such homiletical arrogance, such take-it-or-leave-it assumption of theological finality, such cancellation of the life and words of the historic Jesus by the substitution of a dogmatic Christ. My first contacts with neo-orthodoxy's effect upon the preacher were very disillusioning.

This does not mean that I underestimate the service which neo-orthodoxy has rendered. Karl Barth is a stalwart character and a stimulating, provocative thinker. In 1934 he was removed from his professorship in the University of Bonn because he refused to take an unqualified oath of allegiance to Hitler. Of the eighteen books he wrote during those fateful years in Germany eleven were banned, and in 1935 he was arrested and escorted to the Swiss border where he was released. In Switzerland he became professor of theology at Basel and one of the most influential thinkers in the modern church. Just as the liberals reared in the old orthodoxy had revolted against *that*, so Barth reared in the liberalism of Ritschl and Harnack revolted against *that*. Liberalism was too thin, too optimistic, too blind to the tragic sinfulness and desperate plight of man—so he thought—to represent the gospel's truth or to meet the need of human souls in such a catastrophic age.

The response with which Barth's neo-orthodoxy was greeted surprised no one more than himself. He said that his experience was like that of a man who, climbing in a church steeple, reaches out for support and to his dismay discovers that he has seized the bell rope and has awakened the whole town.

It is not easy for a liberal to describe neo-orthodoxy with objective fairness. Just as some reactionaries are tempted to lump all liberals together, define them en masse into an insane asylum, and then condemn them for being there, so some liberals are tempted to treat the neo-orthodox. Present-day neo-orthodoxy, however, is not a stereotype; it is a doctrinal trend rather than a dogmatic system; far from being static it is fluid; its adherents are not harmonious but are discordantly variant. Karl Barth and Emil Brunner have had famous disagreements—Barth's brochure, *Nein!* was a blistering attack on Brunner—and, as for the camp followers, their opinions scatter far and wide, and the whole movement is becoming increasingly self-critical.

Certainly, neo-orthodoxy must not be identified with fundamentalism. If one wishes to hear a neo-orthodox proponent roar, call him a fundamentalist! And in return the fundamentalists attack the Barthians, for the neo-orthodox accept modern science and modern Biblical scholarship as liberals do.

Moreover, men like Barth and Brunner have not stood still. Barth recently wrote that he did not know whether to "weep or laugh" at the misrepresentations of his position —to which one learned churchman replied that "it was the violence of Barth's own early attacks on liberal theology that led to the violence of the reaction." I think that is a fair statement, but it is also fair to recognize that men like Barth and Brunner have modified and deepened their positions, so that what they said in an early book may be quite different from what they are saying now. So Paul Tillich says about Barth, even while vigorously assailing some of his positions: "Barth's greatness is that he corrects himself again and again in the light of the 'situation' and that he strenuously tries not to become his own follower."

While these wide variations and changing emphases within neo-orthodoxy are real, however, there is one common quality which characterizes the neo-orthodox movement as a whole: its discontent with the liberal theology current in the late nineteenth and early twentieth centuries. I write about this now because that liberal theology saved my Christian faith, and I am intensely interested in what is happening to it.

Liberalism grew up in an era when a utopian estimate of man was in full swing—Karl Marx saying: "The religion of the workers has no God because it seeks to restore the divinity of man"; Samuel Butler predicting that automatically, by the sheer force of evolution, man will become "not only an angel, but an archangel"; Swinburne singing at the top of his voice:

> Glory to man in the highest,
> For man is the master of things.

Marx, Butler and Swinburne were all atheists, but they tried to make up for it by deifying man.

This sentimental man-worship, this blindness to human wickedness, was part of the *Zeitgeist,* and certain extreme forms of religious liberalism were infected by it. In my early ministry the story ran concerning a popular religious book that a friend said to the author: "You did not even mention sin in your book," to which the author replied: "Oh, there ought not to be any such thing." Against this mood and temper neo-orthodoxy has entered a vehement protest. Emil Brunner, in his early book, *The Theology of Crisis,* whose extravagance he has, I am sure, happily outgrown, said: "Liberalism . . . has ever affirmed that the heart of man is not evil. Evil merely clings to man's heart as the barnacles do to the ship's hull." Such a simile seems to me nonsense, and no evangelical liberal I ever knew would have consented to it.

Nevertheless, some liberalism did go to optimistic extremes in its estimate of man, and some of us, quite uninfluenced then by neo-orthodoxy, also entered vehement protests. In one of my early books I said:

A comfortable modernism which, eliminating harsh and obsolete orthodoxies and making a few mental adjustments to scientific world views, contents itself with a sentimentalized God and a roseate optimism will, if it continues, encourage the worst opinions of religion as a pacifying fantasy. Such a lush gospel will claim its devotees, but minds with any sinew in them turn away. Modern Christianity has grown soft, sentimental, saccharine. It has taken on pink flesh and lost strong bone. It has become too much flute and too little trumpet. It has fallen from the stimulating altitudes of austerity and rigor, where high religion customarily has walked. Its preachers have become too commonly religious crooners. In consequence it is called a mere wish-fulfilment because it acts that way.

I cordially agree, therefore, that there are types of liberalism against which neo-orthodoxy was justified in rebelling, but theologians, being nothing if not human, when they rise in revolt against extremes are tempted to go to extremes themselves. In his early book Brunner called men "sinners, always hopeless sinners," standing in "absolute helplessness and despair in the presence of the Holy God"; he affirmed "the ultimate hopelessness of all human activity"; he made a "vehement denial of a divine depth or height in man where communion with God may be effected." Anyone who knows Emil Brunner now and is acquainted with his later books will be sure that were he confronted with those phrases today, he would be the first to deny that they adequately

represent his doctrine of man. What he was trying to say—
so it seems to me—was that man is no automatically evolv-
ing archangel, that man's wickedness is a dreadful, desperate
fact, and that man, left to his own unaided devices in a
materalistic universe empty of the saving grace of God, is
doomed. I thoroughly agree.

At their best the neo-orthodox are saying *that* today much
more clearly and effectively than they did at first. They
are happily discovering that in attacking unhealthy optimism
they do not need to phrase their opinions in terms of unhealthy pessimism. When Reinhold Niebuhr presents the
desperate estate of man, as he sees it, he is not pessimistic
and discouraging. He is provocative, stimulating, shocking,
challenging, sometimes paradoxically bewildering, but he
is not disheartening. He comes at us, like Winston Churchill,
with a message of "blood, toil, tears and sweat" not to dismay but to arouse. Some of the neo-orthodox, however,
especially some of the camp followers, do vilify man in
order to glorify God, reducing man to mere emptiness and
impotence, and that is such a perversion of the truth that,
as another put it, the neo-orthodox "have carried the argument to an extreme which provides its own refutation."

Another emphasis of liberalism in my early ministry was
the divine immanence, God's indwelling presence in the
world and in man. We nineteenth-century Christians were
reared on the idea of God's available inward presence. The
old Newtonian concept of the cosmos—a vast *machine* with
God as the Great First Cause—had gone, and the new
world of evolution, a *process* with God in it as well as above

it, shaped our thinking. Moreover, God's immanence meant
to us especially what the New Testament proclaims: "If we
love one another, God abides in us;" "We are the temple of
the living God; as God said, I will live in them"; ". . . that
Christ may dwell in your hearts, through faith; . . . that you
may be filled with all the fullness of God." This seemed
to us—and still does seem—the very essence of vital religion. To be sure, God is transcendent, above and beyond
the world, not limited by it, but to us his most vital aspect is
inward:

> Speak to Him thou for He hears, and Spirit
>   with Spirit can meet—
> Closer is He than breathing, and nearer
>   than hands and feet.

I vividly recall Arthur Cushman McGiffert lecturing to us
in seminary days on the immanence of God as "the most
characteristic religious doctrine of the nineteenth century."

That some liberals carried their concepts of this doctrine
to exaggerated extremes is obvious. Immanence can be
stretched into pantheism; God's presence in us can be translated into God's identification with us; and the idea of
immanence can be blown up until the idea of God's transcendence disappears. Some liberals so overdid their stress
on God's subjective presence in us that God's presence anywhere else was pretty much lost sight of.

So once more the theological pendulum swung from one
extreme to the other. God's transcendent sovereignty needed
to be recovered and reinstated in Christian thinking. To be
sure, Barth's early description of God as the "Wholly Other"

and his stress on "man's utter distance from God" do not
fairly represent the better balance and more inclusive scope
of his later writings, but they do represent one important
area of doctrine where neo-orthodoxy started out to correct liberalism. Brunner even wrote: "All doctrines of immanence are its [Christianity's] dissolution." Of course,
when he wrote that he was not thinking of immanence as
we evangelical liberals conceived it. He was not denying
John's doctrine of the Logos—the light that "lighteth every
man." He was not denying the Trinity—God revealed as
not only transcendent Creator and historic Character but
as indwelling Comforter. He was not denying the New
Testament's assertion: "Hereby we know that we abide in
him and he in us, because he has given us of his Spirit."
Surely he was not denying his revered St. Augustine: "Why
do we go forth and run to the heights of the heavens and
the lowest parts of the earth, seeking Him who is within
us, if we wish to be with Him?" He was not thinking, therefore, of "all doctrines of immanence," although he said
he was, but he was expressing in extreme terms the recoil of
early neo-orthodoxy against certain extremes in current
"immanentism."

Theologians in revolt against the frying pan commonly
leap into the fire. Facing two aspects of an important truth
they make an either-or out of what ought to be a both-and.
With regard to the matter we are now considering the neo-
orthodox leaders today see this fact, I think, as clearly as
we do, and the two sides are moving toward a just balance.
As for me, I go back to what William Newton Clarke said
to us students over half a century ago, in the very era

which neo-orthodoxy now pictures as going crazy about "immanentism." "The ideas of immanence and transcendence," said Dr. Clarke, "are sometimes set in opposition to each other, and each has ever had its advocates; but this, at least in the present age, is needless and wrong. Each conception needs the other. Transcendence without immanence would give us Deism, cold and barren; immanence without transcendence would give us Pantheism, fatalistic and paralyzing." That is the position which evangelical liberals as a whole have always maintained.

Another aspect of neo-orthodoxy's reaction against liberal extremes is to be seen in what L. Harold De Wolf, in the title of his excellent book, calls *The Religious Revolt against Reason*. We liberals at the turn of the century did exalt reason. We were fed up with dogmatic orthodoxies claiming to be divine revelations, which demanded our acceptance whether they insulted our intelligence or not. We did tend to make human reason a supreme court of appeal. Brunner, in his early book, describes this attitude in its extreme form: "Modern theology, like all modern thinking, is controlled by noncritical faith in reason. . . . The man who has this noncritical faith in reason will accept as valid only what he is able to verify." Liberals, guilty of that exaggeration, deserve his rebuke. The realm in which it is possible to "verify" conclusions, in any exact use of that word, is very limited. Who in his senses ever thought that a cosmic philosophy could be thus verified? Theism, atheism, pantheism, materialism, are not amenable to a neat Q.E.D., and certainly not the Christian God of grace and mercy. Nevertheless, in those troubled days when my generation was fighting for its faith, we were sure that reason should not be shut out. We were determined to gather all evidence, marshal all arguments, consider all possibilities, and make a choice, if we reached one, consonant with what seemed to us rationally true.

Some liberalism, however, did carry its confidence in reason to irrational extremes. For one thing, it was tempted to forget the unfathomable mystery of life, which all our reasoning can never plumb. One of the first articles I ever had published—the *Atlantic Monthly* carried it—was entitled "The Mystery of Life," and now the older I grow the more the incomprehensible mysteriousness of this universe and of our human lives within it chastens my thinking and keeps my theology humble. We liberals too agree with St. Augustine: *"Si comprehendis, non est Deus"*—which freely translated means, I take it: "Anything which your intellect is able to comprehend is too small to be God." Of course, human reason is limited. Of course, the unfathomable depths of life's mystery are beyond the reach of our mental plummets. All our thinking about God is partial, our concepts not literal but pictorial, our language symbolic. Of course, no man "by searching" can "find out God."

Neo-orthodoxy is right, therefore, in stressing the necessity and primacy of God's self-revelation, if we are to know him. In no area of our spiritual life—the love of nature, of friends, of books, of music—is reasoned argument the *initial* factor. Nature first unveils herself to us; friends open their hearts to us; books and music burst upon us—always revelation comes first. As for our faith in God made known in

Christ, our rational arguments are not the primary, creative factor. He himself came first; often against our will and wishes he confronted us and thrust his claims upon us. Our faith is our response to God's self-disclosure in nature, in prophetic characters, in inspired scriptures, in Christ, and in intimate, inward "I-Thou" relationships. That this response should be reasonable has been liberalism's rightful insistence, but some types of liberalism were tempted to forget that it was a *response to a revelation.*

Moreover, some liberalism forgot how corroded with prejudice our reason is. In certain fields, such as physics, reason can be fairly objective, but when a man deals with his ultimate philosophy of life, his scale of values, his idea of life's basic meaning, his reason is never neutral, but is swayed by his own personal quality, his subconscious motivations, his already accepted faiths. Reason, therefore, is not an impartial arbiter when faith in the Christian God is concerned; what a man's reason will say about that is influenced, sometimes determined, by factors deeper than rational processes go. Neo-orthodoxy's criticism of the way certain types of liberalism almost idolatrously trusted reason is justified.

Nevertheless, all this does not mean that reason is to be thrown out the window. Why does Barth say things like this?—"Faith takes reason by the throat and strangles the beast." He actually did say that in his early book, *The Epistle to the Romans*. He does not really mean that. Even in his volume of lectures, *Dogmatics in Outline*—inadequate and irritating to a liberal though it is—he says: "Christian faith is not irrational, not anti-rational, not supra-rational,

but rational in the proper sense." Exactly! It takes reasoning
even to discern the limits and insufficiencies of reason. It
takes better reasoning to correct bad reasoning. Barth himself and his followers are among the most persistent, inde-
fatigable reasoners of our time, using every rational argument they can think of to support their concept of the
Christian gospel. And yet, in their revolt against certain types
of liberal overconfidence in reason, some of the neo-orthodox
go to such extremes that I, for one, share Walter Marshall
Horton's feelings after reading Gustaf Aulén: "I am really
distressed by the apparent implication of Aulén's method,
that to reason about the Christian faith with perplexed en-
quirers is to commit high treason against the faith."

As I recall the critical days when my own mind walked
the thin edge between new theology and no theology, I
am grateful that I did not fall into the hands of men who
represented such an idea. I desperately needed someone
who would talk to me reasonably about religion. Men who
would only pound the table, announce God's revelation as
they understood it, and demand that by faith I accept it
with a decisive act of will, would have made Christianity
impossible for me. Faith does *not* take reason by the throat
and strangle the beast! Faith and reason are not antithetical
opposites. They need each other. All the tragic supersti-
tions which have cursed religion throughout its history have
been due to faith divorced from reason.

One American theologian, Stanley R. Hopper, in his
book, *Crisis of Faith*, compares the saving decisions of
Christian faith with the act of a man who, falling into an
abyss, has a rope thrown to him and desperately seizes
it. He does not first analyze the rope's adequacy and

strength; he cannot know *that* until he has clutched and tested it; his act is sheer unthinking faith and decision. Even Emil Brunner, in an early book, says that the acceptance of Christian faith is a choice made in a crisis, "with the passion of a drowning man who desperately cries for help." Anyone, however, who with the desperation of a drowning man cries for help, is likely to lay hold on anything—on optimistic pantheism, on escapist Buddhism, on Christian Science, spiritualism, astrology, Aimee Semple McPherson, or even on Christian liberalism! The neo-orthodox theology is not the only choice to which a desperate faith can turn. More than one rope dangles near the soul that is falling into the abyss—communism, nontheistic humanism, fundamentalism, and how many more! Granted the decisive choice that is involved in a vital faith, faith alone does not solve the problem. One must choose between faiths, and just as soon as one begins seriously thinking about *that*, one is reasoning.

Well, the situation is improving. Emil Brunner in his later book, *Revelation and Reason*, goes a long way toward re-establishing the rights of reason in dealing with Christian truth. "The question," he says, "can never be *whether,* but *to what extent* and *in what sense,* reason and revelation, faith and rational thinking, can be combined with one another." I cordially agree. Nevertheless, the neo-orthodox "revolt against reason," especially as represented in some of its camp followers, still presents a serious danger to hungry and inquiring souls who are asking questions about Christian faith which require reasonable answers.

Another characteristic of liberalism at the turn of the century was its tolerance, inclusivenes, open-mindedness.

We were disgusted with dogmatic claims to orthodox finality, accompanied by excommunication of dissenters—a temper which, far from being Roman Catholic only, had split Protestantism into warring sects. We were pioneers of the inclusive spirit which has created our interdenominational churches and our national and world councils. Within the Christian fellowship we wanted unity, with tolerance of differences; and, as for the non-Christian religions, we were intensely interested in discovering the truth in them and in establishing with them understanding relationships. In this regard I was then and am still a convinced liberal.

Nevertheless, tolerance carried to extremes can become vague. One can be so open-minded that he is like a summerhouse, through which all ideas are free to pass but where no ideas settle down and live. Gilbert Chesterton once remarked that the object of opening the mind, as of opening the mouth, is to shut it again on something solid. Some liberals forget that. They are long on tolerance and short on convictions. The story runs that a theological student, a stranger to Quakerism, hearing for the first time of the Hicksite-Orthodox split, exclaimed: "I didn't know that you had enough theology to split over." Some liberals doubtless gave that impression. To suppose that evangelical liberals in general thus sacrificed positive conviction to tolerant looseness is preposterous, but certainly the temptation was present.

When, however, World War I brought no peace, when Hitler rose to power, and Stalin too, when World War II broke in fury with its dreadful aftermath, if one was to be an honest-to-goodness Christian and stand his ground, especially in Europe, one had to possess more than tolerance; one desperately needed resolute convictions. This situation is a major explanation of the vogue and influence of neo-orthodoxy. Definite, positive religious convictions became a life-and-death matter.

Admiration, therefore, must mingle with criticism when, thinking of strong, courageous men like Barth and Brunner, one considers neo-orthodoxy's revolt from liberal tolerance to what now seems to many of us a wild extreme. Nevertheless, criticism of Barthian dogmatism is inevitable. Especially at first neo-orthodox excommunications were flung far and wide. All modernists, for example, were read out of the Christian fellowship. Even Brunner—himself a most gracious person, embracing all mankind in his sympathy and good will—said in his early book, *The Theology of Crisis*, that there is "little difficulty in proving that the modernist teaches under a label of Christianity, a religion which has nothing in common with Christianity except a few words, and that those words cover concepts which are irreconcilable with the content of Christian faith." "The modernists," he said, "no longer hold the Christian faith," and "Modernism can no longer be called Christianity."

As for non-Christian religions, the idea of finding in them any revelation of the true God meets with neo-orthodoxy's vehement denial, and behind this attitude lies one of the famous Barthian antitheses: man's search for God set over against God's search for man. Barth does not say, as liberal Christians do, that man has always needed God and tried to find him, and that God always and everywhere has been seeking man, revealing himself to man's clouded understanding as the Scripture says, "in many and various ways," and that in Christ the supreme fulfillment has come to man's long search and God's self-revelation. "The God of the Christian Confession," says Barth in stout denial, ". . . is not a fulfillment, perhaps the last, supreme, and best fulfillment, of what man was in course of seeking and finding." To Barth, all religious faith before Christ appeared is a "world of man's seeking, conjecturing, illusion, imagining, and speculating." That is to say, before Christ and outside of Christ man has been futilely trying to find God, and in Christ the true God for the first time in history entered the world to find man.

Indeed, few things are more distasteful to Barth than a high estimate of what he calls "the long road of human seeking and longing for the divine." What Barth sees in this long road of mankind's religious history, until Christ came, is man's vain quest for a God whom man can never find; he does not, like Christian liberals, see this hunger of the human soul as a response to God's endless search for man and self-revelation to him. For Barth God's self-disclosure is isolated in Christ; suddenly as it were, when Christ came, the God who had always been the merely sought became the seeker. Man, says Barth, "cannot conceive of himself as one who receives and discovers even an *indirect* revelation other than the revelation which is in Jesus Christ."

To the liberal Christian few neo-orthodox positions are more incredible than this insistence, as John Baillie, the Scottish theologian, protestingly pictures it, that "Christ comes vertically into history and he *alone* reveals God; the

history into which he comes does not reveal God *at all.*"
Has not the Shepherd always been seeking for his sheep?
Has not man's spiritual quest always been an answer to this
quest of God? Was Plato merely seeking after God and
never finding him, while Paul was merely found by God
without ever seeking him? Why this extravagant contra-
distinction, this false antithesis between two indispensables?
This, however, is Barth's reiterated position. Except through
revelation there is no knowledge of God, and nowhere else
before Christ or outside of Christ—not in nature or history,
not in the human soul or in any other religious faith—is
there any revelation of the true God. "Only the man who
knows about Jesus Christ," says Barth, "knows anything at
all about revelation"; "the confession becomes inevitable
that Jesus Christ *alone* is the revelation."

It is encouraging to note, however, that at no point is
neo-orthodoxy more self-critical than here. Many who, in
general, belong to the movement would utterly disclaim
the position I have just described. Brunner, in his *Revelation
and Reason,* is obviously troubled by it. Standing in the
great tradition of Protestant theology, he elaborates a
theory of "general revelation" which takes in all mankind.
In creation, in conscience, in prophets and seers, in the moral
law, he portrays God's self-disclosure to all men everywhere.
On this issue he explicitly attacks Barth and sharply re-
bukes him. To be sure, when he estimates the non-Christian
religions he grants them scant value, and as for the redemp-
tion of man, he asserts that "this general revelation cannot
have any saving significance for the sinner." Nevertheless,
he indicates a corrective trend which others in the neo-

orthodox movement carry farther. They too find utterly
unacceptable the limitation of God's self-revelation which
some Barthians have carried to such extremes that, as another put it, "their own friends are appalled."

What saves neo-orthodoxy—true in regard to many a
dogmatic system—is that its theologians are so much better
than their theology. Says Brunner: "How often does a
perfectly faultless orthodoxy go with moral sterility!" That
certainly does not describe Brunner and his colleagues.
Their orthodoxy, I am sure, is very far from faultless—
much of it I find not only incredible but alarming. When
Brunner, for example, belittles the historic ministry of Jesus
in order to exalt the Christ of dogma I am disturbed. In
The Theology of Crisis Brunner says: "How Jesus found God,
how he prayed, how he lived is not divine revelation for us."
In *The Mediator* he says: "The Christian faith has just as
little to do with the influence of Jesus on the history of the
world as it has to do with his historical personality. It is not
interested in the 'Founder of Christianity,' nor in his influence
on history." In *Our Faith* he says: "Jesus as an epoch-making
personality is—like all other world history—dust, mortality."
In *The Word and the World* he says: "The 'historic Jesus' is
a corpse." If *this* is "perfectly faultless orthodoxy" the neo-
orthodox are welcome to it! Nevertheless "moral sterility"
cannot possibly be associated with them. They have seized
the place they now occupy in the theology of Europe, and to
a far less degree in the theology of the United States, by their
aggressive, courageous challenge to the evil of our time, and
by their head-on meeting of its desperate plight with a hard,

dogmatic message which makes any soft type of liberalism seem unrealistic and pale.

My salutations, therefore, to the neo-orthodox whose extreme positions seem to me incredible—especially to Emil Brunner! Thirty years ago he sat for a semester in my lecture room at the Union Theological Seminary—how did he ever stand it! I warmly admire and honor him, but I predict that neither the extremes to which liberalism often went nor the extremes to which neo-orthodoxy goes today will be the final word.

If, presenting thus the false exaggerations of which liberals and neo-orthodox proponents have been guilty, I have seemed to represent my own position as wisely free from mistakes, omissions and unbalanced emphases, I humbly beg the reader's pardon. Of course I shared the exaggerations of late nineteenth-century liberalism. Of course I preached some sermons then which I could not possibly preach now without radical emendation. A preacher who has lived through the tremendous experience of two world wars without learning anything that has added increased depth and realism to his theology should be ashamed of himself. All of us liberals, whose ideas of God and man were inevitably influenced by the slants and biases of the optimistic era before the wars, have been compelled—unless our liberalism is unteachably rigid and hidebound—to welcome new insights, revise old judgments and acknowledge deplorable omissions in our understanding of the gospel.

Speaking some time since at Union Seminary, when I remarked, "Any neo-orthodox teacher here who has not come into his neo-orthodoxy by way of liberalism is not worth his salt," I was greeted with applause; and when I added, "Any liberal professor here who has not gained from neo-orthodoxy some new insights which liberalism had forgotten, is not worth his salt either," the applause was equally hearty. Perhaps, as well as anything I can say, that sums up the matter.

Liberalism cannot remain as it was fifty years ago; neo-orthodoxy cannot remain as it is today; there will be a synthesis.

Chapter 10.

❧

Ideas That Have Used Me

TOWARD THE CLOSE of his life Felix Adler said: "I am grateful for the Idea that has used me." Such a retrospect, combining self-esteem and humility, subordinates one's individual achievements to the ideas in which one has believed and by which one has been used. Despite our egotism the fact remains that our personal arrival on earth was long antedated by varied ideas of life's meaning, contrasting life philosophies, conflicting concepts of personal and social right and wrong; and our life's ultimate significance lies in our choice of the convictions to which we surrender ourselves, and of which in our generation we become the representatives. Whatever satisfaction I can find in retrospect springs primarily from some of the ideas that have used me.

The desire, which lay behind my vocation as a Christian minister, to make a contribution to the spiritual life of my generation has with the years grown more clearly defined and more imperative. Mankind desperately needs what Christianity *at its best* has to offer—that idea has become ever more urgent and commanding. I emphasize *at its best* because Christianity can be and often is perverted, corrupted, degraded, until far from serving good ends it becomes a deplorable evil. I grow weary at times with preachers who, without clarifying definition, set over against each other words like "Christianity" and "secularism," as though secularism were cursing the world and Christianity alone could save it. The fact is that so-called "Christianity" at its worst has produced some of the most hideous persecutions, wars and fanaticisms in history, and that today it is sometimes bigoted, superstitious, intolerant, socially disruptive, while so-called "secularism" is sometimes humane, ethically-minded and socially constructive.

Alfred N. Whitehead at Harvard once said: "It would be impossible to imagine anything more unchristian than Christian theology. Christ would probably not have understood it." I would say the same about more things in historic Christianity than its theological perversions; its ethical perversions have been and still are sometimes monstrous too, giving divine sanction to such evils as slavery, racial discrimination, war and religious persecution as being "the will of God." As for Christianity's all too frequent decadence into moralistic legalism, its proud assumptions of ecclesiastical sovereignty, the arrogance of its clerical hierarchies, its absorption in the search for political power, it has often exhibited at their worst the very evils against which in the religion of his time Jesus most vigorously protested. How often must Jesus Christ have felt that he was not a Christian!

I say this because I do not wish to use the word "Christianity" as though it were an unambiguous term. One needs to define what one means by it. For me the essence of Christianity is incarnate in the personality of the Master, and it means basic faith in God, in the divinity revealed in Christ, in personality's sacredness and possibilities, and in the fundamental principles of life's conduct which Jesus of Nazareth exhibited. I am sure that the world today desperately needs his faith and his way of life, and that without them there is no hope.

This conviction has been forced home on our generation by our disillusionment with some of the reliances in which we trusted for the salvation of the world—science and education, for example. To say that I believe in them is to speak mildly, but they are only instruments and the crucial question on which everything in the end depends is what kind of people—with what undergirding convictions about God and man, with what quality of character and with what ethical standards—are going to use them.

The present generation can hardly imagine the colossal impact of the new science on the mood and temper of the late nineteenth century. Was not man remaking the world? Was there any limit to the possibilities? No wonder that George A. Gordon, in his Boston pulpit, exclaimed: "Life in our time is founded on optimism!"

It has become obvious now, however, that science is not saving the world. Science has given man unprecedented power, only to confront him with the ancient fact that, as Alfred the Great put it, "power is never a good, except he be good that has it." Science has brought mankind proximity, the ends of the earth woven together in intercommunication and interdependence, but it cannot provide the ethical quality which, transforming proximity into fraternal community, saves proximity from becoming tragedy. In one realm after another science has forced on men collective activity, compelling them to do together countless things which men never before had to do together, but it cannot by itself create the character which dedicates collective activity to public good. And science has produced such implements of destruction that war now threatens the very existence of the race.

I sat at dinner recently with Charles Lindbergh, and recalled the drastic change in mankind's mood about science which had caused him to say: "I have seen the science I worshiped and the aircraft that I loved destroying the civilization I expected them to serve, while the lifesaving miracles of medicine are being perverted toward the murderous ends of biological warfare." In my early years I never expected to hear anything like *that* from the scientific side of the fence. Science has indeed changed the world; its achievements have been magnificent; but today its stunning, climactic effect is to confront man with his own perversity in using his new powers. As Arthur H. Compton, Nobel Prize winner in atomic physics, exclaimed: "Science has created a world in which Christianity is an imperative."

Along with science, education has appeared to many as the world's savior. Certainly, as a nation, we have accomplished wonders with it. When I was graduated from Colgate the total undergraduate population of all the colleges and universities in the United States was one hundred and fifty thousand; now it is three million. Never has any country invested so much in education and counted so much on it as we have done in America.

Today, however, education—indispensable and inexpressibly valuable though its contribution to human welfare has been—has become an aider and abettor of some of mankind's worst evils. To paraphrase a saying of George A. Buttrick, there is only one thing worse than a devil and that is an educated devil. That emphasis is a newcomer in America. We are not used to it. Education with us has had a halo over it. Ignorance is bad; education is good— that has been our simple formula. Our attention has been obsessed by the danger to democracy inherent in illiteracy, ignorance, stupidity. Of course they are dangerous to democracy. But when today one asks what we are *most* afraid of, what makes the shivers run up and down our spinal columns, it is not ignorant but educated devils, whether in Moscow or anywhere else—men with the know-how, the techniques of modern science in their grasp, the psychological skills for propaganda purposes, and all the rest, with the question rising: In heaven's name, what are they going to do with it? It is not primitive peoples who terrorize the world today, but educationally advanced peoples who have made learning a road to power without bringing that power under ethical control.

So I have lived into a generation where not science alone but education too "has created a world in which Christianity is an imperative." Facts without values, fragmentary specialties with no integrating philosophy of life as a whole, data with no ethical standards for their use, techniques either with no convictions about life's ultimate meaning or with corrupting convictions—here, too, a panacea has turned out to be a problem. What quality of faith and character is going to use our educated minds?

Now in my elder years, therefore, I am even more convinced than I was at the beginning that the truths about God and man, about right and wrong, for which the Christian gospel stands are man's indispensable necessity. Insofar as that idea has used me—I am grateful.

As I recall my endeavors to relate Christian faith and ethic to social problems, one conviction has been central: that the ultimate criterion of any civilization's success or failure is to be found in what happens to the underdog. I came from a family whose own history made us feel close to the poor, and what Lord Asquith said seems to me basic: "The test of every civilization is the point below which the weakest and most unfortunate are allowed to fall." This does not mean sentimental glorification of the underprivileged. "Essential human nature," I said in 1936, "is much the same wherever it is found, and it is as false and dangerous to glorify the proletariat as it is to play sycophant to the privileged. Sin is 'no respecter of persons.' Its demonic, corrupting power runs through all classes, and no realistic mind can suppose virtue to be preponderant in any special group, even the downtrodden." Nevertheless, the downtrodden reveal the unjust wrongs and cruelties of any social order, and what happens to them is, in the long run, any social order's test.

This conviction makes impossible the glorification of any *laissez-faire* economy—every man for himself and the devil take the hindmost. Only a short generation before I was born Lord Shaftesbury's Factory Laws in England were fought tooth and nail both by reactionary industrialists and by erudite economists who feared that any interference with the supply of labor, even laws to save little children from working fourteen hours a day in the factories, would disrupt the social order. They fell back on Darwinism's picture of the world—ruthless competition and the survival of the fittest—as the law of human society, and brooked no interference by government with this brutal fight. Stated in terms as camouflaged and beguiling as possible, that philosophy was pretty much ascendant when I was young, and still its belated advocates oppose one endeavor after another to make government the servant of all the people, especially of the underprivileged.

This position has seemed to me anti-Christian and anti-democratic. Did we not see long ago that a democratic nation cannot be maintained by a population of illiterates, and did not government assume responsibility at public expense for public education? If the preservation of democracy demands at least a minimum of literacy, does it not also demand at least a minimum of economic security? The idea that that government is best which governs least is long outdated. On the basis of that idea vast aggregations of power and wealth in an industrialized nation seize control, and the masses of the people are at their mercy. What good does their *political* liberty do them? In 1890 one-eighth of the families in the United States owned seven-eighths of the nation's wealth. Even bypassing humane motives and thinking only of an adequate consumers' market for agricultural and manufactured products, that is an insane situation. Franklin D. Roosevelt was surely right when he saw that no democratic state can survive on freedom of speech and freedom of worship alone; there must be also freedom from want and freedom from fear; and all alike demand the support of government.

Woodrow Wilson I knew well. The hours I spent in his home in Princeton, on my visits there, are vivid in my recollection, and especially one conversation, after he became Governor of New Jersey, in which he blazed out with indignation at the powerful corporations which were asking government for everything that they could get—tariffs, subsidies, concessions of land, franchises and rights of way —while fighting every extension of governmental control on behalf of the workingman.

In the long fight, therefore, to make government the servant of all the people, I have been on the liberal side. The perils involved in the assumption of governmental responsibility for the welfare of the people are obvious— expanding bureaucracy, wild expenditures, crazy subsidies under political pressure, dependence on government as an exhaustless cornucopia, and many more—but the cure is not a return to Adam Smith's economic doctrines. One of the most important changes in public policy which I have lived through is illustrated by the fact that in 1895 the Illinois Supreme Court invalidated an eight-hour law as "an unwarrantable interference with the right of both the employer and employee in making contracts"; that in 1905 the United States Supreme Court declared unconstitutional a ten-hour law for bakers in New York State; that the courts then began reversing themselves. In 1908 an Oregon ten-hour law and in 1915 a California eight-hour law were sustained. At last the law had begun to catch up with the facts.

When Franklin D. Roosevelt was inaugurated President
in 1933, the concern of government about the down-and-out
became a matter of crucial emergency. With seventeen million people unemployed, agriculture prostrate, banks
closed, privation harrowing and panic frightening the nation, something immediate and radical had to be done. Like
almost everyone else, I had my ups-and-downs with regard
to Roosevelt's policies, approving and disapproving, blow-
ing hot or cold on this move or that, but as to his total aim
and achievement, they have in my judgment stood the
test of time. Our grandchildren may not understand, as
we oldsters can, how indispensable and heartening his
gospel was:

Democracy has disappeared in several other great nations—
not because the people of those nations disliked democracy, but
because they had grown tired of unemployment and insecurity, of
seeing their children hungry, while they sat helpless in the face
of government confusion and government weakness through lack
of leadership in government. Finally, in desperation, they chose
to sacrifice liberty in the hope of getting something to eat. We
in America know that our own democratic institutions can be
preserved and made to work. But in order to preserve them we
need . . . to prove that the practical operation of democratic
government is equal to the task of protecting the security of the
people.

I talked with President Roosevelt only once. A small
group of us was given an appointment at the White House
to discuss the treatment of conscientious objectors in World
War II. We were received by Mrs. Roosevelt with informal
hospitality such as one might meet in any typical American
home; we had tea with her, her daughter Anna and two

grandchildren; and then were ushered into Mr. Roosevelt's office by Mrs. Roosevelt, saying: "Franklin will be here in a minute." He came in his wheel chair, and during the next hour I saw why an ardent Republican leader, who had similarly talked with him, swore that he would never come again for, if he did, he would surely become a Democrat. The President was charm incarnate. He did most of the talking— fascinating talk—giving us hardly a chance to get in a word edgewise. He radiated confidence, assurance, courage. It is, I suspect, typical of his hypnotic effect that we were so charmed by him that we almost—not quite—forgot what we had come to see him about.

President Roosevelt was more than charming, however. He proclaimed a policy that enraged the defenders of old *laissez-faire* doctrines. A government, he said, "that cannot take care of its old, that cannot provide work for the strong and willing, that lets the black shadow of insecurity rest on every home, is not a government that can or should endure." On that point, I am confident, history will endorse his stand. He stood for laws concerning minimum wages and maximum hours, for old age and unemployment insurance, for reducing farm tenancy, for the ending of child labor, for the support of private home building, for the breaking up of utility monopolies, for flood control, drought control, water conservation, assistance to farm co-operatives, for the resettlement of farmers from marginal lands, and for reciprocal trade agreements with other nations. He stood for the principle which Abraham Lincoln had put into a single sentence: "The legitimate object of government is to do for a community of people whatever they need to have done, but cannot do at all, or cannot do so well for themselves, in their separate and individual capacities."

I am not a socialist but it seems to me obvious that with the development of modern technology, some things that once were done individually can now best be done communally. Once every family could have its own well, but a modern city must have municipal waterworks, not because of any ideology but because of an utterly new technological situation. Whenever, because of modern conditions of life and modern inventions, a situation develops where an indispensable result can be better obtained by communal action than by individual action, the community must step in. Granted that it is often difficult to decide just when that situation emerges! Granted the sometimes frightening danger of concentrated power in Washington, and the necessity of decentralizing governmental control, so that everything which can be adequately done on local and state levels is done there! Yet the principle of communal responsibility under modern conditions is clear. I am all for free enterprise but the only hope of maintaining it lies, I believe, in the amazing capacity of capitalism—amply illustrated in the last half century—to change its old methods to meet the demands of new times. Capitalism is not static but fluid, and in its adaptability to changing conditions lies its strength.

In one sermon after another I said things like this:

There is only one way ultimately of keeping the government out of any area of business enterprise: namely, to prove by actual performance that by some other means we can achieve the complete dedication of the economic processes not primarily to private gain but to public welfare. If our capitalism can so adjust itself to the new circumstances that it can achieve such devotion of economic processes to the welfare of all the people, even the least of them, then capitalism can go on. If not, there is nothing on earth that can save it, and nothing in heaven that will try.

At any rate, the conviction that the basic test of any society is what happens to the underdog has haunted my preaching. I have just looked over some of my sermons to see what I actually said at the Riverside Church and I have run repeatedly on statements such as these:

I fear for a church like this where, from the pulpit to the pew, we come from privileged backgrounds, when I remember how often in history the underdog has been right.

The major movements of social progress in history have commonly had their source and sustentation in people who were being hurt. They felt the intolerable social wrongs, not with their wits but with their pulses. . . . William Ewart Gladstone, who was certainly privileged, said, while campaigning for Irish home rule, that "during the preceding half century the privileged classes, the aristocratic classes, the educated classes, have been on the wrong side of every great social issue and, if their opinion had prevailed, it would have been to the detriment or even the ruin of the country."

It is not the underprivileged, the whipped and beaten, who have brought on the world its greatest evils. No! Privilege is power, and privilege consolidated in a social class is prodigious power, and the misuse of *that*, especially to sustain an unjust *status quo* grown obsolete, has been, I suspect, responsible for the worst wrongs that have cursed mankind.

Once the principle of *laissez faire* was liberating; it worked a magnificent emancipation for the mercantile and industrial classes against the oppressions of a landholding aristocracy. It is a tragic sight, however, to see the loyal friends of liberty, having in one generation won a victory for their cause with weapons suited to their time, now in a later generation insisting on fighting their battle with the same weapons, forgetting that they are in another age, which has made those instruments as obsolete as bows and arrows at Verdun.

The disinherited, the underprivileged, the hard-hit, the restless, dreaming of a better day for their children, whom they love as much as we love ours, are trying to do something about the situation. To be sure, they often turn to crazy panaceas, yet they are planning, hoping, working for a better day, and in the best and most intelligent areas, mark it, they forge ahead—the best social conscience of our times set on such a reformation of the social order as will make impossible the continuance or recurrence of our present inequities.

The conviction that Christianity is no "simple gospel," applicable to the private needs of individuals alone, but involves social change as well, is now taken pretty much for granted in the ministry. It had some hard sledding in my youth, however, and still there are plenty of pulpits which tone it down, side-step it, confess it in theory but do nothing about it in practice. Surely, however, it is sheer hypocrisy for the church to say that it cares for personality as sacred and then to do nothing about social conditions that impinge on personality with frightful consequences.

As a preacher I found myself constantly on a two-way street. If I started with the social gospel I ran into the need of better individual men and women who alone could create and sustain a better social order, and so found myself facing the personal gospel; and if I started with the personal gospel, I ran straight into the evils of society that ruin personality, and so found myself facing the social gospel.

The practical implementation of this matter in the pulpit is not easy. On Sundays the preacher faces men and women holding varied political and economic convictions, honestly holding them and trying to be Christian about them. What preacher is wise enough to tell them which of the conflicting views are Christian and which are not? He occupies a privileged position in the pulpit, where they cannot talk back at him. Does that not impose on him an obligation to refrain from partisan statements on controversial issues? Have they not a right to worship God without hearing a plea for one set of economic or political opinions against another?

I have never found a formula to answer that question. Certainly the preacher must be able to say what the King of England said: "I would have you understand that no political party has me in its pocket." Fair play with the congregation, freedom from narrow partisanship, humility about one's own judgments, good sense and good taste in making one's position clear—such criteria are obvious and, accepting them, one must do one's best, but one must not keep still on public issues that affect the welfare of human souls. One typical Sunday morning in my early ministry I proclaimed the social gospel in general and everybody liked it; then—that subject at the time being hot—I spoke up for the eight-hour day in the steel industry, and there were lifted eyebrows. One must expect that.

Fortunately I have had a free pulpit at Riverside Church. I do not mean that there have been no objections to my utterances; I should be ashamed to have preached to such congregations without awakening hostility. When the Supreme Court by a five-to-four decision—a bad decision, now in effect rescinded—denied citizenship to Professor Douglas Clyde Macintosh of Yale, because he would not promise to support unscrupulously any war the country got into, whether he thought it just or unjust, I vigorously protested, praised Justice Charles E. Hughes' minority opinion supporting Macintosh, and lost from the church one of our leading lawyers, who stalked out and never came back. Such incidents, however, have been rare, and the church as a whole has consistently taken the position once voiced to me by the president of the Board of Trustees: "If anybody tries to limit your liberty, he will do it over my dead body."

Strange as it seems now, one occasion for distressed misgiving on the part of some of the members was an attack of mine on Hitler in 1933. His atrocious anti-Semitic campaign was sending a stream of refugees to the United States. The American people as a whole took it for granted that these refugees were Jews, and our Christian churches were leaving the entire burden of relief and assistance to be carried by the Jewish people, while, in fact, a considerable proportion of Hitler's fleeing victims were Christians. The meeting which launched the American Christian Committee for German Refugees—including, as it did at first, both Roman Catholics and Protestants—was held in the Riverside Church. It took a long time and some strenuous propaganda to persuade the American public that the refugee problem, far from being exclusively Jewish, was Christian also, and in the course of our endeavor James G. MacDonald—later American ambassador to Israel—and I put on a movie in which we used plain language about what the Nazis were doing. A few of the members at Riverside Church were quite upset. Even though our movie had been cleared with the State Department, they were afraid we were too politically aggressive. Later they were ready enough to go to war with Hitler; in 1933 they had begged me to speak more softly even in talking about him.

We began our work in the Riverside Church as the great depression was starting, and the background of my ministry there was the grim era before we entered World War II, followed by the terrific struggle itself, and its disillusioning and chaotic aftermath. Controversial questions were tumultuous, differences of opinion inevitable, preaching both exciting and difficult. What I said, my printed sermons represent; as Samuel Butler remarked: "My books are me." My congregation was often called on for patience with their preacher, but as I look back, I am chiefly impressed by the harmony that prevailed at Riverside and by the scrupulous protection of the pulpit's liberty for which the whole church stood.

Were I to list the social causes with which liberals of my stripe have been concerned, many of them would be meaningless names to my grandchildren. The Sacco-Vanzetti case in Massachusetts, the Mooney case in California, the Scottsboro case in Alabama—all of them in my judgment miscarriages of justice—aroused our righteous indignation. I vividly recall the day when Ruby Bates, one of the two girls who had sworn at the first trial of the Scottsboro boys that they had been raped by the Negroes, crept into my study at the Riverside Church and confessed to me that she had lied, that she had lain with a white boy the night before, but that the Negroes had not touched her. I appealed to her troubled conscience, and sent her back to confess her perjury at the second trial, lest she be in effect a murderer of the innocent. This she did, but with no effect upon the Alabama jury. Said the prosecuting attorney with scorn concerning one of the falsely accused boys: "If you free him, put a ring of roses around his neck, give him a dinner and ship him to New York; there let Dr. Fosdick put him in a high hat, a morning coat, fancy trousers, and a pair of spats." Nevertheless, the boys were not executed as the first jury's infamous verdict required. A new trial was granted, but it was over nineteen years before the last of those falsely accused boys was released from prison, thanks to the tireless labors of a committee headed by Allan Knight Chalmers.

Some of our social loyalties, I trust, have worked results which the next generation can take for granted. The mitigation of the iniquitous misuse of child labor, for example, cost a harder fight, not only against economic greed but also against old-fashioned economic theory, than our posterity will find it easy to imagine. So, too, our granddaughters will take the right to vote for granted, but even when I began my ministry I was cool about woman suffrage, and it was only when my first pastorate was well on its way that I became its advocate. Then, with the zeal of a convert, I entertained utopian dreams of what the votes of women would accomplish. Those dreams have been disappointed. Woman suffrage was inevitable and right, but the consequences have not been as revolutionary as we hoped.

I was associated with the planned parenthood—birth control—cause early in Mrs. Margaret Sanger's campaign, and on a few occasions have had opportunities to serve it. One of the most basic issues in the world today, on whose solution even our hopes of ending war depend, is the population problem. Until mankind can be educated out of its careless, casual, unthinking, unpurposed, merely animal propagation of children into thoughtfully planned parenthood, many of man's dearest hopes are impossible. The planned parenthood movement is sometimes misunderstood; it is associated exclusively with the phrase "birth control." But birth control is only a tool, an implement, and like any tool it can be used for unwise and evil purposes. The planned parenthood movement, however, is socially constructive; it offers an indispensable factor in solving one of mankind's profoundest problems; its central aim is family life at its best. Against the opposition of human ignorance and casual lust and of powerful obscurantist forces—such as Roman Catholic hostility, which that church will someday be compelled to regret—it demands liberty to use contraceptive control for the building of thoughtfully purposed, wisely planned homes. I believe in it with strong conviction.

In recent years the Euthanasia Society's endeavor to find some way of preventing the needless prolongation of agonizing existence of those doomed to die of incurable disease has had my support. It is a contentious issue; the problem will not be easily solved; I do not expect to see it solved in my lifetime. It will have to be handled in a more merciful way than now obtains, however, for the present situation is intolerable. The old argument still runs that only God has the right to decide the terminus of any life. But God alone is not determining how long men and women shall live. Man himself is determining that, with his scientific medicine prolonging the average span of life from the thirties in early colonial days to nearly seventy now, and in individual cases extending the hopeless suffering of those whom nature, left to herself, would release. Man must shoulder the responsibility thus thrust upon him, and must devise some way of mercifully liberating the hopelessly ill from needless agony.

As for politics, I wonder if our grandchildren will still face the rotten municipal government which in my time has cursed our American cities. I lived through the days of Jimmy Walker's regime in New York City, under whose mayoralty I said once in a sermon:

There is something so disgraceful about the spectacle of this great community held in the grip of a confessedly corrupt machine, which generation after generation has robbed us and today, in ways so well known that they can be set down in specific detail, has worked out the most ingenious devices of political thievery in the history of municipal government—there is, I say, something so intolerably shameful about our helplessness and supineness in the presence of this disgrace that I should suppose that the hour would strike before long when we would stand it no more.

I hope that venture of faith may turn out to be justified.

Some good causes with which I have been allied have fortunately been all success without contention—Alcoholics Anonymous, for example. I teamed up with that movement in its early days, and count my acquaintance with Bill W., whose experience helped to launch this remarkable society, a very rewarding association. We ministers are not uncommonly thought of as needlessly prudish and puritanical about the use of alcoholic beverages, but I challenge anyone to be a parish pastor very long without hating the prevalent misuse of liquor with implacable indignation. We have the devastating results of alcoholism dumped in our laps day after day—individuals and families ruined by drink, men and women enslaved by a habit they are powerless to break, children humiliated, shamed and irretrievably harmed by drunken parents. In dealing with this problem I often found myself utterly frustrated. What could I do? To be sure, even before Alcoholics Anonymous arrived we had our victories. Once a young journalist, ruined by drink, bought a bottle of poison, and on a Sunday morning headed for Washington Square where he planned to commit suicide. Passing the First Presbyterian Church, where I was then preaching, and seeing the crowds waiting to get in, his journalistic curiosity was aroused. Why on earth, he wondered, were so many people going to church? So he postponed his suicide long enough to join the congregation and listen to the service. Afterward he poured the poison down a manhole, and the next day he came to see me. He won his battle, but alas! that young man was only one victory among many defeats.

Since then Alcoholics Anonymous has grown to its present astonishing strength, and it is a godsend to us ministers. How can we understand an alcoholic—his compulsive desire for liquor, the hopeless captivity against which he futilely contends, one determined decision after another to stop drinking ending in collapse? When we talk to an alcoholic, he knows that never having been in his place we cannot understand his plight. But when an ex-alcoholic, who has been in the depths himself and has taken the Twelve Steps to freedom, talks to an alcoholic, amazing results can follow and have followed in countless thousands of lives.

Month after month I read *Grapevine*, A.A.'s official journal—about the most moving collection of testimonies to the possibility of personal transformation of which I know. Moreover, these testimonies bear witness to religion's reality, for Alcoholics Anonymous is deeply religious. That Eleventh Step is an essential factor in its program: "Sought through prayer and meditation to improve our conscious contact with God, as we understand Him, praying only for knowledge of His will for us and the power to carry that out." The meetings of Alcoholics Anonymous are the only place, so far as I know, where Roman Catholics, Jews, all kinds of Protestants and even agnostics get together harmoniously on a religious basis. They do not talk theology. Many of them would say that they know nothing about it. What they do know is that in their utter helplessness they were introduced to a Power, greater than themselves, in contact with whom they found a strong resource which made possible a victory that had seemed incredible. I have listened to many learned arguments about God, but for honest-to-goodness experiential evidence of God, his power personally appropriated and his reality indubitably assured, give me a good meeting of A.A!

The endeavor to deal with the liquor problem by a prohibitory amendment to the federal Constitution I watched with foreboding, as it rose to furious intensity during World War I and then, after a transient victory, petered out. I never believed in prohibition. I vividly recall one occasion during World War I when at Gondrecourt in France, twenty miles behind the front lines, Daniel Poling, an ardent Prohibitionist, joined me in a billet, and bundled up on our cots to keep warm, we discussed prohibition far into the night. He had just come from America, full of enthusiasm about the passage of the prohibition amendment of which he was assured. I told him that it would be a major national catastrophe. I believed in local option but not in what the Prohibitionists were fighting for. In January, 1919, however, the Eighteenth Amendment was passed and a year later it was put into active operation. Along with many others, I saw nothing to do except to back it up and try to make a success of it. I certainly tried hard, endeavoring to see all the good I could in it, pleading for the observance of the law, and wanting desperately to avoid the setback and disillusionment bound to follow the breakdown of so well-intentioned an effort to destroy the liquor traffic. In one sermon especially I vigorously presented prohibition in the best light I could throw on it, but even in that sermon I stated my judgment that "such sumptuary legislation, written into the Constitution," was a "mistake in strategy," and I expressed regret that this "peremptory handling of the liquor question has undoubtedly landed us in an unsatisfactory position." What happened is notorious history now. There are some things that federal legislation cannot do.

The struggle against racial discrimination in general and against mistreatment of Negroes in particular has been a lifelong concern of mine. One of my vivid recollections from early boyhood days in Lancaster is Billy Greenfield, an ex-slave who did odd jobs for the villagers and whom we boys liked. He used to tell us that he was not a human being, like white folks; that he was an animal and had no soul; that was what his white masters had taught him and that he believed it was so. We vigorously protested with all the arguments we could think of, but I can still see him with his stooped shoulders, his grizzly hair and whiskers and his deeply lined black face, insisting that he had no soul. He little guessed what an unforgettable impression he was making on at least one boy. I had not heard then about John Wesley's saying that American slavery, with which he had lived in Georgia, was "the vilest that ever saw the sun," but in my boyhood that judgment was early in the making.

In my family any kind of racial discrimination was anathema. We were reared on firsthand stories of escaping slaves —one of them, hidden in my grandfather's home in Buffalo while waiting to be taken across the Niagara River to Canada, died of fright because mistakenly he thought he heard the footsteps of federal officers searching the house for him. I vividly recall, while I was in high school, attending a public dinner with my father and sitting at table close to Booker T. Washington. I little thought then that some fifty years afterward it would be my privilege, as one of the electors, to help choose him as the first Negro to be given a place in the American Hall of Fame, and that at Riverside Church a statue of him, carved in stone, would stand among the sculptures in the chancel.

This is no place to expand my convictions on the Negro problem. In my youth it was still thought of as almost exclusively a southern issue, but it is no longer that. Such has been the northward migration of Negroes that as early as 1940 the six cities in the United States with the largest Negro population were all north of the Mason and Dixon's line. Moreover, this national problem—one of the most insistent and crucial that we face—is now a matter of world-wide concern. As Samuel Higginbottom, after fifty years of missionary service in India, has said, everyone in Asia knows the worst about our treatment of Negroes here, and it is a major reason for the success of communistic propaganda there.

In my lifetime great progress has been made, and as today in one realm after another, from sports to music, science and statesmanship, Negroes move up to positions of unquestioned leadership, hope is justified for better days ahead. At a recent commencement at Columbia University, the most stirring moment came when Ralph Bunche, "the grandson of a slave," was given an honorary doctorate as one of America's outstanding diplomats, and he has now received the Nobel Peace Prize. With all our faults, a larger proportion of American Negroes now go to college than is true of the British population as a whole. Nevertheless, the policy of segregation still obtains, explicit in the south, camouflaged but disgracefully real in the north, and laws to give equality of treatment to Negroes face shameful opposition. On this issue the churches have, to a shocking degree, conformed to current practices, and President Charles Spurgeon Johnson of Fiske University has even said: "The church is the most segregated institution in America." This, too, is changing and interracial congregations are increasing across the country. I hope that my grandchildren will take a hand in this continuing battle against racial prejudice and discrimination. It is, as H. G. Wells said, "the most evil thing in the world."

Meanwhile, I take comfort from long-range contrasts. A hundred and fifty years ago, Maury de St. Mary wrote: "The present population of New York is 40,000 free people and 2,500 slaves." We have come a long way since then. In 1945 the University of Cincinnati enrolled a thirteen-year-old freshman—a Negro, who could read when he was three, who graduated from grammar school at nine and from high school at twelve, and whose parents are both graduates of the University of Chicago. Indeed, Mrs. Edith Sampson, a colored woman, one of the American delegates to the Assembly of the United Nations, when heckled at a public meeting in India, said that she would "rather be a Negro in the United States than a citizen of any other land." I wonder at her saying it, but I thank God that we have come on far enough so that it could be said. And now I have lived to see the day when in a unanimous decision the Supreme Court has declared segregation in the nation's public schools to be unconstitutional.

The most critical and contentious social problem of my generation, for the ministry as for all mankind, has been war. Concerning that, I have been forced to a complete reversal of the opinions which I held at my ministry's beginning. "Any man," said Macaulay, "who held the same view of the French Revolution in 1789, 1804, 1814 and 1834, must either have been a divinely inspired prophet or an obstinate fool." I certainly was not divinely inspired about war in my early years, and I am glad that I decided not to remain obstinate.

In my high school days I heard without question Judge Tourgée, a public figure and successful novelist of the time, say in one of our student assemblies: "Every nation needs a good war about once in thirty years." That may have been unusually candid, but it expressed a not unusual idea. John Ruskin seems ancient history now, but he died in the year I graduated from college, and he said: "War is the foundation of all the arts . . . of all the high virtues and faculties of men. . . . All great nations learned their truth of word, and strength of thought, in war; they were nourished in war and wasted by peace; taught by war and deceived by peace; trained by war and betrayed by peace."

No about-face in my time is more remarkable than the reversal of opinion about the meaning of war. Recalling the unanimity of many otherwise diverse nineteenth-century minds in praise of war—Nietzsche saying: "A good war halloweth every cause"; Renan saying: "War is in a way one of the conditions of progress, the cut of the whip which prevents a country from going to sleep"; Lester Ward, outstanding American sociologist, saying: "War has been the chief and leading condition of human progress"—an older man like myself hears with amazement what is being said now. General Eisenhower declares: "I hate war as only a soldier who has lived in it can, only as one who has seen its brutality, its futility, its stupidity." General MacArthur says: "With present weapons there no longer is any advantage to winning a war. Everyone loses, with the victor only losing a little less than the vanquished." A statement from the United States Defense Department says: "The end of an atomic war may find both victor and vanquished in a state of almost complete ruin. It follows that winning the war may well not be preserving national security."

I shared with my generation this revolutionary change of opinion, but as a Christian my revolt went deeper and raised issues with which the Christian conscience today everywhere is struggling. In the first world conflict I saw war at firsthand, and went through the disillusionment of its aftermath, confronting with increasing agony the anti-Christian nature of war's causes, processes and results. I could not dodge my conscience: I must never again put my Christian ministry at the nation's disposal for the sanction and backing of war.

So I became a pacifist. To be sure, there are various kinds of pacifism, some of them negative, individualistic, sentimental, anarchistic, and anyone who accepts a foregone definition of pacifism in such terms and then applies it to all who bear the name is dealing in caricature. In my sermon, "An Interpretation of Pacifism," I definitely disclaimed "doctrinaire pacifism of the absolutist sort." Here again I am not a good partisan and dislike being represented by a

tag. I do not think that any pacifist position contains a neat
solution of the problem confronting the Christian conscience
in wartime. There is no neat solution. Every position, pacifist
or nonpacifist, that a Christian can take in war involves him
in an inner agony of self-contradiction. Any position plunges
him into sinful compromise with evil, whether he supports
war and gives it his Christian blessing or refuses support
and stands aloof from a conflict where great issues are at
stake. Nevertheless, since Christian ministers under present
circumstances are willy-nilly known either as pacifists or
nonpacifists, I wish to be numbered among the former. It is
true that some pacifists are so wrongheaded and some nonpacifists are so right-spirited that I can work more easily
with the latter than with the former, but I do not want to
bear the nonpacifist name. For that group, too, is made up
of various types, many of them, so it seems to me, grossly
betraying the Christian faith, prostituting their ministry to
the service of a false god, until the distinctive elements
of the Christian ethic are obliterated. Wrongheaded many
pacifists may be, but history, I am convinced, will say of
them what it now says of the more extreme abolitionists of
slavery days, that while they were often wrongheaded, they
were "wrongheaded in the right direction."

When World War II broke in Europe and every day more
ominously threatened to become global, I dreaded it as
one might dread perdition. I recall those months, when
America's belligerence was becoming more and more probable, as among the darkest of my life. I threw whatever
influence I had against our belligerent participation. I joined
a Ministers' No-War Committee, made up of both pacifists

and nonpacifists, and remember especially two addresses I made in Cleveland and Detroit, pleading against our military entrance into the war. I was no neutral—I made that plain—but I hoped, as an overwhelming proportion of the American people did, that we might be able to stay out of war. Then one Sunday afternoon I went up to my study in the Riverside Church tower for my weekly broadcast, and to my horror was stopped in the midst of my sermon, told that I was off the air because the Japanese were attacking Pearl Harbor.

In the meantime, I had made many of my congregation at Riverside Church unhappy by my attitude. They stood by me but they were worried; and, anticipating what war, if it came, would do to my ministry, I worried too. I expected that it would mean, of course, my withdrawal from broadcasting, and beyond that I prepared myself inwardly for the possible necessity of resigning from the church. In that case, my plan was clearly in mind—to join the Quakers and spend the rest of my life in their fellowship. If any one term best describes my position on war, it is to call me a Quaker. From its start I have been a member of the Wider Quaker Fellowship, and in the positive, constructive, socially-minded type of pacifism of the Society of Friends I find myself most at home.

That my plan to become a full-fledged Quaker did not materialize was due not to change in my attitude, but to the very great change in the public attitude toward war which took place between the first world conflict and the second. In ways deeper than I had supposed the statement of the Oxford Conference in 1937 had taken hold on the conscience

of Christians, and in the Riverside Church even the passions
of wartime did not demand that a Christian minister forget
it. That statement had declared: "War involves compulsory
enmity, diabolical outrage against human personality, and a
wanton distortion of the truth. War is a particular demon-
stration of the power of sin in this world and a defiance of
the righteousness of God as revealed in Jesus Christ and
him crucified. No justification of war must be allowed to
conceal or minimize this fact."

Quite apart from my pacifism, ominous foreboding about
Russia was involved in my hope that the United States
could avoid active belligerency. I had begun attacking communism from the pulpit at least as early as 1928, when in a
sermon on revolutionary spirits who see plainly what they are
revolting from, but not what they are revolting to, I used
Russia as an illustration:

What Russia was fleeing *from* is clear. Russia wanted to get
away from capitalism. . . . But when we see what Russia has
come to—with thousands of political prisoners still in custody,
with Siberia opening wide her maw for those who disagree with
the ruling classes, with freedom of speech, freedom of assembly,
freedom of the press gone, with a small oligarchy ruling a vast
nation—even extreme radicals in the West, like Bertrand Russell,
have no interest in introducing Bolshevik communism here. One
looks at Russia and says with Amos, "As if a man fled from a
lion, and a bear met him."

Even when Russia was our wartime ally, my fears of her
were not allayed by the popular hopefulness about postwar
co-operation with her. What seemed to me more probable
was a chaotic, exhausted world, with Stalin—so I wrote in

1941—"hoping to become the residuary legatee of a ruined continent." As for what that meant, I said privately, when it could not be said publicly, that "Stalin was carved off the same piece of meat as Hitler." I never was tempted to any sympathy with communism. Indeed, J. B. Matthews— later notorious as a member of Senator Joseph McCarthy's staff, who was forced to retire because of his irresponsible attack on supposed communists among the Protestant clergy —was a left-wing agitator himself in the middle-thirties, and in his book, *Partners in Plunder,* he scornfully wrote: "Reverend Harry Emerson Fosdick comforts the Rockefeller dynasty with this declaration: 'Personally, I dread the thought of collectivism which Russia represents as I would dread the devil.'" War came, however, making us Russia's ally despite all such premonitions, and even a pacifist knows that while he may utterly distrust the old arguments about a "just" war, nations can so mismanage their affairs that there is no way of escaping inevitable conflict.

I did not avoid, nor did I try to avoid, controversy during World War II. When, for example, ruthless, indiscriminate, obliterative bombing of civilians got under way, Vera Brittain, the English novelist, published a thoughtful, carefully documented statement on the matter, some twenty thousand words long, soberly presenting the facts and pleading against this deliberate "mass murder of civilians" and "bombing of women and children." Twenty-eight of us republished this statement and commended it to the attention of the American public. As late as January 27, 1940, Winston Churchill had denounced obliterative bombing as "a new and odious form of attack," and even on September 8, 1943, President Roosevelt assured Congress that Americans would never be guilty of it, but would "blow to bits carefully selected targets—factories, shipyards, munition dumps."

War, however, ruthlessly repeated itself in its inevitable persuasion of each side to copy the atrocities of the other, and by 1942 Winston Churchill was saying over the radio, albeit with humane reluctance: "I hail it as an example of sublime and poetic justice that those who have loosed these horrors upon mankind will now in their homes and persons feel the shattering strokes of just retribution." Concerning this vicious cycle of reciprocated horrors one of our leading religious journals said: "Admitting that the insane logic of war requires that all things be done which are necessary to win victory, yet millions of Christians find themselves tormented with the question: Is such horror as this indiscriminate slaughter of civilians necessary?"

It was this question which Miss Brittain raised in her moderate and thoughtful statement and which we commended to the attention of our people. The response was an outburst of vitriolic denunciation. To be sure, letters of commendation poured in, but in general the Noes had it, as the *New York Times* reported, 50 to 1. Ministers, like my belligerent friend, Daniel Poling, burst into emotional tirades. He called our protest a "squawk," accused us of being "mushy," and said he could not think of a "more foolish or dangerous attitude"; and Bishop William Manning of the Episcopal Diocese of New York, writing, so he said, "as a minister of the Christian church," threw the weight of his ecclesiastical leadership on the side of continuing unabated the indiscriminate bombing. As for the religious press, inter-

estingly enough, our support came mainly from Quaker and
Roman Catholic papers, as though in these two far-separated
movements, the one guided by an "Inner Light" and the other
by the historic tradition of Christian ethics, there was enough
moral insight left to see that the Christian conscience, unless
it was to be utterly apostate, must pass judgment on this new
and horrible manifestation of war's brutality.

Of course, I never supposed that our protest would stop
obliterative bombing. It certainly did not. The process went
terribly on, culminating in the use of the atomic bomb on
Hiroshima. Saturation bombing was ghastly when the Japanese perpetrated it on the Chinese; it was equally ghastly
when we, in turn, were the perpetrators. It foretells the utter
destruction of all civilization if war is not stopped.

An excellent editorial in the *New York Times* said in part:

> The argument which Miss Vera Brittain and twenty-eight
> clergymen and other leaders have made against "massacre by
> bombing" is not in reality an argument against bombing. It is
> an argument against war. Miss Brittain and those who have
> associated themselves with her view are perfectly right when they
> say that "in our time, as never before, war is showing itself in its
> logical colors." Attempts to humanize it have utterly failed. . . .
> It is a hideous business. . . . War is, as Miss Brittain says, "a
> carnival of death." It tortures the "Christian conscience." Nothing
> that we value in our collective lives can endure if the war
> system endures.

That goes to the pith of the matter. I should have blamed
myself if I had lived through this hideous development of
war's "insane logic" without voicing my protest. One of our
prominent internationalists, far from being a pacifist himself,

remarked to me concerning it: "Ten years from now almost everybody will be glad that someone said that."

My ministry during World War II was not confined to protests against war's iniquities. About two hundred of our own congregation were in active service, and we kept in constant touch with them by letter, doing all in our power to keep track of their whereabouts and their good or ill fortune. Opportunities for ministering to the men and women associated with the armed forces who came to New York were almost endless. Hundreds of our members were organized for a great variety of wartime services. With special satisfaction I recall our relationships with the Naval Reserve Midshipmen's School, whose headquarters were at Columbia University. For three and a half years thousands of men, training at that school, used the facilities of the Riverside Church for many purposes, from gymnasium workouts and bowling to worship. Each Sunday evening some two thousand young midshipmen, along with many guests and visitors, worshiped at the Protestant service. The chaplain, C. Leslie Glenn, and the choir director, Grover J. Oberle, did a magnificent job, and those services were among the most moving I ever attended.

During World War I, I had learned from grateful responses to letters which I wrote from France what it meant to a family to receive a message from someone who had seen their son and could report that he was well and going strong. So we wrote thousands of letters to the families of men and women in service, who were finding their opportunities for recreation and worship at the Riverside Church. Nothing we ever did was more gratefully appreciated. And when the young ensigns were ready to leave for active service, hundreds of brides came to New York and were married in the church—the record, as I recall it, was twenty-seven weddings in one day.

In this endeavor personally to serve the young men whom the fortunes of war brought to the Midshipmen's School we had the cordial backing of the commandant, John K. Richards, and when the war was over, at the school's generous insistence, the following inscription was engraved on the wall of the church:

INSCRIBED IN GRATITUDE TO
THE RIVERSIDE CHURCH
FOR ITS FRIENDLY MINISTRY
TO THE THOUSANDS OF MEN
IN TRAINING AT THE
UNITED STATES
NAVAL RESERVE MIDSHIPMEN'S SCHOOL
IN THE CITY OF NEW YORK
AND FOR THE INSPIRATION GIVEN THEM
BY THE PRIVILEGE OF WORSHIPPING
AT THE MIDSHIPMEN'S VESPER SERVICE
MAY 1942 TO NOVEMBER 1945

To one holding my convictions concerning the essentially unchristian nature of war, preaching during World War II was a disturbing problem. Week after week speaking to crowded congregations in the Riverside Church and to multitudes over the air, I was often perplexed as to what I ought to say. Nevertheless, as I recall those strenuous years, their challenge and opportunity loom larger than their difficulty.

Two major aims controlled the content of my sermons.

First, I tried to help individuals. That, at least, a preacher could do—help individuals to stand their ground, keeping their faith despite the world's violent horror and finding inward resource, not only to endure strain and bereavement, but to translate the appalling experience of war into stronger character, clearer vision, more loyal dedication to the service of mankind. Recently a letter has come to me, over a decade after the war's end, which encourages me to hope that once in a while I succeeded in this endeavor:

During World War II, as a young naval lieutenant just back from a tour of duty with a P.T. Boat in the Pacific, I heard you preach at Riverside Church. Strangely enough I disagreed with most of the things you said. Yet that experience did something to me that nothing else had ever done before—it made me think about religion. In fact the only impression I now have of the service is that you said in effect: "This is what I believe and why I believe it; what do *you* have to say about it and *why*?" Moreover, you seemed to be saying it directly to me.

Prior to that time I had been primarily interested in wine, women and money—each in liberal doses. I had seen religion as something external—medicine that preachers were continually urging the sick to take, but which I had no need of because I was healthy. You changed that. Thinking begets thinking. When you challenged me to think about religion, you started a chain reaction which ended with my thinking about life in general and my life in particular.

To make a long story short, in 1946 I entered a theological seminary and in 1949 became a minister.

I might curse you for disrupting my well-laid plans to be successful, for causing me to turn down a business opportunity which would have given me ulcers and made me modestly wealthy. Instead I want to thank you for twelve-hour days, discouragements, criticisms, and the most altogether satisfying life I could hope to lead.

Beyond helping individuals I was deeply concerned in my preaching with a second purpose: to keep the church Christian despite the unchristian nature of war. Arguments about a "just war" have for centuries beguiled Christians into baptizing bloody slaughter in the name of Christ. In the present evil estate of the world bloody slaughter may sometimes be unavoidable, but it is blasphemy to degrade Christ into giving it his benediction as though it represents his will and way of life. In World War II, for example, one preacher argued that because God sends men to hell—obviously a coercive process!—therefore Christians may use violence in war; and another preacher, laboring with the text "God is love," concluded that saturation bombing of enemy cities may be one expression of the divine compassion, and that "men may be forced at times, *in the service of love* [the italics were his] to use weapons to strike down the innocent as well as the guilty." Such preaching, obliterating all difference between Christ and Mars, and making the church a mere adjunct to the war department, seems to me a complete negation of Christ's teaching.

It is true that this wicked world confronts us with situations where our choice lies, not between the Christian ideal and satanic evil, but between two evils, one of which is better than the other. That kind of choice faced this nation after Pearl Harbor; the only other alternative, Gandhi's nonviolent strategy, would have been inconceivable as national policy in the United States. The fact remains, however, that while war may sometimes be defended as the lesser of two

evils, war is never under any conditions *Christian*, and if
the church is to remain the church of Christ she must not
prostitute her influence to the sanctifying of war as though
that were the meaning of Christ's gospel and ethic. In World
War I, I came perilously near being guilty of such prostitu-
tion. In World War II, to the best of my ability, I kept the
pledge I had made as the conflict came closer and closer to
our doors:

I can never use my Christian ministry for the support and
sanction of war. . . . When I picture Christ in this warring world
I can see him in one place only, not arrayed in the panoply of
battle on either side, but on his judgment seat, sitting in con-
demnation on all of us—aggressor, defender, neutral—who by
our joint guilt have involved ourselves in a way of life that
denies everything he stood for. The function of the church is to
keep him there, above the strife, representing a manner of living,
the utter antithesis of war, to which mankind must return if we
are to have any hope.

This did not mean that I withdrew from the manifold
opportunities for personal and public usefulness in wartime.
I thoroughly disapprove that type of pacifist who, concerned
only with keeping his own skirts lily-white, retreats from the
world's problems in wartime to a kind of monastic and irresponsible seclusion. From that sort of merely negative pacifism may the good Lord deliver us! But I did try to keep the
gospel of Jesus Christ from being degraded to the service of
Mars, and of course I labored to foresee the kind of strategy,
personal and governmental, that would make another war
impossible.

With some surprise I note that I entitled the volume containing sermons preached during the war, *A Great Time To Be Alive.* Well, it was a great time—the like of which may I never see again! Meanwhile, with the coming of the H-bomb and intercontinental missiles, Jesus' words, which for centuries have been treated as unrealistic idealism, have now become the most momentous realism that confronts the world: "They that take the sword shall perish with the sword."

The idea that mankind is inevitably becoming "one world," so far as the conquest of distance and the intensifying of economic interdependence can make us one, has had a major influence on my thinking and preaching. We take that for granted now, but I have seen that idea's emergence and development in my lifetime from very small beginnings. I remember yet the impression made on me when William C. Redfield's book, *Dependent America,* came out in 1926. It was one of the first clear, detailed statements showing that the United States required even for her industrial existence resources and materials from all over the globe. The book put factual foundations under my slowly growing sense of world-wide indebtedness and our inescapable international responsibilities. An electric lamp involved the use of materials from Greenland, Germany, China, India, Spain, Indonesia, Brazil, Chile and the Caucasus! As for larger and more vital matters concerning the nation's welfare, it was becoming more evident every year that what happened in some remote land, of which we had barely heard, might affect us more profoundly than what happened here at home. Isolationism was impossible.

In the old days one American citizen had said that his first and most sacred duty was to Maryland, and his second to the United States. He meant *that* to sound like a declaration of loyalty to his state, but it really was treachery even to Maryland, for it never can be well with any state unless it is well with the nation. And now it can never be well with any nation unless it is well with the world. Today being an internationalist is an essential part of being a patriot.

At this point my autobiography becomes a family matter, and I detour for a moment to express my satisfaction that ours has been a wholeheartedly internationalist family. One of the most venturesome careers in world-wide service was my sister Edith's. She taught in Kobe College in Japan, at Ginling College in China, at the American College for Girls in Greece, and ended with eleven years on the faculty of the American College for Girls in Istanbul. She saw more of the world than any of us. In World War I she served as a canteen worker under the Y.M.C.A., in the American Army in Italy, and in World War II, retiring because of health, she left Turkey by way of the Euphrates Valley and India, and sailed home around the Cape of Good Hope.

My brother, Raymond, has had a distinguished career in international service, as everybody knows—that is, almost everybody. Some people never have been able to understand that there are two of us, not one, and in consequence each of us is not uncommonly credited with the good deeds or blamed for the delinquencies of the other. Raymond once wrote an excellent article on postwar problems, and received a scathing letter from an isolationist, denouncing him not only for being an internationalist, but for being a minister, believing in revealed religion and thinking baptism necessary for salvation!

I cherish especially two letters which Raymond wrote me, the first dated August 13, 1919, when, as Under Secretary General of the nascent League of Nations, he was in London, enthusiastic about the prospects:

Everything here is going well—far better than I anticipated. I am tremendously encouraged by the progress that is being made in shaping the plans for the League of Nations. . . . With just a little goodwill and intelligence we can shove this thing over the top, as far as its initial stages are concerned, and start it on its way with growing momentum, as it gathers the support of what Wilson called "the conscience of mankind."

The second letter was written March 29, 1920, after the United States Senate had declined to enter the League:

It's hard to be an American in Europe these days—hard to hold your chin up. For we have to face this inescapable fact: We left Europe in the lurch in the middle of the game after imposing on her our ideas and our procedures. In a single year we have lost the confidence and affection of the people of all nations —people who believed that under our leadership this war-weary world could find a way out. We didn't lose this position; we deliberately threw it away. We let cynicism and lies and partisan politics get the better of us, and we chucked the League out of the window to satisfy a miserable political quarrel. . . . Our generation in America has betrayed its own children and the blood of the next war is on our hands.

A lawyer by profession, Raymond was always mainly absorbed in public and humanitarian movements of one sort or another, and in the end they took him out of professional legal work altogether. As president of The Rockefeller Foundation, he has had a creative share in some of the most exciting forward movements of our time.

As for our daughters, Elinor became a doctor of medicine, specializing in pediatrics, and she married a fellow physician, Roger Downs, who, enlisting as a medical officer in the navy, died while on active service in World War II. After that tragic loss, one of the most severe that ever fell upon our family, Elinor chose public health as her major interest. Her two years of service on the staff of the World Health Organization in Geneva were especially exciting and rewarding—helping to set up maternal and child health clinics at key centers around the globe. Feeling that two years of residence abroad were enough for her children, if they were to grow up to be Americans, she returned home and is now on the staff of the American Public Health Association in New York. At our dinner table, when international politics look gloomy, we get some comfort from an inside view of a kind of international service which does not commonly make the headlines—the outreach of public health programs across all frontiers to make available everywhere the best that modern medicine knows.

Our daughter Dorothy took her doctorate in political science at Columbia, and after teaching for four years at Smith College, was called to the State Department in Washington, where she served for twelve years, four of them on the Policy Planning Staff. From Dumbarton Oaks on, she had been active in every conference leading to the establishment of the United Nations. When she flew to London as Technical Adviser to the American Delegation at the sessions of the Preparatory Commission charged with the task of setting up

the machinery of the new world organization, Raymond
wrote her:

Twenty-six years ago this month I sailed to London on this
same identical errand, i.e., to set up the provisional organization
of the League of Nations. . . . Only this time the chances of
success are so much greater than they were a quarter of a century
ago. We have learned through bloody disaster what the price of
failure is—and this new generation will put the thing over
where my generation fell down on the job. So you see what it
means to me personally to have you go on this assignment. In
some mystical way I feel as if my own hopes and ambitions were
about to be fulfilled through you.

Well, despite frustrations and defeats, the United Nations
is still our best hope of organizing a peaceful world, but it
obviously faces a rough road to its goal. Dorothy has recently
written a book, *Common Sense and World Affairs*, which
sums up the situation, so it seems to me, in a wise, well-
balanced fashion. I suspect that, having resigned from the
State Department to write this book, she will for the present
go on writing about international affairs.

As for me, I do not see how a Christian, believing in
God's fatherhood and man's brotherhood, can escape the
fact that Jesus' saying, "The field is the world," takes on
intensified meaning with every passing year. Nationalism can
have noble meanings but when it is used as an enemy of
internationalism, it becomes what I called it in one of my
sermon titles: "Christianity's Supreme Rival."

The towering problem now, whose solution no one can
foresee, is the relationship between the communist and non-
communist portions of the globe. It would be presumptuous

in me to prophesy. One thing, however, seems to me clear: we cannot meet communism's challenge by reactionary policies. Granted the priceless traditions of democracy and liberty which we must defend, they cannot be preserved by refrigeration, but by progressive development into new forms and fresh applications.

Communism is a false philosophy and the world's prodigious menace, but it does at least proclaim a gospel of change. This world is all wrong, it says, and we are out to transform it. In consequence, along with some starry-eyed idealists, millions of impoverished, discontented, exploited people around the world welcome communist propaganda, if only because it promises them the one thing they want most—a change. I certainly am anticommunist—anti its totalitarianism, its atheism, its Marxism—but I am also sure that the only way to beat the communists is to match and surpass them in proclaiming a new day for the world's common people.

Many anticommunists in our country are so absorbed in being "anti" that they present no positive, constructive alternative to the transformed world which the Reds promise. The Kremlin is turning too many Americans into Tories. "Stay put!" some of our anticommunists seem to be saying, "We are all right as we are! Resist all change!" That attitude turns over to communism the vast advantage of being the sole sponsor and backer of progressive change. In one area of the world after another we have thus been jockeyed into appearing as the champions of standpattism against a ringing gospel of social change; whereas the fact is that if we are to beat the communists, we must prove ourselves their betters as pioneers of a juster social order, with liberty and democracy implemented as they have never been, and made real as even in this country they never have been real.

In private conversation one congressman made a statement so hopelessly Tory that I exploded. "That is incredibly reactionary," I said; to which the congressman replied: "In these days is it possible for anyone to be *too* reactionary?" The answer to that seems obvious: if we want successfully to meet the challenge of what Stalin called his "new order," it is fatally possible to be too reactionary. Does not democracy inherently involve a "new order" too? Is not the welfare of all the people a central tenet of democracy, and does not its realization involve forward-looking social change?

Such was the spirit of our democratic ancestors. *They* were the progressives; *they* stirred the world with a gospel of revolutionary change; *they* were the apostles of a new day. We betray our forefathers if we let the desire for security and static changelessness, in so stormy an era, crush out that spirit. As Jean Jaurès put it: "Take from the altars of the past the fire—not the ashes."

These, then, are some of the ideas that have used me. I wish they could have used me to better effect. Sometimes, looking at the sorry spectacle of our chaotic world, I am tempted to apply to myself Al Smith's admonition to a self-important politician: "Go stick your finger in a pail of water and take it out again, and see what a hole you have made."

Epilogue

W HEN MY GRANDCHILDREN were little, they always referred to the Riverside Church as "Gramp's church." Once, when Patty was about five years old, I rode with her on top of a bus down Riverside Drive to a point from which both the church tower and Grant's Tomb were visible. "Look," I said, "what do you see there?" "Oh," said Patty, "there's Gramp's church and Gramp's tomb." Feeling as I do today, that seems a bit previous, but undoubtedly I am now an old man, and I must add that I am enjoying it.

I retired from the active ministry at Riverside Church in 1946, and following a session with a surgeon and its recuperative aftermath, I plunged into a heavy schedule of itinerant speaking. I recall with mingled pleasure and dismay a visit to the Panama Canal Zone where I made fourteen addresses in ten days, but I soon had to stop that kind of schedule and have now settled down to calmer living.

Nevertheless, I have carried into my retirement association with many worth-while causes which make life exciting, so that expectancy about tomorrow looms larger than nostalgia about yesterday. To be sure, "Youth longs, and mankind strives, but age remembers," and I am endlessly grateful for my memories—especially about my early home. My father and mother are still among the most vital influences in my life. My father carried his work in Buffalo until his seventy-fifth year, and then retired. His second marriage, three years after my mother's death, to a lifelong friend of the family brought him satisfying companionship in his later days, and my half-sister, Ruth, and her household are near us every summer in Maine. My father lived to see his professional services widely recognized, and no man in Buffalo, I think, was better loved by more people than was he. He never stopped growing. He did not propose, he said, to let the younger generation get ahead of him; he intended to keep one jump ahead of it. In his later years I saw him mostly in the summertime, where on the Maine coast he had a cottage not far from ours. To the very end he was alert and vigorous, a tireless deep-sea fisherman, full of good stories and salty humor, always admirable in my eyes, not simply because he was my father, but because he was a real man. If I believed in reincarnation and could select my father and mother for my next appearance, I would choose them again.

Nevertheless—in large measure, I suspect, because I am their son—I am finding plenty of tasks to make the present interesting and the future expectant. The matter of public interest, in which during recent years I have made my largest investment of time and energy—and I must add, anxiety—has been the endeavor to halt and reverse the deplorable deterioration of the Manhattanville-Morningside neighborhood. It is not people only who grow old; cities grow old, and that fact today constitutes one of the most serious internal problems which this country faces. For thirty years I lived on Morningside Heights, surrounded by its galaxy of educational and religious institutions, and with a disturbed mind and conscience watched the deterioration of the community immediately to the north of us—Manhattanville, extending roughly from 123rd Street to 135th Street, and from St. Nicholas Avenue to the Hudson River. In 1892, when the movement of institutions such as Columbia University and the Cathedral of St. John the Divine to the Heights was assured, the *New York Times* waxed a bit lyrical. "The College and the Cathedral together," it said, "will attract . . . a community of quiet and scholarly people who will convert the neighborhood into a 'close.'" Doubtless some quiet and scholarly people do live in the neighborhood, although many of them have fled to the suburbs, but something else has happened, characteristic in one degree or another of all our aging American cities, which the *Times* did not foresee.

The change began in the valley a few blocks north of the Heights. In the early nineteen-hundreds, when I first saw the area, only about eighteen thousand people lived there, predominantly Irish and German. Then the influx of many nationalities rapidly increased; old-style tenements sprang up like mushrooms; in the late nineteen-thirties the Negroes moved in, and then, after World War II, the Puerto Ricans. When the crowded tenements overflowed southward and, one after another, higher grade apartments were made over so as to accommodate whole families in single rooms, it became evident that unless something were done about it,

Columbia University and all the rest of our institutions would be located in a slum.

Two motives played with increasing urgency on all of us who were concerned about the community. One was the need of self-protection for our institutions against the deplorable conditions which were making our neighborhood a public disgrace and shame. The other was humane care for the helpless people who were being victimized by slum conditions which they hated but could not change. It was this latter motive which first started our work in Manhattanville. The residents there were commonly fine people—about one-third Negroes, one-third Puerto Ricans, and the other third made up of over twenty different nationalities—and they and their children needed help. So in 1944, after several fine-spirited enterprises, too poorly supported and with too small a scope, had proved inadequate, an endeavor was started to get something done on a more ambitious scale.

World War II was still on when a group of public-spirited citizens—I dare not start naming them, for there is no place to stop—opened a child care center in Manhattanville for the children of working mothers. Although inadequately housed, the center soon enrolled in its program a hundred teenagers in addition to the little children, and the community's needs, increasingly evident and clamorous, were being loudly advertised on the "Hill." So in 1946 at the Riverside Church, a meeting of neighborhood leaders approved accepting from Teachers College, for the purposes of a welfare center, the abandoned building of the old Speyer School in the heart of Manhattanville, which, unoccupied for ten years, had been ravaged inside and out by vandals. It would take fifty thousand dollars to recondition the building, we were told. When a few months later, just after my retirement, I accepted the chairmanship of the committee, we soon found that it would cost much more—one hundred and sixty thousand dollars in the end. John D. Rockefeller, Jr. came handsomely to our aid, and after many anxious months the Manhattanville Neighborhood Center was officially opened in 1948. A unique feature of the center was the fact that all the major institutions on the Heights appointed representatives on our official boards and began making substantial annual contributions to our budget.

Meanwhile, the whole Morningside community was waking up to the dangerous situation of the neighborhood, and in 1947 Morningside Heights, Inc., under the able chairmanship of David Rockefeller, with Lawrence Orton of the City Planning Commission as executive director, was founded, and the institutions on the Heights joined in a united effort to eliminate the miserable housing of our fellow citizens, to secure adequate schools for the children, and to achieve proper police protection from the mounting criminality."The improvement and redevelopment of Morningside Heights as an attractive residential, educational and cultural community" was the stated aim of this new organization. The results in which we now rejoice are hopeful evidence of what can be done in the renovation of deteriorated urban areas when the citizens make up their minds to reverse the downward trend and to redeem slums from their misery and juvenile delinquency to respectability and decency.

Today three large-scale, interracial housing projects, displacing many of the worst of the old tenements, are assured

—two for low-income and one for middle-income residents —and work on them has already begun. There are plenty of difficulties still to be met. As a member of the Mayor's Committee on Better Housing, I am fairly staggered by the complexity of the problems which a city like New York faces in enforcing laws against unscrupulous landlords and in securing new and decent living accommodations for its people. Nevertheless, we are now confident that at least Morningside Heights will not be a slum area. As for the Manhattanville Neighborhood Center, we have now combined with the much older Manhattanville Day Nursery, and under the able leadership of our executive director, Clyde E. Murray, we are expanding our program, turning street gangs into constructive groups, dealing directly with some seven hundred children in our activities, looking forward to the social welfare facilities which we shall operate in the new housing projects, and helping to organize the citizens of the area for service to the neighborhood.

As I recall what I have learned from participation in this civic enterprise, one experience asks for emphasis: deep satisfaction in the loyal and effective co-operation among Jews, Roman Catholics and Protestants, and among all the varied racial groups involved. The best way to get together across dividing lines is to work together on common tasks, and we have proved that in Morningside-Manhattanville. I venture that nowhere in America are the three religious fellowships living together with more mutual understanding and respect, and nowhere is interracial good will more taken for granted. There is not a racially segregated institution on the Heights, and a racially segregated new housing project would not be tolerated. As for the three religious communities, my long-standing respect for President Louis Finkelstein of the Jewish Theological Seminary and Father George Ford of the Corpus Christi Roman Catholic Church has deepened into warm friendship. When, under the Riverside Church's hospitable roof, a convocation of Columbia University, celebrating its bicentennial anniversary, recently conferred an honorary doctorate on Father Ford, even he could not have been much more pleased than I was.

A friend of mine tells me that many years ago he heard me say in a sermon: "It is magnificent to grow old—if only one stays young." To this challenging adventure in renovating a city area which was on the skids I am grateful for some of the zest which has helped me to handle retirement with youthful relish.

As for the world's future, I am not so discouraged as many are. Granted that the old, easygoing optimism is impossible! William Allen White, rereading the files of his *Gazette* from 1896 to 1905, was shocked, he says, "at the intrepid complacency with which I viewed the universe." So would many of us say. Today, however, complacency is out. To be sure, a sensible man's life is not all anxious tension. One does not go about all day exclaiming with Polycarp in A.D. 156: "My God! In what a century have you caused me to live!" There are escapes. There is golf and reading and nature's beauty and human friendship and Beethoven's Concerto in D Major. My grandson, Steve, wrote for his school class a poem about the ocean, whose closing lines run:

> Ah, thou Neptune! Thou dost govern
> All the stormy sea around;
> But even in thy strength and fury
> Sleepy harbors can be found.

That is a sage observation for an eleven-year-old. But, despite the tranquil harbors, this generation has no place for "intrepid complacency."

Nevertheless, at threescore-years-and-eighteen I find this generation the most stimulating, exciting, provocative—yes, promising—era I have ever seen or read about. I am not yet ready to die. I want to see what is going to happen next. Like the French editor, carried in a tumbrel through the streets of Paris to the guillotine, I would say: "It is too bad to cut off my head; I want to see how all this is coming out." Prophetic, germinative ideas are here; there are open doors of possibility for good as well as evil, which did not exist when I was born; and though I am an old man, I share at least a little the hopeful spirit of the young, facing life, as Lowell sang, with "the rays of morn on their white Shields of Expectation!"

Index

Abbott, Lyman, 64
Adams, James Truslow, 47
Adler, Felix, 20, 267
Agnosticism, 20, 21
Alcoholics Anonymous, 286-88
Alexander, Dr. George, 132, 133, 162
Alfred the Great, 269
Alger, Horatio, Jr., 43, 46
American Christian Committee for German Refugees, 281
American Friends' Service Committee, 111
American Public Health Association, 308
American Revolution, 1
Amos, 296
Anarchism, 26
Andrews, Newton Lloyd, 55
Anti-Semitism, 281
"Apologetics," 119
Armitage, Thomas B., 183, 189
As I See Religion (Fosdick), 242
Asquith, Lord, 272
Assurance of Immortality (Fosdick), 89
Atheism, 20, 21, 250
Atomic bomb, 299
Atonement doctrine, 231, 232
Augustine, 254, 256
Aulén, Gustaf, 258

"Back to Christ" movement, 64
Baillie, John, 262
Baker, Ray Stannard, 45, 101-2
Baldwin, Arthur, 153
Ballard, Edward L., 181
Baptism, 22, 198
Barth, Karl, 236, 247-48, 249, 253, 257, 258, 261, 262, 263
Barton, Clara, 27
Bates, Ruby, 283
Bellamy, Edward, 26
Bernadotte, Count, 187
Best, Nolan R., 159
Bible, liberal position on, 243; use of, in preaching, 95, 117-19
Biblical criticism, 20, 64
Birth control movement, 284
Blain, Jacob, 12
Books, boyhood, 36-37; by Fosdick, 75, 87-88, 89-91, 118, 119, 121, 134-35, 186, 220, 233, 238, 242, 305
Boothbay Harbor, Maine, 113-16
Bowery, New York, 70-71

Bowne, Borden P., 22, 64
Breasted, James Henry, 183
Breen, John J., 105
Brewster, Elder, 5
Briggs, Charles H., 229
Brigham, Albert Perry, 55
Brittain, Vera, 297, 298, 299
Brooks, Phillips, 100
Brown, Francis, 77
Brown, William Adams, 77
Browning, 1, 41
"Bruce, Father," 28
Brunner, Emil, 248-49, 250, 251-52, 254, 255, 259, 261, 263, 264, 265
Bryan, William Jennings, 147-48, 160, 164, 170, 171
Buddhism, 241
Bull Moose party, 108
Bunche, Ralph, 290
Burns, Robert, 1
Butler, Nicholas Murray, 70
Butler, Samuel, 250, 282
Buttrick, George A., 271

Cadman, S. Parkes, 221
Calvinism, 63
Canby, Henry S., 44
Candid Examination of Theism (Romanes), 20
Capitalism, 277-78
Carder, Eugene C., 191, 192, 193, 195, 209
Carlyle, 1, 155
Carnegie, Andrew, 46
Carter, Thomas, 139
Castlemon, Harry (Charles Fosdick), 25, 43-44
Challenge of the Present Crisis (Fosdick), 121
Chalmers, Allan Knight, 283
Channing, 168
Charity Organization, of Buffalo, 27; of Riverside Church, 205
Chautauqua Literary and Scientific Circles, 30
Chesterton, Gilbert, 260
Chiang Kai-shek, 138
Child labor, 273, 283
China, 135, 136-39
Chou En-lai, 137
Christianity, essence of, in Jesus, 269; perversion of, 268; see also Religion and Theology
Christianity and Progress (Fosdick), 238
Christianity and the Social Crisis (Rauschenbusch), 109
Church(es), "class," 102, 199; institutional, 201-2; as

mother of all Christians, 77-78; present and past, 227-28; segregation in, 291; in wartime, 303-4
Churchill, Sir Winston, 125, 252, 297, 298
Clark, John Bates, 102
Clarke, James E., 159
Clarke, William Newton, 55-56, 61, 65-66, 79, 254-55
Coffin, Henry Sloane, 83, 158
Colgate, James C., 76, 180-81
Colgate University, 48-49, 52-62, 65, 67, 76
College preaching, 88-89, 119
College years, 48-62
Collier, Jeremy, 156
Columbia University, 70, 102, 188, 290
Common Sense and World Affairs (D. Fosdick), 309
Communism, 103, 104, 105, 137, 138, 211, 290, 296-97, 309-11
Community Service Society, 205
Compton, Arthur H., 270
Comte, Auguste, 20
Cooke, Jay, 25
Cooper, Clayton, 87
Counseling, personal, 93-95, 99-101, 135, 212-21
Coxey's "army," 44-45
Crawshaw, William Henry, 55
Crisis of Faith (Hopper), 258
Crockett, David, 9
Culture, theology and, 244, 245-46
Cyprian, 58

Darwin, 20, 273
Death Not Life (Blain), 12
Deism, 255
Deland, Margaret, 63
Dependent America (Redfield), 305
Depressions, of 1873, 25; of 1893, 44-45; of 1933, 275, 282
Detmers, Arthur, 41
De Wolf, L. Harold, 255
Dieffenbach, Albert C., 165-67, 182
Doctrinal controversies, 229-66
Dogmatics in Outline (Barth), 257
Douglass, H. Paul, 210
Downs, Mary, 205
Downs, Roger, 308
Dreiser, Theodore, 44, 71
Drummond, Henry, 35
Dryden, 156

322

Duffield, Dr. Howard, 132
Dynamic of Manhood, Gu-
lick), 91

Ebina, Dr., 140
Economic problems, domestic,
see Finances, family; na-
tional, 25-26, 44-45, 272-82
Edison, Thomas, 2
Education, 269, 270-71; clas-
sical tradition in, 41; pub-
lic, 12-13, 273
Edward VII, 74
Egypt, 183
Eighteenth Amendment, 288
Einstein, Dr. and Mrs. Al-
bert, 192
Eisenhower, Dwight D. 293
England, 74, 140-41
Epistle to the Romans
(Barth), 257
Erie Canal, 8-9
Ethical Culture, Society for,
20
Ettor, 104, 105
Euthanasia Society, 284-85
Evangelistic campaigns, 11, 35
Evolution, 20, 49, 252
Experience, Christian, 64, 66-
67, 234-35

Faith, 256-57, 258-59, 269
Faunce, W. H. P., 160, 183
Feminism, 14
Field, Rachel, 117
Finances, family, 37, 49-50, 61
Finkelstein, Louis, 318
Finley, John, 160, 161
Fiske, John, 54
Flushing Remonstrance, 7
Ford, Father George, 318
Fosdick, Amie Weaver, 13-16,
18, 19, 22, 30, 31, 60, 79-80,
313
Fosdick, Anna Thorne, 7-8
Fosdick, Charles (Harry Cas-
tlemon, 25, 43-44
Fosdick, Dorothy, 113, 308-9
Fosdick, Edith, 17, 61, 73,
306
Fosdick, Elinor, 113, 308
Fosdick, Ethel, 17
Fosdick, Florence Whitney,
68-69, 81-82
Fosdick, Frank, 9-10, 13, 15-
16, 17-18, 30, 31-33, 36, 37,
41, 45, 49, 50, 60, 61, 313
Fosdick, grandmother, 12, 51
Fosdick, Jesse, 7
Fosdick, John, 5
Fosdick, John Spencer, 7, 8,
9-12, 13, 43
Fosdick, Lewis L., viii
Fosdick, Morris, 7
Fosdick, Raymond, viii, 17,
61, 73, 142, 179, 306-7, 309
Fosdick, Ruth, 313
Fosdick, Samuel, 5-6

Fosdick, Samuel, II and III,
6
Fosdick, Silas, 6
Fosdick, Solomon, 7
Fosdick, Stephen, 3-5
Frame, James Everett, 77, 118
Freeman, Judge, 154
Freud, 213
Fundamentalism, 51, 134, 135,
143, 225, 244, 246, 249; vs.
Liberalism, 144-76

Gandhi, 91, 303
Gates, Frederick T., 178-79
George, Henry, 26
Giddings, Franklin H., 102
Gilkey, Charles and Geraldine,
115, 116
Giovanitti, 104
Gladden, Washington, 26, 63
Gladstone, 1, 63, 278
Glasgow, University of, 141-42
Glenn, C. Leslie, 300
God, faith in, 256-57; fear of,
34; immanence of, 252-55;
as immediate Resource, 75;
Kingdom of, 239, 240, 242;
personal experience of, 234;
revelation of, 236, 256-57,
262-63; revolt against, 20
Gordon, George A., 64, 269
Great Time To Be Alive (Fos-
dick), 305
Greece, 184
Greene, John, 55
Greenfield, Billy, 289
Grenfell, Sir Wilfred, 207
*Guide to Understanding the
Bible* (Fosdick), 119
Guillet, Mrs. Alma, 205
Gulick, Luther, 91

Hall, Charles Cuthbert, 77
Hall, Thomas C., 238
Harnack, 248
Harris, Frederick, 87, 91
Harris, James Rendel, 67
H-bomb, 305
Hegel, 64
Heidt, George, 195
Hell, fear of, 33-34, 35, 36
Hellstrom, C. Ivar, 195, 204
Henty, G. A., 43
Hibben, John Grier, 160
Higginbottom, Samuel, 290
Hillis, Newell Dwight, 237
Hiroshima, 299
History of European Morals
(Lecky), 41
*History of the Warfare of Sci-
ence with Theology in
Christendom* (White), 52
Hitler, 281, 282
Holland, J. G., 38
Holmes, Oliver Wendell, 12,
63
Holy Land, 184-86
Home life, 16, 30-31, 36-44, 61

Homiletics, 83; *see also*
Preaching
Hopkins, James, 4
Hopper, Stanley R., 258
Horton, Walter Marshall, 258
Housing projects, 316-17
How the Other Half Lives
(Riis), 71
Howe, Frederick C., 69
Huggins, Mr. and Mrs. G.
Ellsworth, 114
Hughes, Charles Evans, 101,
120, 207
Humanism, 20, 244
Husseini, Grand Mufti, 187

Illness, 72-75
Immanence of God, 252-55
Immortality, 89, 240-41
Individualism, 45-47
Industrial Workers of the
World, 103, 105
Ingersoll, Robert G., 21-22
Institutional church, 201-2
Interdenominationalism, 196-
97, 260
International House, 188, 200
Internationalism, 305-9
Interracialism, 199-200, 318
Irving, Sir Henry, 111
Islam, 234
Isolationism, 25, 305

James, William, 45, 73, 110,
232
Japan, 135, 136-37, 139-40
Jaurès, Jean, 311
Jenkins, Edward and Eliza-
beth, 115
Jesus Christ, 236, 269; "back
to Christ" movement, 64;
ministry of, 264; revelation
of God in, 262-63; revolt
against, 20
John Ward, Preacher (De-
land), 63
Johnson, Charles Spurgeon,
291
Jones, Rufus, 110-11
Jordan, David Starr, 120
Jung, 213

Kagawa, Toyohiko, 210-11
Kapital, Das (Marx), 26
Keats, 241
Kelman, John, 125, 158
Kingdom of God, 239, 240, 242
Kingsley, 26
Knox, George William, 77, 238
Kreisler, Fritz, 111

Labor Movement, 26, 102-7
Lanier, Sidney, 235
Latimer, Hugh, 226-27
Laud, Archbishop, 4
League of Nations, 122, 134,
142, 307, 309
Lecky, 41

Lee, Ivy, 146, 167
Legalism, 35, 36
Lew, Timothy T., 138
Liberalism, 63-66, 144, 145-76; causes espoused by, 274, 282-311; and neo-orthodoxy, 231-66; reactionary, 246-47; social, 109-11
Lincoln, Abraham, 276
Lindbergh, Charles, 270
Lloyd George, 124
Lobenstine, Edwin, 139
Looking Backward (Bellamy), 26
Lorimer, George C., 76, 78-79, 80, 85
Lotze, 64
Lowell, Lawrence, 89
Lyman Beecher Lectureship on Preaching, 168-69, 243

MacArthur, Douglas, 293
Macartney, Clarence Edward, 146
Macaulay, 292
McCarthy, Joseph, 297
McCracken, Robert James, viii, 228
MacDonald, James G., 282
MacDonald, James Ramsay, 141
McGiffert, Arthur Cushman, 77, 229, 253
Macintosh, Douglas Clyde, 281
McKinley, William, 108
Magnes, Rabbi Judah, 186
Maine coast, 113-17
Manhattanville - Morningside neighborhood improvement, 313-18
Manhood of the Master (Fosdick), 90-91
Mann, Horace, 13
Manning, Bishop William T., 152, 298
Mao Tse-tung, 137
Mariners' Temple, 70-71
Martineau, 168
Marx, Marxism, 20, 26, 250, 310
Materialism, 47, 58
Matthews, J. B., 297
Matthews, Dr. Mark, 171
Maurice, 26
Meaning of Faith (Fosdick), 119
Meaning of Prayer (Fosdick), 75, 91
Meaning of Service (Fosdick), 134-35
Mediator (Brunner), 264
Merrill, William P., 158, 170
Meyer, Adolf, 213
Midshipmen's School, 300-301
Military training, 40-41
Ministers' No-War Committee, 294-95

Ministry, decision to enter, 56-57; in Montclair, 84-87, 111-12; in Old First Church, 132-35, 174-76; in Park Avenue Baptist Church, 177, 178, 181-83; preparation for, 63, 65-67, 69-72, 75-79; radio, 221-26; in Riverside Church, 178, 182, 187-228, 281-82, 290, 312; in World Wars, 120-32, 297-305
Missionaries, 24, 135-36, 138-39
Modern Use of the Bible (Fosdick), 118, 168, 233
Moody, Dwight L., 35
Moore, Robert, 55
Morals, religion and, 242-43
Morgenthau, Mr. and Mrs. Henry, Sr., 184
Morris K. Jesup Professorship, 112, 117-19
Morrison, Charles Clayton, 156
Mott, John R., 87
Mott, Lucretia, 14
Mouse Island, Maine, 113, 115
"Muckrakers," 101-2
Munger, Theodore, 63
Municipal government, 285
Munkácsy, 43
Murray, Clyde E., 317
Music, 16, 30

National Guard, 40-41
"National Vespers," 222-26
Nationalism, 309
Naval Reserve Midshipmen's School, 300-301
Negroes, mistreatment of, 289-91
Neo-orthodoxy, 134, 239, 244-45, 247-66
Newton, Joseph Fort, 130
Niebuhr, Reinhold, 144, 239, 247, 252
Nietzsche, 292
Northfield student conference, 87
Nye, Bill, 181

Oberle, Grover J., 300
Old First Church, 132-35, 174-76
On Being a Real Person (Fosdick), 220
"One world," 305-9
Optimism, philosophy of, 58-59, 237-38, 241-42, 269
Ordainment, 79
Oriental Exclusion Act, 139
Origin of Species (Darwin), 20
Orton, Lawrence, 316
Osaki, Yukio, 139
Our Faith (Brunner), 264
Outline of Christian Theology (Clarke), 55
Oxford Conference, 295

Pacifism, 293-96, 304
Page, Walter Hines, 126
Palestine, 184-86
Pantheism, 253, 255
Park Avenue Baptist Church, 177, 178, 181-83
Parker, Joseph, 130
Parkhurst, Charles Henry, 71-72, 132, 171
Partners in Plunder (Matthews), 297
Pastoral service, 212, 214, 218
Peabody, Francis, 167-68
Pekin Union Medical College, 138
Penn, William, 116
Personalism (Bowne), 64
Philosophy courses, 57-58
Picket, Mercy, 5
Pilgrimage to Palestine (Fosdick), 186
Planned parenthood, 284
Poling, Daniel, 288, 298
Polycarp, 318
Prayer, 75, 91
Preaching, 83-89, 92-101; Bible in, 95, 117-19; college, 88-89, 119; co-operation in, 96-98; expository, 92; itinerant, 119; personal counseling approach to, 93-101; popular, 216; radio, 221-26; topical, 92-93, 95
Progress, belief in, 237-38, 239, 241-42
Progress and Poverty (George), 26
Prohibition, 288
Psychology, 213-14
Psychotherapy, 218-19

Quakers, 7, 111, 202, 295

Racial discrimination, 289-91
Racial good will, 318
Radhakrishnan, Sarvepalli, 116
Radio preaching, 221-26
Rauschenbusch, Walter, 109-10
Reason, 255-56, 257; faith and, 258-59
Recreation, 111, 114-15
Red Cross, 27
Redfield, William C., 305
Reed, Melbourne Stuart, 58
Reform movements, 27, 101, 108-9
Religion, co-operation within, 317-18; finding new possibilities in, 54-59; freedom of, 4, 5, 15; fundamentalist-liberal controversy in, 144-76; morals and, 242-43; psychology and, 213-14; revolt against, 19-21, 51-54, 63-64; social thought and, 237-38; in youth, 19-22, 33-36, 42-43, 56-57; see also Theology

324

Religious Revolt against Reason (De Wolf), 255
Renan, 292
Republicanism, 24-25
Revelation of God, 256-57, 259, 262-63
Revelation and Reason (Brunner), 259, 263
"Revisionists," 187
Richards, John K., 301
Ridgeway, E. J., 101
Riis, Jacob, 71
Ritschl, 64, 248
Riverside Church, 178, 182, 187-96, 228, 281-82, 290, 312; finances of, 208-10; interdenominational membership of, 196-99; interracialism of, 199-200; personality-centered policy of, 211-21; program of, 200-208; public usefulness of, 210-11
Robert Elsmere (Ward), 63
Rockefeller, David, 316
Rockefeller, John D., Jr., 177-80, 191, 207, 316
Rockefeller, John D., Sr., 46
Rockefeller Foundation, 179
Romanes, George John, 20
Roosevelt, Mrs. Eleanor, 275-76
Roosevelt, Franklin D., 273, 275-76, 297-98
Roosevelt, Theodore, 71, 108-9
Rufus Jones Speaks to Our Time (Fosdick, ed.), 111
Ruskin, John, 1, 26, 292
Russell, Bertrand, 296
Russian Revolution, 137

St. Mary, Maury de, 291
Salmon, Dr. Thomas, 218
Sampson, Mrs. Edith, 291
Samson, 51-52
Sanger, Mrs. Margaret, 284
Sankey, Ira, 35
Sato, Lieutenant-General, 139-40
Schindall, Henry, 217
Schleiermacher, 64
Schurman, Jacob Gould, 89
Science, 269-70
Scotland, 141-42
Scott, Albert L., 181
Scottsboro case, 282-83
Sears, Charles Hatch, 67
Second Mile (Fosdick), 88
Secularism, 268
Sedgwick, Ellery, 90
Segregation, 291
Shaftesbury, Lord, 272
Shepardson, Professor and Mrs. Frank L., 68
Sin, social and personal, 239-40
Slavery, 11-12, 289
Smith, Adam, 274
Smith, Al, 311

Smith, Sir George Adam, and Lady Smith, 125
Social gospel, 26, 279-80
Social Law in the Spiritual World (Jones), 110
Social problems, 26-27, 44-45, 70-72, 101-8, 272-82
Social service, 134, 204-5
Societies for the Prevention of Cruelty to Animals, to Children, 27
Sockman, Ralph, 84
Soulen, Henry, 184
Speer, Robert E., 87
Speers, Guthrie, 133, 162
Spencer, Herbert, 20
Stalin, 296-97, 311
Stanton, Elizabeth Cady, 14
Steffens, Lincoln, 101
Stiles, Ezra, 231
Straton, John Roach, 153
Streeter, Canon B. H., 234
Strikes, 25, 44, 102, 103-7
Stuart, John Leighton, 138, 139
Student conferences, 87
Stuyvesant, Peter, 7
Success, worship of, 45-47
Sun Yat-sen, 136, 137, 138
Sunderland, Clyde, 49
Swinburne, 250

Taft, William Howard, 108, 122
Tarbell, Ida, 102
Taussig, Admiral, 130
Taylor, James M., 55
Taylor, Jeremy, 235
Tennant, Elder, 22
Theology, culture and, 244, 245-46; dogmatic, 231, 233, 234; factual basis for, 64; fluidity in, 229-30; liberal, 63-66; perversions of, 268; study of, 232; *see also* Fundamentalism, Liberalism, *and* Neo-orthodoxy
Theology of Crisis (Brunner), 250, 261, 264
Thomas, Ralph, 55, 57
Thompson, Dorothy, 34
Thompson, Francis, 236
Thompson, Peter, 34
Thorne, Anna, 7-8
Tibbetts, Norris L., 195, 207
Tillich, Paul, 249
Tolerance, Liberal, 259-61
Tolstoi, 73
Tourgée, Judge, 292
Transcendence, 253, 254, 255
Travel abroad, 74, 135-42, 183-87
Twain, Mark, 73

Underground railroad, 11-12, 289
Union Theological Seminary,

67, 74, 76-77, 80, 112, 117-119, 188
Unitarian movement, 165
United Nations, 308-9

Vance, Myra, 205
Van Dusen, Henry, 110
Van Dyke, Henry, 158
Vester, "Brother Jacob," 184
Victoria, Queen, 1
Voltaire, 46

Waith, William, 34
Walker, Jimmy, 285
War, 270; defense of, 121; opposition to, 292-305
Ward, Mrs. Humphry, 63
Ward, Lester, 292
Washington, Booker T., 290
Watson, Sir Angus, 141
Weatherhead, Leslie, 131
Weaver, Albert, 31
Weaver, Amie. *See* Fosdick, Amie Weaver
Weaver, Andrew Jackson, 14, 15, 17
Weaver, Caroline, 23
Weaver, Clement, 15
Weaver, Florence, 23, 31
Weaver, grandmother, 14, 17, 23, 31
Wells, H. G., 291
Wesley, John, 289
White, Andrew D., 52, 89
White, William Allen, 318
Whitehead, Alfred N., 268
Whitman, Walt, 41, 60
Whitney, Florence. *See* Fosdick, Florence Whitney
Wider Quaker Fellowship, 295
Williams, Maynard Owen, 184
Wilson, Admiral, 129
Wilson, Woodrow, 89, 120, 122, 142, 274, 307
Winthrop, John, 4
Woelfkin, Cornelius, 171, 177, 182, 183, 195
Women, equal rights for, 14; suffrage for, 27, 283-84
Women's Christian Temperance Union, 27
Woods, Vice-Admiral, 108
Word and the World (Brunner), 264
Wordsworth, 41, 50
Work, Edgar Whitaker, 150, 151
World Health Organization, 308
World War I, 120-32, 136, 300, 304, 306
World War II, 297, 298-305, 306

Y.M.C.A., 127

Zionism, 186-87